D1595227

A Chronology of Islamic History

570–1000 CE

A Chronology
of Islamic History
570–1000 CE

H.U. Rahman

G.K.HALL&CO.
70 LINCOLN STREET, BOSTON, MASS.

Published 1989 in the United States of America and Canada by
G.K. Hall & Co., 70 Lincoln Street, Boston, Massachusetts 02111, U.S.A.

First published 1989 by Mansell Publishing Limited.
A Cassell Imprint
Artillery House, Artillery Row, London SW1P 1RT, England

Library of Congress Cataloging in Publication Data
Rahman, H. U. (Habib Ur), 1940–
    A chronology of Islamic history, 570–1000 CE.
    Includes index.
    1. Islamic Empire—History—Chronology.   2. Muhammad,
Prophet, d. 632—Chronology.   I. Title.   II. Series.
DS38.3.R35   1988   909′.097671   88-12710
ISBN 0-8161-9067-4

Printed and bound in Great Britain

Contents

Introduction

In less than one century after the death of the Prophet Muhammad in 632, Muslim rule covered more of the earth than had the Roman Empire at its peak. The empire of the desert dwellers from Arabia stretched for 4,500 miles and over three continents, from the frontiers of China in the East to Spain and southern France in the West. These conquests united the ancient civilizations of the Middle East, to say nothing of North Africa and Spain, under a single rule for the first time since the days of Alexander the Great (356–323 BCE). Under the Muslim rule came Greeks, Berbers, Copts, Armenians, Arabs, Persians, Turks, Sogdians, Indians and Chinese. The banner of Islam made a strong impact on the world, an impact that has remained considerable to this day, extending from Morocco to Idonesia.

It is not enough, however, merely to acknowledge Islam for its role in military history, considerable and enduring though it was. Under the spiritual unity it offered, Arab language and culture became dominant in the civilized world. The most striking effect of the unification of such a vast area was the breaking down not only of political, but also of linguistic and intellectual frontiers which had hitherto been closed. The two mighty empires of the Byzantines and the Persians had been at war with each other for centuries, but under Islam, a medical student from the ancient academy of Jundishapur could meet in Baghdad, his counterpart from the philosophical schools of Alexandria sharing a discussion with a Turk or an Arab. The centres of power in the Muslim Empire also became centres of learning, where scholars of many cultures, religions and languages came together to exchange ideas in their shared devotion to inquiry. In addition to the capital, Baghdad, the provincial centres, such as Bukhara, Samarqand, Shiraz, Damascus, Aleppo, Cairo, Tunis, Fez, Cordova, etc., competed with each other in intellectual attainment. After the seventh Abbasid Caliph al-Mamun had established the famous House of Wisdom in Baghdad in 830, Greek gave way to Arabic as the recognized language for scientific and philosophical expression in international scholarship. Classical Greek works were translated into Arabic to support the Muslim quest for knowledge. Muslims had been actively enjoined by such *dicta* of the Prophet as 'Seek ye learning, though it be in China'. As these intellectual activities intensified in the Muslim world, Europe was passing through the so-called Dark Ages, when science was dead and theology (then 'queen of sciences') was the main preoccupation. A large part of European culture had been destroyed by the barbarian invasions; whereas only a fraction of Aristotle's work was known in Europe in the post-classical period, most of his work was translated into Arabic and keenly studied by Arab philosophers in the East. Alpharabius (al-Farabi), who died in 950, is said to have lectured on Aristotle's *Physics* forty times and his *Rhetoric* eighty times, and wrote a number of commentaries on him and other Greek philosophers. Thus, when awakening came in mediaeval Europe, the scholars first turned to the Arabs, from whom they gained a large part of the Hellenistic legacy, in the form of Arabic translations (and commentaries by Arab scholars) of the works of Aristotle, Euclid, Galen, Ptolemy and many others. These works had to be re-translated into Latin—chiefly in Spain and Sicily—before they could enrich scientific, medical and philosophical studies in Christian Europe.

The transmission function of the Arabs was important, but it must not be allowed to obscure Arab originality as evidenced by such scholars as Geber (Ibn Hayyan), al-Kindi, al-Khwarizmi, Albategnius (al-Battani), Rhazes (al-Razi), Alhazen (al-Haytham), Avicenna (Ibn Sina) and Averroes (Ibn Rushd). Much of the work of Arab scholars, after it was translated into Latin, served as text books in Europe for centuries. Avicenna's *Canon of Medicine* dominated the teaching of medical science until at least the end of the sixteenth century. It went through sixteen printed editions in the fifteenth century (one being in Hebrew), twenty editions in the sixteenth, and several more in the seventeenth. Of the works of the philosopher al-Kindi more have survived in Latin translations than in the Arabic original. It was through al-Khwarizmi's work that Arabic numerals, including zero, and important branches of mathematics—algebra and algorism (forerunner of modern arithmetic)—were introduced into Europe. The Arabic word *al-jabr,* meaning transposition, in the title of al-Khwarizmi's book became *algebra* in Latin transliteration, and his own name was distorted into algorism.

Yet the Islamic world is not homogeneous. Even in its first century there were a number of schisms, and Muslim history is not without its upheavals. There were periods of strife and periods of peace and prosperity, splits and realignments among various factions and sects, and wars with the infidel. The unity of the vast Muslim Empire remained unbroken till the fall of the

Umayyad dynasty in 750, but thereafter the peripheral parts of the empire started to break away from the centre; the first to do so was Spain in 756 and, in 800, Ifriqiya became virtually idependent under the Aghlabids. In spite of its majestic record, no Muslim state was ever again to provide unity for Islam after the tenth century; by then the process of fragmentation had become irrevocable. Yet Muslim unity has remained a cherished dream to this day.

One's perception of historical events may naturally be influenced by one's own background, which has had its impact on the writing of Islamic history as much as on history in general. The student of Islam is, therefore, faced with a mass of historical data into which have been built the biases of the writers and their own intellectual heritage. The search for a single, historical framework upon which to develop religious, political, economic or social analysis is hindered by much historical confusion and ambiguity.

This book, nevertheless, is an attempt to construct such a chronological framework, avoiding, as far as possible, any particular bias other than that of my own pursuit of objectivity. Thus, there is a focus on the known facts with a minimum of interpretation. Even in the statement of facts there is an economic use of language which betrays my background as a mathematician. As far as possible, each entry is self-contained and complete, so that the reader does not have to go through the whole to understand the events of a particular year or period. Repetition, therefore, sometimes occurs, but only when necessary in order to cross-reference information being dealt with with other happenings in the Islamic world and elsewhere. The emphasis is on dates, people involved and the exact locations of events, since some of the places no longer exist or are known by different names. Chronology is sometimes a matter of controversy; wars can be dated from the moment they are declared, yet the true date might be the first clash of arms. Generally, laws are dated by their enactment, yet it is at their vesting date that they come into effect. The signing of treatises and their dates of ratification present similar problems as do the founding of cities and the completion of buildings. The dates used here are those accepted in the most authoritative sources available; any disagreements among them are indicated. The period covered in this work ranges from the birth of the Prophet himself to the expeditions of Mahmud of Ghazna into India in the beginning of the eleventh century. The chronology is an attempt to cover the main social, intellectual and political developments in the world influenced by Islam during this period.

I am very grateful to Dr Rosemary Douglas and Dr John N. Young for their continual encouragement during the project and for reading parts of the manuscript. Generous help was given by Mr Ian Morrison of the University of Edinburgh in overcoming some of the problems encountered in putting the text on a word processor. I thank my wife, Naseem, and son, Tariq, for their support; they had, at times, to bear the inconvenience on family routines when Dad was busy doing Islam, if not doing maths. Tariq also helped me in preparing the Index.

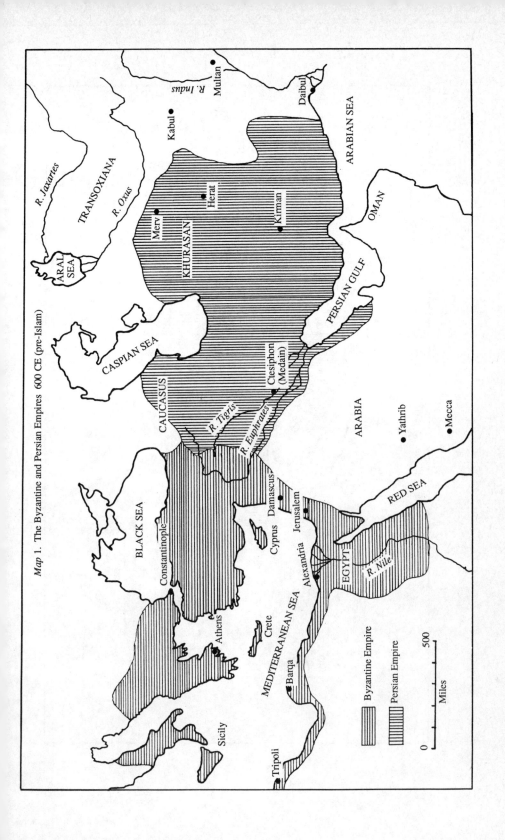

Map 1. The Byzantine and Persian Empires 600 CE (pre-Islam)

Byzantine Empire

Persian Empire

Miles

0   500

TRANSOXIANA

R. Jaxartes

R. Oxus

ARAL SEA

CASPIAN SEA

Merv

KHURASAN

Herat

Kabul

Multan

R. Indus

Daibul

ARABIAN SEA

Kirman

OMAN

PERSIAN GULF

Ctesiphon (Medain)

R. Tigris

R. Euphrates

CAUCASUS

ARABIA

Yathrib

Mecca

RED SEA

Damascus

Jerusalem

EGYPT

R. Nile

Alexandria

Cyprus

Crete

MEDITERRANEAN SEA

Barqa

Tripoli

Sicily

Athens

BLACK SEA

Constantinople

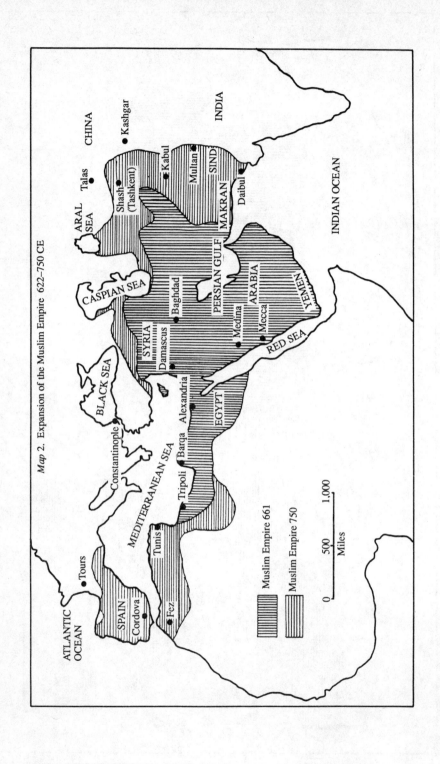

Map 2. Expansion of the Muslim Empire 622–750 CE

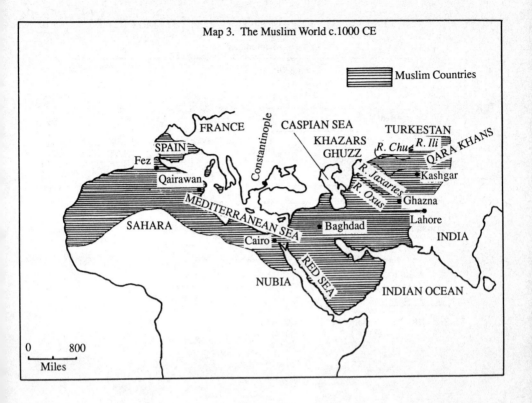

Map 3. The Muslim World c.1000 CE

Muslim Countries

FRANCE

SPAIN

Fez

Qairawan

SAHARA

MEDITERRANEAN SEA

Constantinople

CASPIAN SEA

KHAZARS

GHUZZ

TURKESTAN

R. Chu

R. Ili

QARA KHANS

Kashgar

R. Jaxartes

R. Oxus

Ghazna

Lahore

Baghdad

INDIA

Cairo

NUBIA

RED SEA

INDIAN OCEAN

0   800

Miles

Table 1. Genealogy of the Umayyads 661–750 CE

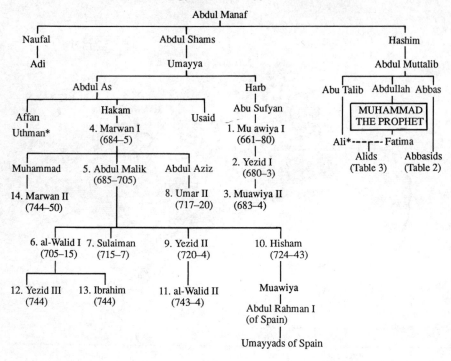

Abdul Manaf

Naufal — Abdul Shams — Hashim

Adi

Umayya

Abdul Muttalib

Abdul As — Harb

Abu Talib Abdullah Abbas

Affan   Hakam   Usaid

Uthman*   4. Marwan I
           (684–5)

Abu Sufyan

1. Mu awiya I
(661–80)

MUHAMMAD
THE PROPHET

Ali*----Fatima

Alids   Abbasids
(Table 3)   (Table 2)

Muhammad   5. Abdul Malik   Abdul Aziz
           (685–705)

2. Yezid I
(680–3)

14. Marwan II
(744–50)

8. Umar II   3. Muawiya II
(717–20)   (683–4)

6. al-Walid I 7. Sulaiman   9. Yezid II   10. Hisham
(705–15)   (715–7)   (720–4)   (724–43)

12. Yezid III   13. Ibrahim   11. al-Walid II   Muawiya
(744)   (744)   (743–4)

Abdul Rahman I
(of Spain)

Umayyads of Spain

* Orthodox or 'Rightly-guided' Caliphs: Uthman (644–56), Ali (656–61)

Table 2. Genealogy of the Abbasids 750–1258 CE

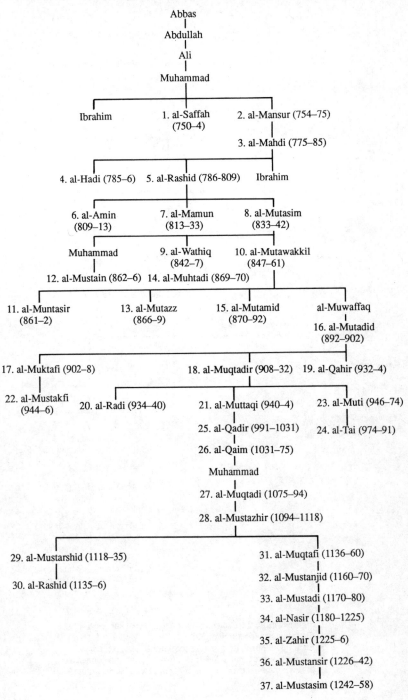

Abbas
|
Abdullah
|
Ali
|
Muhammad

Ibrahim   1. al-Saffah (750–4)   2. al-Mansur (754–75)

3. al-Mahdi (775–85)

4. al-Hadi (785–6)   5. al-Rashid (786-809)   Ibrahim

6. al-Amin (809–13)   7. al-Mamun (813–33)   8. al-Mutasim (833–42)

Muhammad   9. al-Wathiq (842–7)   10. al-Mutawakkil (847–61)

12. al-Mustain (862–6)   14. al-Muhtadi (869–70)

11. al-Muntasir (861–2)   13. al-Mutazz (866–9)   15. al-Mutamid (870–92)   al-Muwaffaq

16. al-Mutadid (892–902)

17. al-Muktafi (902–8)   18. al-Muqtadir (908–32)   19. al-Qahir (932–4)

22. al-Mustakfi (944–6)   20. al-Radi (934–40)   21. al-Muttaqi (940–4)   23. al-Muti (946–74)

25. al-Qadir (991–1031)   24. al-Tai (974–91)

26. al-Qaim (1031–75)

Muhammad

27. al-Muqtadi (1075–94)

28. al-Mustazhir (1094–1118)

29. al-Mustarshid (1118–35)   31. al-Muqtafi (1136–60)

30. al-Rashid (1135–6)   32. al-Mustanjid (1160–70)

33. al-Mustadi (1170–80)

34. al-Nasir (1180–1225)

35. al-Zahir (1225–6)

36. al-Mustansir (1226–42)

37. al-Mustasim (1242–58)

Table 3. Genealogy of the Shi'ite Imams

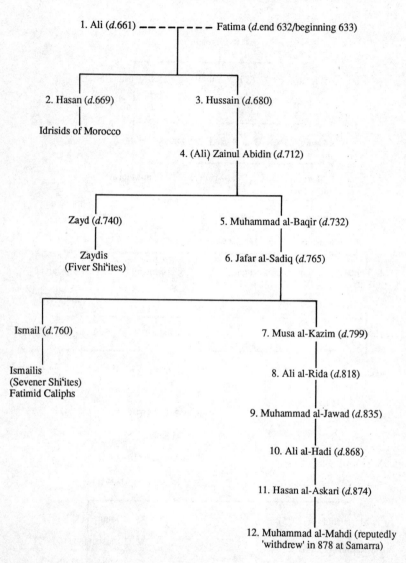

1. Ali (*d.*661) ── ── ── ── ── Fatima (*d.*end 632/beginning 633)

2. Hasan (*d.*669)   3. Hussain (*d.*680)

Idrisids of Morocco

4. (Ali) Zainul Abidin (*d.*712)

Zayd (*d.*740)   5. Muhammad al-Baqir (*d.*732)

Zaydis
(Fiver Shi'ites)   6. Jafar al-Sadiq (*d.*765)

Ismail (*d.*760)   7. Musa al-Kazim (*d.*799)

Ismailis
(Sevener Shi'ites)   8. Ali al-Rida (*d.*818)
Fatimid Caliphs

9. Muhammad al-Jawad (*d.*835)

10. Ali al-Hadi (*d.*868)

11. Hasan al-Askari (*d.*874)

12. Muhammad al-Mahdi (reputedly
'withdrew' in 878 at Samarra)

NOTES

1. Figures before the names indicate the order of succession
of the Imams of the Twelver Shi'ites.
2. Each Imam has a title, such as the Truthful, the Accepted,
the Generous, etc., and some are known by more than one name.
3. In some cases, the exact year of death cannot be ascertained.

Islamic and Christian Dating

The Muslim Calendar

The starting date of the Muslim calendar is the Hijra or migration of the Prophet Muhammad from Mecca to Yathrib (later known as Medina), about 250 miles to the north. The Prophet Muhammad left Mecca on the date corresponding to 16 July 622 CE in the Julian calendar and arrived at Medina on 22 September 622 CE. About seventeen years later, the Muslim calendar was introduced by the second Caliph, Umar ibn al-Khattab, who was faced with the practical problems of administering a rapidly expanding empire in which correspondence between distant places had to be accurately dated. The introduction of the new calendar also gave expression to the feelings of all Muslims that a new era began with the migration to Medina. Caliph Umar ordered that the Muslim calendar should be held to have begun on the day the Prophet Muhammad left Mecca, i.e., 16 July 622 CE.* In English this is usually abbreviated in the Latin form AH (Anno Hegirae: 'in the year of the Hijra'.)

The Muslim year is purely lunar, consisting of twelve months containing, in alternate sequence, thirty and twenty-nine days. Thus it is approximately eleven days shorter than the solar year, with the result that in each cycle of 32.5 years, the individual months pass through all the solar seasons. If, for example, the Hajj (which takes place in the last month of the Muslim calendar) occurs at the height of summer, it will occur in the coolest season 16.25 years later, and the same time in summer again after another 16.25 years.

The twelve months forming the Muslim year are known as Muharram, Safar, Rabi I, Rabi II, Jumada I, Jumada II, Rajab, Shaaban, Ramadan, Shawwal,

1

Dhu al-Qada and Dhu al-Hijja. Thus, 16 July 622 CE was officially declared as 1 Muharram AH 1.

The common year, therefore, has 354 days. But the mean length of a lunar year is 354 days, 8 hours, 48 minutes, 36 seconds, and the period of mean lunation is 29 days, 12 hours, 44 minutes, 3 seconds. This difference of 8 hours, 48 minutes, 36 seconds (which is almost equal to 11/30th of a day), by which the astronomical lunar year is the longer, is compensated by the intercalation of eleven days in every cycle of thirty years at the stated intervals. The most commonly used method of intercalation is to make years 2, 5, 7, 10, 13, 16, 18, 21, 24, 26 and 29 in the cycle into leap years, called *kabisha*. The intercalary day itself is always added to the twelfth month, i.e., the month of Dhu al-Hijja which has twenty-nine days in the common year—in a kabisha year it has 30 days. Thus, to determine whether a Muslim year is common or kabisha, divide it by 30. If the remainder is 2, 5, 7, 10, 13, 16, 18, 21, 24, 26 or 29, the year is kabisha, having 355 days; otherwise, it is a common year consisting of 354 days. AH 1400 gives a remainder 20 and is a common year. AH 1406 (remainder 26) is a kabisha year.

The day in the Muslim calendar is twenty-four hours in length. However, it is reckoned to commence not from midnight (as in the Christian calendar) but from the sunset preceding it, because the first day of the month is fixed by the first sight of the new moon observed at sunset. As a result, the Muslim and Christian days do not cover exactly the same twenty-four hours, which can lead to an incorrect dating of an event if this difference is overlooked.

Although in modern times mathematically calculated calendars are widely available and used, some Muslims still use the ancient practice of actually observing the new moon to establish the beginning of a month, especially the fasting month of Ramadan and the following month of Shawwal.

The Christian Calendar

In the Christian or Julian calendar, named after Julius Caesar, who introduced it at the suggestion of the Egyptian astronomer Sosigenes as a reform of the old Roman calendar, the years are reckoned from the birth of Christ, and so are known as years AD (Anno Domini: 'in the year of the Lord'), or simply CE (Common Era) as non-Christian usage in place of AD. It fixed the average length of the year as 365.25 days, each fourth year being a Leap year, making up the omitted quarters by having 366 days. The new calendar officially began on 1 January 45 BCE.

Since the time which the earth takes to complete its orbit is 365 days, 5 hours, 48 minutes and 46 seconds, in the Julian calendar a year was about eleven minutes longer than a solar year. The resulting cumulative error became about ten days by the close of the sixteenth century, which was rectified in 1582 by Pope Gregory XIII, who ordained that 5 October in that year be called 15

October. In order to prevent further accumulation of error, he also ordered that while each year divisible by four should contain 366 days, as in the Julian calendar, centenary years should be counted as Leap years only if they are divisible by 400. Thus, 1600 was a Leap year but not 1700, 1800 or 1900, while 2000 CE will be a Leap year. It is this modified version, known as the Gregorian calendar, which is in use now. Different countries adopted the calendar at different times. Great Britain (including her Dominions), for instance, did not adopt it until 1752, by which time she found herself eleven days behind the rest of Europe which was rectified by 3 September being reckoned as 14 September. It was adopted by Japan in 1872, China in 1912, Turkey and Soviet Russia in 1918, and by Greece as late as 1923.

Conversion Formulae

To ascertain an approximate date of the commencement of a given Gregorian year (CE) in relation to Hijra year (AH), subtract 622.5643 from CE and then multiply the resultant figure by 1.030684:

$$AH = 1.030684 \, (CE - 622.5643)$$

Likewise, to convert a Hijra to Gregorian year, multiply AH by 0.970229 and then add 621.5643 to it:

$$CE = 0.970229 \, AH + 621.5643$$

As an illustration of the second formula, consider AH 1408; $1408 \times 0.970229 + 621.5643 = 1987.6467$, the decimals corresponding to seven months and twenty-four days, i.e., 24 August. The year AH 1408, in fact, began on 26 August 1987.

The following chronology is given according to the Gregorian calendar, but it can be converted into the Muslim calendar by using the first formula. However, there is no simple one-to-one correspondence between the Christian and Muslim years, because the beginnings of the two types of years do not coincide and are of different lengths. In general, the Muslim year overlaps parts of two consecutive Christian years: AH 133 began on 9 August 750 CE and ended on 29 July 751 CE. In the primary sources on Islamic history, dates are given according to the Muslim era. In the present chronology, the convention has been followed that, when only the Muslim year is known, the Christian year in which it began is regarded as the equivalent.

*There is a doubt about the date on which the Prophet Muhammad left Mecca, and according to some traditions, this date was chosen not because it was the date of the

Prophet's departure but because it was the first day of the Arab year in which the Hijra took place.

Chronology

570

The Birth of Muhammad

The Prophet Muhammad was born in Mecca of the Hashim clan, belonging to the tribe of Quraish. His mother, Amina, was the daughter of Wahb, and his father was Abdullah, who died before his birth. He came under the care of his paternal grandfather Abdul Muttalib, who was about seventy years old. At the age of six, he lost his mother. After the death of his grandfather, when Muhammad was eight years old, he was entrusted to his uncle, Abu Talib, who had become the new head of the clan, and grew up in his home.

The Byzantine and Persian Empires Bordering Arabia

After the death of Emperor Theodosius I in 395, the Roman Empire was partitioned into western and eastern halves between his sons Honorius and Arcadius respectively. In 476, however, the western Roman Empire collapsed, abandoning Britain, Gaul, Spain and part of Italy to the barbarians. In contrast, the eastern half of the empire, comprising the wealthier and more civilized provinces of Greece, Egypt, Syria and Asia Minor, was not only able to sustain the loss of the West but had flourished independently since then. The eastern Roman, or Byzantine, Empire had its capital at Byzantium (Constantinople). The other Great Power was Persia, and the boundary between the two ran from the Caucasus to the Upper Euphrates (roughly coinciding with the present border separating Turkey and Syria from Persia and Iraq), leaving the Arabian Peninsula in the south sharing frontiers with both empires: the Byzantine on the north-west and the Persian on the north-east. The Arabian Peninsula, which is mostly tractless desert, is the largest in the world. The capital of the Persian Empire was at the ancient city of Ctesiphon (known as Medain in Arabic) on the Tigris, some twenty miles south-east of the site where the city of Baghdad was later to be founded in 762.

The Byzantine Empire was founded on Roman law and administration, Greek language and civilization and Christian religion and moral values. The Church played a powerful role but it also became a weakening factor in the Empire because of the dogmatic conflict of Christology within it. Greek became the official language of the Roman Empire during the reign of the Emperor Heraclius (r. 610–41); Christianity was made the state religion by the Emperor Theodosius I (r. 379–95). Constantine I (r. 306–37), the first Christian Roman Emperor, had, of course, already paved the way for a Christian state by a number of important steps such as the Edict of Milan in 313, declaring Sunday as a rest day in 321, presiding over the ecumenical Council of Nicaea in 325, and founding Constantinople (formerly Byzantium) in 330 as a Christian city and his permanent capital. But, contrary to a common belief, he did not make Christianity the religion of the Empire, which was done later by Theodosius I. Constantine himself was baptized shortly before his death.

Mecca, Centre of Caravan Trade Route

There had been a long struggle for territory between the two mighty and rival empires, the Byzantine and the Persian or Sasanid (Zoroastrian), as a result of which the overland trade routes through Persia had been broken. An alternative route, though not a direct one, had been found through Arabia for trade between the East and the Mediterranean. A part of this route was by sea to the Yemen port of Adan and a part overland to Damascus and Gaza, via Mecca, along the west coast of the peninsula. There was extensive caravan trade between Yemen and the markets of Syria, and Mecca, which was a staging post, became a prosperous commercial centre and the metropolis of Arabia. It also had a sanctuary called the Kaba, which was famous throughout Arabia and assured the safety of those who came to buy and sell at the trade fairs held there. The Kaba, a pagan shrine at that time, is an almost cubical building with the Black Stone embedded in one corner. It attracted a large number of pilgrims to perform idolatrous rites. In this way, the shrine, situated a few steps away from the famous spring Zamzam, played an important role in the economic and commercial life of Mecca which was run by a small group of rich merchants.

Geography and Chief Clans of Mecca

Mecca itself stood in a narrow, barren valley, surrounded by steep, bare hills. Its food supply came from the fertile fields of Taif, a town forty miles to the south-east. Water was also scarce, its main source of supply being the Zamzam, although there were other wells located outside the town. The free air of the open desert was thought to be healthier than the suffocating heat of this dusty and congested little town. It was, therefore, a widespread custom for people to give their children to be suckled by women of the neighbouring tribes in the desert. Muhammad thus spent his early childhood in the care of a woman of the Sa'd tribe outside Mecca, after which he returned to his mother, but she died within a year, leaving him an orphan.

Mecca was inhabited mainly by the tribe of Quraish, which consisted of, among others, two prominent clans—the Hashim, headed by Abdul Muttalib, and the Umayya. The Hashim clan was entrusted with the duties related to the maintenance of the Kaba and the management of the Pilgrimage, while the Umayya clan had the hereditary leadership in war. It was in the exercise of this last right that the shrewd Abu Sufyan (d. circa 652), leader of the Umayya clan, had overall command of the Meccan forces against the Muslims in later battles. The two clans were great rivals and this later became a dividing force in the choice of a successor to the Prophet Muhammad. Both clans were engaged in trade, the Umayya clan much more so than the Hashim.

Christians and Jews in Arabia

After Christianity became the official religion of the Roman Empire in the fourth century, it began to penetrate Arabia, slowly, but still posing a challenge to Arabian paganism. However, in the succeeding centuries, the Byzantine Orthodox Church no longer remained a religious unit but was bitterly divided into mutually hostile groups differing in their interpretation of the Incarnation. The Nestorian Christians were persecuted and driven out of the Roman Empire altogether in the middle of the fifth century. These Greek refugees were welcomed in Persia as victims of the Byzantines, whom the Persians regarded as their main enemies. The Nestorians conducted a vigorous missionary campaign along the Euphrates and the northern part of the Persian Gulf and succeeded in converting many Arabs in those regions. Even the last ruler of the Arab Lakhmid dynasty, Numan III (r. circa 580–605), who ruled the north-eastern periphery of Arabia, became a Nestorian Christian. On the north-western side, the Ghassan Arab, tribe living along the border with Syria, had also become Christian by the middle of the sixth century, but they professed Monophysite Christianity, which was condemned as heretical by the Orthodox Church and bitterly opposed by the Nestorians.

In fact, both the Persian and Byzantine Empires maintained the Arab satellite states of Lakhm and Ghassan respectively to protect their open southern flanks from Bedouin attacks. The Lakhmids and the Ghassanids were recognized as clients by these governments around the years 300 and 500 respectively. These rival tribes not only provided buffer states for their respective paymasters, but also engaged themselves in endless desert warfare, carrying out raids against each other. Christian communities were also founded in Yemen and Najran. In addition to the Christians, there were many much older Jewish colonies in Arabia, found mainly in Yemen and Khaybar. There were three clans in Mecca who professed the Jewish faith. Thus, while the tribes of the peninsula were still pagan and worshipped idols, Judaism and Christainity had already established a foothold in the peninsula and penetrated some communities, particularly along the fringes of the desert.

An Abyssinian Attempt to Destroy the Kaba

Abraha, the Christian Abyssinian governor of Yemen, invaded Hijaz in 570 but retreated in disarray from a place a few miles from Mecca, abandoning the original aim of the expedition, which was to destroy the Kaba. Abraha himself died on returning to the Yemenite capital, Sana. Thus the Kaba was saved, which was regarded as the fulfilment of the prayer which its Keeper and Muhammad's grandfather, Abdul Muttalib, had made to God to defend His own House.*

It is this incident which is referred to in sura ('The Elephant') 105 in the Quran, so-called because of an elephant being present in the Axumite army. The Arabs of Hijaz were greatly impressed, because they had never seen an elephant before. So much importance is given to this event that the year 570 is described as the 'Year of the Elephant' in some Arab chronicles.

574

The Capture of Yemen by the Persians

The Abyssinians were expelled from Yemen by the Persians after fifty-two years of occupation, and Yemen came under Persian rule.

581

Exposure of Byzantine Border to Arabia

The ruling Prince of the Ghassan tribe, being a Monophysite Christian, was arrested and taken to Constantinople for alleged treason. The Byzantines withdrew their recognition of the Ghassan dynasty, which had been living along the Syrian border and protecting it in return for a subsidy and other privileges. This left the tribe in defiance and the desert border exposed to Bedouin attacks from Arabia.

595

Muhammad's Marriage to Khadija

At the age of twenty-five, Muhammad married Khadija, a forty-year-old wealthy widow, who was his only wife until her death in 619. This gave him financial security, enabling him to pursue his own inclinations, which included long periods of introspection in solitude and involvement in trade. They had two sons, who died in infancy, and four daughters named Zaynab, Ruqayya, Fatima and Umm Kulthum. Of these, Ruqayya married Uthman ibn Affan and Fatima married the Prophet's cousin Ali ibn Abi Talib; Uthman and Ali later became the third (644–56) and fourth (656–61) Caliphs respectively. Muhammad was survived only by Fatima (d. end 632/beginning 633), and her marriage to Ali was of lasting importance, since the Prophet's descendants from this line have been especially revered. The Shi'ites were later to look upon the descendants of Ali and Fatima as the true heirs to the Caliphate.

605

Exposure of Persian Border to Arabia

Numan III, the Lakhmid ruler, quarrelled with the Persian Chosroes, who abolished the privileges which had been enjoyed by his family in return for defending the desert frontier. As a result, the Arab tribes along the Euphrates rebelled against the Persians and left the border with Arabia unguarded. The same had happened previously in 581 along the Syrian border of the Byzantines.

610

Muhammad's Call to Prophethood

In the seclusion of a little cave on Mount Hira outside Mecca, Muhammad had his first revelation through the angel Gabriel that he was the Prophet of God. This was the beginning of the new faith, Islam, which means 'surrender' (to the Will of God). The first group of people who were converted to a belief in his preaching were his wife Khadija, his ten-year-old cousin Ali ibn Abi Talib, the ex-slave but now adopted son Zayd ibn Haritha, and his friend Abu Bakr.* This new faith attracted intense hostility from the local pagan community, especially from those with wealth and position, because its teaching, although basically religious, criticized implicitly the conduct and attitude of the rich merchants who had a complete monopoly in Mecca. They equated the success of the new faith with their own downfall. Consequently, the converts were subjected to contempt and ostracism by their fellow citizens.

*The Sunnis and the Shi'ites differ with each other, out of dynastic considerations on the sequence of these Believers.

615

Emigration of First Muslims to Abyssinia

As a result of persecution, some eighty Meccan Muslims emigrated to Abyssinia (Ethiopia) to take refuge with the Christians there, who disliked the pagans of Mecca.* The party included Uthman ibn Affan, the future third Caliph (644–56), and his wife Ruqayya, the Prophet Muhammad's daughter, but the Prophet himself stayed behind in Mecca to continue preaching in the face of fierce opposition.

The Negus of Abyssinia treated them with consideration, allowed them to practise their religion and refused to hand them over to their oppressors, who demanded their return. This had an influence on the Prophet Muhammad's future attitude towards the Christians, who were termed the 'People of the Book' and were accorded special treatment. The tradition was to be followed in subsequent times by the Prophet's successors in their treatment of a subject population of different faiths in the conquered territories.**

*According to some records, the emigration took place in two groups, one after the other, with an interval of about two months. The first group consisted of fifteen people and the second one of ahundred.

**The Prophet distinguished between mere pagans and the possessors of a revealed (or holy) scripture. The latter included Christians and Jews, who were promised protection and allowed to practise their religion if they submitted without fighting and payed a poll-tax at a prescribed rate.

616

Umar's Acceptance of Islam

The conversion to Islam of Umar ibn al-Khattab, Muhammad's bitter opponent and a forceful personality in Mecca, took place. He later became the second Caliph (634–44).

619

The Death of Khadija; Muhammad's Unsuccessful Visit to Taif

The Prophet suffered two personal misfortunes; Khadija and Abu Talib, the Prophet's uncle and protector, both died. Although Abu Talib never accepted Islam, he always stood in defence of his cousin, whom he had brought up in his own home. Now, another uncle, Abu Lahab, succeeded as head of Muhammad's clan, but he withdrew the clan's protection from him. As a result, Muhammad, accompanied only by his adopted son Zayd ibn Haritha, left for Taif, a town forty miles south-east of Mecca, but failed to find the support he had hoped for. Instead, he was subjected to public scorn and ridicule, and decided to return to Mecca dejected but determined to carry on with his mission.

The 'Night Journey'

Muhammad's reputed 'Nocturnal Journey' (The *Miraj*) took place from Mecca to Jerusalem and thence to the Seventh Heaven. He was charged with the command that all Muslims were to offer prayer five times a day.

620

Muhammad's Marriage to Aisha

The Prophet Muhammad married Aisha*, daughter of a close friend and rich merchant, Abu Bakr.** Aisha later played an active role in the choice of successors to the Caliphate. Together with two prominent Meccans, Talha ibn Abdullah and Zubair ibn al-Awwam, she strongly opposed Ali's succession as the fourth Caliph (see **656**, Battle of the Camel).

*Apart from Aisha, all the Prophet's other wives were widows and seem to have been chosen for political reasons. For twenty-five years he was married only to his first wife, Khadija, who was considerably older than himself. All his remaining marriages took place in his fifties and after Khadija's death.
**According to some historical sources, the marriage was not consummated until after the Hijra in 622.

622

The Hijra; Beginning of the Muslim Era

At the age of fifty-two, the Prophet Muhammad secretly migrated to the fertile northern oasis of Yathrib, which was not on the caravan trade route from southern Arabia to the north. This was the famous Hijra. Some Muslims had already left for Abyssinia to escape persecution, but it was largely unknown territory to them. On the annual Pilgrimage to the Kaba (still a pagan shrine) about seventy inhabitants of Yathrib had accepted Islam and invited Muhammad to their city, where he and his followers would be given sanctuary. Before his own departure, his followers, some seventy in all, had already, on his instructions, left Mecca for Yathrib in small groups, eluding the vigilance of the Quraish.

   The people of Yathrib received with enthusiasm the Prophet and his Meccan followers, who had abandoned their homes for the sake of their new faith. To mark the occasion, the ancient name of the city was changed to Medinat un-Nabi (the City of the Prophet) or Medina, for short. The inhabitants of Medina proved to be far more receptive than the Meccans had been to Muhammad's teaching, and soon the Medinese Muslims (termed by the Prophet 'the Helpers') greatly exceeded the Meccan immigrants in numbers. He severed kinship ties in Mecca and started a new life as the leader of a religious community, acknowledged to possess divine authority. Here he settled and built his house, which served as a gathering place for his followers and as a model for a mosque which would later be built on the site.* The Hijra proved to be a decisive event in the life of Muhammad and the development of Islam. A part of the population of Medina was Jewish.

The Prophet's Mosque in Medina is the second holiest shrine of Islam, next in sanctity to the Kaba in Mecca.

624

The Battle of Badr

Muhammad decided to hit the Meccans where they were most vulnerable. Their whole economic life was dependent on camel caravans with the main trade centres in the north. Thus, if he were successful in making these trade routes unsafe, he would not only have an economic stranglehold on the Meccans but it would bring badly needed booty for his followers, who had migrated to a new place leaving their possessions behind.

In command of little more than 300 Muslim converts, he went out in the middle of March to a place called Badr to attack a Meccan caravan which was being led by the head of the Umayya clan, Abu Sufyan. It was on its return journey from Syria. Badr, a small town about eighty-five miles south-west of Medina, was on the caravan route connecting Mecca and Damascus. Abu Sufyan skilfully eluded the Muslims by devious routes and led the caravan to safety. But a force was rushed from Mecca to defend the caravan. It consisted of 950 men with 700 camels and 100 horses, led by Abu Jahl, the Prophet's uncle and head of the Mukhzum clan, who decided to seek a real fight. In the ensuing battle, at least 45 Meccans, including Abu Jahl and many other leading Meccans, were killed and about 70 taken prisoner, while the Muslims lost 14 killed.

The complete victory for the Muslims, though outnumbered by three to one, in this battle was a milestone in the early history of Islam. This was the first time that the young Muslim community became conscious of its own striking power, which was destined in the years to come to grow into an unstoppable avalanche. The event took on an immense religious significance, too, since, according to the Quran*, God himself helped the Believers in sustaining the cause of Islam. The Prophet Muhammad recognized it as a divine vindication of his mission. As a consequence, it brought new converts and increased the prestige of the Muslim community.

Reference to the name Badr is made in sura ('The Imrans') 3:123. Indirect references to this battle also appear in the Quran in some other suras.

Change of *Qibla* to Mecca

The *Qibla*, the direction to which the Muslims turn in praying, was changed from Jerusalem to the Kaba in Mecca.

Fatima's Marriage to Ali

The Prophet Muhammad's daughter, Fatima, was married to his cousin and future Caliph (656–661) Ali ibn Abi Talib.*

According to some historical accounts, the marriage took place after the battle of Uhad in 625.

625

The Battle of Uhad

To avenge the year old defeat in the Battle of Badr and also to make their trade route safe, the Meccans mobilized about 3,000 men and entered the oasis of Medina in the month of March. In response, Muhammad could muster a force of about 700 only, and a pitched battle took place near the hill of Uhad, about three miles to the north of Medina. The Muslims repelled the Meccan infantry at first but were then thrown into disarray by a sudden attack from the rear led by Khalid ibn al-Walid. This was the first time that Khalid, who was later to become the most famous of all Arab generals, displayed his brilliant talent for leadership on the battlefield. The Prophet himself was wounded, which added to the confusion. Yet strangely enough, the Meccans, who were again commanded by Abu Sufyan, did not pursue their advantageous position by attacking the town itself, which remained undefended; instead, they marched towards home. Perhaps they only wanted to prove their chivalry or simply teach the enemy a hard lesson. Whatever the reason, the battle did not produce a clear victor or loser. The Muslims and the Meccans lost 70 and about 20 men respectively. The Prophet lamented the death of his uncle Hamza, a great hunter and mighty warrior, whose body was mutilated by Abu Sufyan's wife Hind as an act of revenge for her father whom Hamza had killed at Badr.

627

The Battle of the Ditch

Medina was besieged by a Meccan army of 10,000, perhaps the largest force ever seen in Arabia, under Abu Sufyan who had now become Muhammad's arch-enemy. Repeated attempts to cross a trench, especially dug to protect the town, failed and the army drifted away after about a fortnight. This was partly due to the Meccans' lack of knowledge of regular warfare involving long seiges, and partly due to bad weather conditions and falling supplies. Another factor was the dissension in the invading army, skilfully fomented by Muhammad's agents, in this long and restive seige. Muhammad had a wide and efficient intelligence network which he always employed in planning his strategy. The numbers killed on both sides added up to no more than ten. The Prophet Muhammad's position was greatly strengthened by this outcome, which he used as a clear demonstration of the impregnability of his city, where he had established his civil and religious authority. The Meccans had pooled all their resources in arranging this vast army, but their efforts to dislodge or destroy Muhammad had obviously failed. And both their trade and prestige had suffered badly.

628

The Pact of Hudaybiya

In February, the Prophet led a group of about 1,600 men, intending to perform the Pilgrimage at Mecca, but was prevented from doing so. After some negotiations, a pact was drawn up at Hudaybiya (which later came to bear its name), a settlement about ten miles west of the town. Although some of the leading Muslims were not satisfied with the final outcome, Muhammad did get a number of concessions from the Meccans regarding the right for him and his followers to make the Pilgrimage in the following year. This was yet another indication of the weakening resolve of the Prophet's old adversaries to oppose him.

One of the most significant consequence of the Prophet's increasing prestige at this point in time was the conversion of Khalid ibn al-Walid (d. 641) and Amr ibn al-As (d. 663), who later proved themselves to be the greatest military commanders of the Muslims. They took part in many famous victories crucial to the expansion of the Islamic empire. At about the same time, the hereditary custodian of the keys of the idol shrine, the Kaba, also became Muslim, which gave a political boost to the missionaries of the new Faith.

Conclusion of Perso-Byzantine Peace

Chosroes Parwiz, who had come to the Sasanid throne in 590, was assassinated and peace was concluded in 628 between the Persians and the Byzantines after twenty-six years of devastating wars. The two forces pulled back to the old frontiers, and neither side, in the end, gained any new territory in this long and costly conflict which had left both sides utterly exhausted militarily and financially. The wars had brought heavy taxation on the subject populations in the two empires and had undermined their loyalty to their oppressive and alien overlords. This resentment among the populace later helped the conquering Arabs, who, though untrained and ill-equipped, were completely dedicated to spreading their religion.

629

Conversion of Abbas to Islam

While Muhammad was in Mecca for the pilgrimage, his uncle, Abbas (d. 652) accepted Islam. The descendents of Abbas later established the second Islamic dynasty, the Abbasid (750–1258).

630

The Fall of Mecca; the Dedication of the Kaba as the Symbol of Islam

Now the tide had turned and Mecca was in decline with no competent leader. After the humiliating failure of their siege of Medina, they lost the will and the strength to fight. Muhammad marched on Mecca, his birthplace which drove him into exile eight years earlier, with 10,000 men and the city surrendered with virtually no resistance.

Muhammad, instead of being vindictive, ordered a general amnesty from which only four or five persons were excluded. The Prophet won over the Meccans by showing magnanimity on the day of triumph even to those who had persecuted him in the past. This led to a large number of local people accepting Islam. Idols kept in the Kaba (said to have numbered 360) were destroyed, and it became no longer a pagan shrine. Instead, the Kaba was dedicated afresh to the worship of the One and Only God, according to the new Faith, and from now on it became the spiritual centre of Islam.

The Kaba

The structure of the present Kaba (lit. 'cube'), located in the centre of the courtyard of the Great Mosque in Mecca, is approximately 40 feet long, 35 feet wide and 50 feet high, with the Black Stone built into the south-eastern corner near its door, which is about seven feet above the ground level. It dates back to 683, when Abdullah ibn Zubair rebuilt it. Apart from some alterations carried out by Hajjaj ibn Yusuf in 693, the building has survived in this form to the present day. It is the holiest shrine and 'religious pole' of the Islamic Faith; Muslims all over the world orient themselves toward it during prayer, bury their dead facing its meridian, and cherish the ambition of visiting it on a Pilgrimage.

The Black Stone—the exposed side of which is an oval shape a little more than a span across—is set in a thick silver casing of oval shape. The sacred rock is the only remaining relic from the building which existed in the Prophet Muhammad's time. The silver casing protrudes from the building about five feet from the ground, a convenient height for the pilgrims to kiss, touch or otherwise greet the Black Stone during their ritual circumambulation of the Kaba.

Acceptance of Islam by Abu Sufyan

Abu Sufyan, the Prophet's most feared opponent, made his peace with Muhammad and accepted Islam. His son, Muawiya, became one of the secretaries of the Prophet, and later (661) the first Caliph of the Umayyad dynasty (661–750).

Muhammad returned to Medina, where he continued to live for the rest of his life.

632

The Death of Muhammad

By now, the Prophet Muhammad had united a larger part of Arabia than anyone had done before, and pagan cults died out as the number of converts to Islam increased everywhere. He led a Pilgrimage to the Kaba in the month of March, in a form according to Islamic belief. Three months after returning to

Medina from what was later to be called his 'Farewell Pilgrimage', he fell ill and died on 8 June.

Abu Bakr as First Caliph

The Prophet's death took the Believers completely by surprise and created uncertainty about the future. No arrangements had been made for his succession*, and it was the first main problem the Muslim community had to face without its leader. Abu Bakr, the Prophet's father-in-law (through the marriage of Aisha) and his closest friend, was nominated to lead the prayers. He was two years younger than the Prophet, and was elected the first Caliph or 'successor' (632–4). However, it was understood that the Caliph would succeed only to the temporal role of the Prophet and that he could in no way claim those powers of Divine Revelation which belonged only to the latter. The Caliph's relation to the religion would be no more than that of a guardian.

Apostasy Overcome

Many Arabs had come to associate the new religion with Muhammad personally, and to them he had become the symbol of Islam. This fact was demonstrated in a number of tribes renouncing their allegiance soon after his death. Moreover, he did not live long enough to consolidate the Bedouin tribes into a nation, and loyalties were still divided on tribal lines. During his lifetime, he managed to establish the new community of Muslims on the basis of religion rather than tribal kinship, but the idea had not taken deep root, and nomadic instincts reasserted themselves. This presented itself as the most challenging problem to Abu Bakr, threatening to destroy all that the Prophet had achieved in a remarkably short time. Most of the early period of Abu Bakr's reign was taken up in administrating the new-born Muslim state and at the same time dealing with these revolts against Medina's rule in different parts of Arabia. In addition to these political and economic revolts (some tribes refused to pay the *zakat*, or poor tax), there were uprisings to become known as 'wars of apostasy', led by false 'prophets'. The success of the Prophet Muhammad's mission had inspired many people with ambition, and several pretenders claiming to have a divine mission had arisen. The most notable of these was Musailima of the tribe of Hanifa in Yamama in central Arabia. He had a large following of his own tribe and, through his wife Saja, of the neighbouring tribe of Tamim. Musailima, however, was quelled in January 633 by an army under Khalid ibn al-Walid. Other such revolts were also put down and eventually the whole of Arabia was united, by the prudence of Abu Bakr and the sword of Khalid, under the rule of the first Caliph.

According to a Shi'ite Tradition, the Prophet had nomimated his cousin and son-in-law, Ali ibn Abi Talib, as his successor.

The Accession of Yazdijird III

In the period of anarchy and civil war following the murder of Chosroes Parwiz by his son and successor Siroes in 628, there had been a number of quick successions to the Persian throne. As a result, the empire was badly shaken in the absence of any strong government. Soon after the Prophet's death, Yazdijird III (d. 651), a boy of fifteen, was made king of Persia, which included Iraq* and was one of the greatest powers of the world.** The new king, though a mere youth, managed to command the loyalty of most of the princes and generals and started to reorganize the state and the army. It was during his reign that the Muslims overthrew the Persian Empire, he being the last ruler of the Sasanid dynasty.

Iraq at that time was the southern part of the Euphrates-Tigris basin, i.e., lower Mesopotamia, and much smaller than the modern state of Iraq.
**Some historical accounts give the date of Yazdijird's enthronment as two years later.*

633

The Surrender of Hira

Muthanna ibn Haritha, a new convert to Islam after the Prophet's death, from the north-eastern Arab tribe called Bakr, was sent on a campaign in Iraq with Khalid ibn al-Walid and later took over the command. After the victory in the so-called Battle of the River of Blood at Ullais (near modern Samawah in Iraq), the two Muslim generals gave the enemy no respite and Hira was captured in May with only a small and, in part, locally recruited force. Hira was a Persian outpost but largely inhabited by Arabs, and an important city in Iraq. It was also the first aquisition of the Muslim ouside the Arabian Peninsula. Hira was spared military occupation and its Arab inhabitants were allowed to remain Nestorian Christians (this sect was bitterly hostile to the Monophysite form of Christianity prevailing among the Egyptians, Syrians and Abyssinians) on payment of a large sum of money. Next year Khalid was suddenly ordered to go and take over command of the Muslim armies in Syria who needed help, and Muthanna was left behind in charge of the campaign on the Persian front.

The Military Expedition to Syria and Palestine

While the campaign in Iraq against the Sasanids was going on, at home major apostasy was stamped out by the revolting tribes being brought under control. Abu Bakr now turned his attention to the conquest of Syria and Palestine on the Byzantine frontier which he regarded as more important. Through their commercial activities, the Arabs were much more familiar with, and interested in, this region than Persia, which was largely unknown to them. Even the Prophet Muhammad in his lifetime showed interest in it and sent an expedition under his adopted son, Zayd ibn Haritha, to the Syrian border in 629. But the vastly superior Byzantine army had no difficulty in crushing the raw soldiers of early Islam. Zayd died fighting, and the expedition ended in disaster.

In 633, Abu Bakr organized three armies of 3,000 soldiers each and put them under the command of Yezid ibn Abi Sufyan (his father, Abu Sufyan, the Meccan leader in many battles against the Muslims, was then governor of Najran and Hijaz), Shurahbil ibn Hasana and Amr ibn al-As (who was later to become famous for his conquest of Egypt in 640–2 and three times its governor). The first two columns entered Jordan, while Amr led his troops to south-eastern Palestine, and near Gaza he annihilated in February a small army under the local governor, Sergius.

634

The Battle of Ajnadain

After the defeat near Gaza, the Byzantine Emperor Heraclius (r. 610–41) realized the seriousness of the situation and sent down a large amry. Abu Bakr heard about it, and it was at this point that Khalid ibn al-Walid was recalled from Iraq and ordered to rush to the aid of his fellow-generals on the Syrian front. He was to become famous for a perilous eighteen-day march with 900 warriors from Iraq across the waterless and trackless desert of Syria to Damascus. Khalid appeared unexpectedly, assumed supreme command of the army in Jordan and then came to Amr's help. The Byzantine army and the combined Muslim armies met in July at Ajnadain, some thirty miles south-west of Jerusalem, and the Byzantines were decisively beaten. Their army was completely destroyed; only a few escaped with their chief and found refuge within the walls of heavily garrisoned Jerusalem. But a large number of other towns submitted one after another and practically the whole of Palestine was laid open to the Muslim army.

The Accession of Umar to the Caliphate

Shortly after the victory at Ajnadain, Caliph Abu Bakr died on 23 August at the age of sixty-two and was buried beside the Prophet Muhammad. He was succeeded by Umar ibn al-Khattab, another father-in-law of the Prophet (through the marriage of Hafsa), as the second Caliph (634–44), with the additional title of Amir al-Mu'minin, meaning 'Commander of the Faithful' or 'Prince of the Believers'. The distinctive title became a permanent designation for future Caliphs for the next thirteen centuries.*

He belonged to the politically unimportant Meccan clan of Adi ibn Kab, but was a man of strong determination, a keen sense of duty and a remarkable gift for administration. Umar's accession to the Caliphate turned out to be of immense value to Islam. Throughout his reign of ten years of expanding empire, he remained a man of sincere religious convictions, deep personal humility and extreme austerity. He made up for his lack of experience in dealing with the practical problems of government by shrewd judgement of men and motives, and political acumen. However, being an authoritarian, he was feared rather than loved. He laid the foundations of what was later to become the classical Islamic state, the glorious decade of his rule seeing the first phase of its vast expansion before the Umayyads (661–750) expanded it still further.

The Foundation of the New Administration

The conquest of foreign lands was a new experience for the Muslims and raised the important question for the second Caliph of deciding for the first time on what principles the conquered territories were to be governed. He had to pronounce on many fundamental issues encountered for the first time, and his innovative decisions set precedents for his successors. Under Umar, the primitive Arabs took on simultaneously the two ancient and most powerful empires of the time, the Persian in the east and the Byzantine in the west. The former was overthrown while the latter suffered crushing defeats at the hands of the Arabs, losing a number of its territories.

Umar established a highly developed fiscal system in which the public treasury raised its revenue through various forms of taxation including personal and land, and administered a register of those entitled to a state pension. It included the relatives of the Prophet Muhammad, those who had served the cause of Islam and the soldiers with their wives and children. Previously, the tithes and the spoils of war had been distributed directly among those entitled to them, as and when they had come into the treasury.

This system of distribution was found to be unwieldy in practice and was now commuted to fixed allowances. In this way, he established for the first time the principle that it was the state's duty to provide for these groups of people.

The conquered territories were divided into compact provinces so that their resources could be developed separately under their respective governors, who were appointed by the Caliph. But he retained the old political divisions, currency and machinery of civil administration; the Muslim law now prevailed everywhere, but only for Muslims. The non-Muslims were dealt with according to their own laws and by their own religious leaders who were also responsible for collecting and paying the communities' taxes to the government. Greek, Coptic, Persian and to a less extent Aramaic-Syriac were retained as the languages of administration in different provinces of the empire. In order to prevent contact between the conquering troops and the local population, he ordered the former to live in camps outside the conquered towns. The idea was to keep the army prepared for every emergency and available at short notice. Also, the soldiers were now assigned a fixed stipend from the public treasury so that they could devote all their time to military training, which had not been possible when their remuneration was only a share of the booty acquired in a battle. Such military camps were later to grow into important cities of the empire. Some examples of these are Fustat in Egypt, near which the city of Cairo was built three hundred years later, Basra and Kufa in Iraq, and Jabiya in Syria.

The Battle of the Bridge

Umar ordered that the campaigns in Syria and Iraq, started by his predecessor, be carried on and reinforcements were dispatched. However, the Persian king Yazdijird III, though young, proved himself to be energetic and competent. He had managed to unite his subjects behind him in the face of the Arab threat and raised a large army to defend his territory. The Euphrates divided the two armies; the Muslim army was camped on the western bank and the Persian on the eastern. The Muslims decided to cross the river and offer battle to the enemy, but this turned out to be a grave mistake. They found themselves in a closed country unsuitable to their usual war tactics and with their backs to the river. Also, the Persians in their attack employed a number of elephants, which created fear and panic among the Arabs, who were mounted on horses, and unaccustomed to the sight of these huge creatures. The Muslims suffered a heavy defeat (November) in this Battle of the Bridge (so called because Muthanna saved the army from complete destruction by his heroic rearguard action to keep a bridge open over the Euphrates near the city of Hira). Some 4,000 Arabs were killed or drowned in the Euphrates while retreating and half that number deserted in dismay after the battle. This was a shattering blow to the strength and morale of the Arab army on the eastern front.

The title of Caliph remained in use till March 1924 when it was formally abolished by the Turkish nationalist leader Mustafa Kemal Ataturk (1881–1938), and the last Ottoman ruler, Abdul Majid II (r. 1922–4), deposed.

635

The Surrender of Damascus

After decisively defeating the Byzantines at Ajnadain in the previous year, in March the Arabs laid seige to Damascus, which capitulated after six months. The significance of this event went far beyond the immediate military and stategic gain, considerable though that was. It posed the important question of how to deal with the non-Muslim subject population in a conquered territory. The treaty which the Arab commander, Khalid ibn al-Walid, concluded with the inhabitants of Damascus—Christians and Jews—set precedents for many similar situations in different lands for decades to come; those who surrendered without a fight would get full protection of their lives, property and places of worship in return for payment of a tribute.

636

The Battle of Yarmuk—Conquest of Syria

After strenuous effort, Emperor Heraclius (r. 610–41) assembled a large army, under the imperial commander-in-chief Theodorus at Antioch, from various regions of his empire, to take a decisive stand against the intruders and to rid his domain of the 'desert vermin'. In the face of this massive threat and with no prospect of reinforcements from Medina, Khalid ibn al-Walid withdrew south to the bank of the River Yarmuk, an eastern tributary of the River Jordan, a few miles south of the Sea of Galilee. He abandoned even Damascus in order to secure a stategic position. The Byzantine army, though very large, suffered from dissensions among the various nationalities of which it was composed, so that morale was low. In the month of August, the two armies faced each other on the banks of the Yarmuk, and the Byzantines were routed in a pitched battle lasting several days. After the crushing defeat, in which Theodorus was killed, Heraclius returned to Constantinople in despair, and town after town fell into Muslim hands without resistance, sealing the fate of the whole of Syria in an incredibly short time. Only Jerusalem, strongly fortified by the Romans, escaped the conquerors' wrath; the rest of Palestine went the same way as Syria.

The Removal of the Muslim Commander Khalid from His Post

Soon after the brilliant victory at Yarmuk, Caliph Umar removed Khalid from the supreme command and replaced him by Abu Ubaida ibn al-Jarrah, a respected Companion of the Prophet but a comparatively undistinguished soldier; he kept Khalid as his deputy. Different interpretations are put on the sudden dismissal of the most successful of all the Arab commanders, the 'Sword of God', as the Prophet Muhammad had called him. Whatever the reason behind this decisive action on the part of Umar, it clearly demonstrates his complete authority over the army. Khalid later died in oblivion in Hims (Syria) or Medina in 641.

c. 637

The Battle of Qadisiya—The Capture of Iraq

On the Persian front, Muthanna ibn Haritha, who took over the supreme command from Khalid ibn al-Walid after the latter's sudden departure to Syria, died soon after the Battle of Buwayb in 635. The new commander-in-chief was Sa'd ibn Abi Waqqas, one of the Prophet's Companions and a seasoned soldier who had taken part in the famous battles of Badr (624) and Uhad (625). Meanwhile the Persians made a final effort to overcome their internal differences and gathered a large and well-equipped army under an imperial marshal, the nobleman Rustam. The two armies confronted each other at Qadisiya, about twenty miles south-west of Hira and near (the future city) Najaf c. 637*, and the Muslims inflicted a severe defeat on the Persians. Rustam was killed and the retreating army left behind the imperial standard, the sacred palladium of the mighty Sasanid Empire, and the whole of Iraq fell under Muslim control. The Iraqis were of Semitic origin and spoke an Aramaic dialect. They look upon their Persian rulers—who were Aryans and spoke the Pahlavi** language—as aliens and felt more akin to the invading Arabs, and showed their preference by welcoming them as liberators. This was especially so in rural areas, where the peasants were oppressed by heavy taxation which was partly due to the long and costly Perso-Byzantine wars (602–28). These peasants also bitterly resented the widespread excesses of their landlords.

The Foundation of Garrison Town of Kufa

After the decisive battle of Qadisiya, the conquerors then sacked the capital

Ctesiphon, which stood on the Tigris some twenty miles south-east of (the future city) Baghdad, and found themselves in a fairyland of untold riches and splendours such as they had never seen before. Ctesiphon (seat of the Imperial government) was made its headquarters by the invading army. These desert tribesmen were now occupying the luxurious palaces of the capital city of this ancient empire, and the austere Caliph Umar became deeply apprehensive about the possible corrupting effect which these fabulously rich and comfortable surroundings might have on the army. He, therefore, ordered Sa'd to build a military camp to accommodate the army away from the civilian population. This was how the military station of Kufa on the western bank of the Euphrates, three miles south of Hira, came into being, becoming a few years later a populous city and the capital of the Muslim empire in the reign of the fourth Caliph (656–661), Ali ibn Abi Talib.*** Kufa also remained the main intellectual centre of Muslim Iraq until the Abbasid Caliph al-Mansur (r. 754–75) built, in 762, his famous city, Baghdad, when its importance decreased. It became especially renowned for the study of Arabic grammar—a core subject for the study of the Quran—and produced many famous grammarians. An early script of Arabic writing, Kufic, derived its name from the city. Politically, it later grew into the main centre of anti-Umayyad rebellion, both Alid legitimism and Kharijite puritanism.

The battle of Qadisiya did the same for the Iraqi campaign as that of Yarmuk did for the Syrian in 636. And, like Yarmuk, it was a decisive battle and a turning point in the history of the early conquests of Islam, this one opening the way to the east.

The chronology of conquests in Iraq and Persia is uncertain.
**An earlier form of the modern Persian language, also referred to as 'Middle Persian'.*
***As with the important and decisive battle of Qadisiya itself, the year in which Kufa was founded is not certain. According to some sources, it was around the year 640.*

638

The Surrender of Jerusalem

Jerusalem was besieged and its Greek Patriarch, the 'honey-tongue' Sophronius, who had been appointed by Emperor Heraclius (r. 610–41), soon capitulated, so that Umar ibn al-Khattab, who was on a visit to the military camp of Jabiya (some twenty miles north of the Sea of Galilee) after the battle of Yarmuk, came in person to accept the submission.* The terms of surrender were drawn up and the Caliph set out for the Holy City.** Christians were to be given protection and allowed to follow their religion in return for payment of a poll tax which was less heavy than that which the Byzantines had imposed upon them. Umar visited the site once occupied by the Temple of Solomon, and ordered that a mosque be built there which later came to bear his name.***

According to some historical sources, Caliph Umar was still in Medina when Abu Ubaida ibn al-Jarrah sent him a message to this effect, after which the Caliph decided to visit the Syrian front himself. He first proceeded to the military base of Jabiya to settle some civil matters regarding the newly acquired territory and then left for Jerusalem.
**To emphasize the utterly simple life-style ofUmar and the teaching of the concept of human equality in Islam, Muslim historians relate with pride how the barefoot Caliph entered Jerusalem clad in his usual rags and sharing a camel ride with his slave. This caused a great deal of astonishment among the local Greek Christian population, who were used to seeing the pompous ceremonies of Byzantine Emperors.*
***Not to be confused with the magnificent building, the Dome of the Rock, which was built later in 691 by Caliph Abdul Malik (r. 685–705) and which is wrongly referred to as the Mosque of Umar by some European writers.*

639–40

The Introduction of the Muslim Calendar

Caliph Umar ibn al-Khattab (r. 634–44) introduced c. 639 the Muslim calendar, consisting of twelve lunar months, and was reckoned to have commenced on 16 July 622 CE.

The Outbreak of Plague in Syria and Palestine

In 639, there was an outbreak of bubonic plague in Syria and Palestine which had disastrous consequences. About 25,000 Arabs were said to have perished and many took refuge in the desert from the plague-infected cities. Among the dead were the commander-in-chief and Syrian governor Abu Ubaida ibn al-Jarrah, and Yezid ibn Abi Sufyan who had played a distinguished role as a column commander throughout the Syrian campaign. The irrepressible Umar himself visited Syria to reorganize the administration, which became badly disrupted following the death of so many prominent leaders. In place of Abu Ubaida, Umar appointed Muawiya, the eldest surviving son of Abu Sufyan and a former secretary of the Prophet, governor of Syria. A man of exceptional qualities, Muawiya wasdestined to become the founder of the Umayyad dynasty (661–750) and its first Caliph (661–80). He played a prominent but controversial role in the early history of Islam.

The Famine in Hijaz

In addition to the plague in Syria and Palestine, there was severe famine in

Hijaz as a result of drought. The Caliph reacted to the problem with his characteristic energy and skill and alleviated the public distress.

Violent Christological Controversies within the Byzantine Empire

The status of Christianity in the Roman Empire was raised to the level of state religion in 381 by Emperor Theodosius I, previously having been recognized by Constantine I in 313 only as a lawful religion to be tolerated (Edict of Milan). However, ever since the Council of Nicaea (325), there had been fierce controversies concerning the vexed question of the relation of Jesus Christ to God and to man. Furious arguments split the Church and developed into schism. Two sects with diametrically opposed views were the Nestorians and the Monophysites. Nestorius exaggerated the human aspect of Christ and in 420 denied that Mary could be the mother of God, claiming that she could only be the mother of the man Jesus. At the other extreme was the Monophysite (meaning 'one nature') sect which believed that Christ had only one nature—the Divine. Both these sects had been condemned by the Church Councils as heretical. After the Council of Ephesus branded the Nestorians as heretics in 431, their persecution followed and many of them took refuge in Iraq under the Persians (Zoroastrians), where they spread their form of Christianity among the Arabs. The Monophysite doctrine was rejected by the Council of Chalcedon in 451, and by this time its adherents were concentrated mainly in Egypt, Abyssinia and Syria.

Ever since the Byzantines had recovered Egypt from the Persians in 629, Emperor Heraclius (r. 610–41) had been ambitiously trying to reconcile the Monophysite Copts with the Imperial Orthodox Church. At the height of his glory, he drew up a theological statement which omitted the question of the nature or natures of Christ but emphasized his one 'divine will'. In 631, he appointed Cyrus (a Greek by birth, known as Muqawqis to the Arabs) Bishop of Phasis in the Caucasus, Patriarch of Alexandria and civil governor of Egypt, and assigned him the difficult task of persuading the native Copts to accept the new religious dogma. But even after brutal persecution of the Monophysites, the object was not achieved; the attempt only created bitter resentment against Byzantium. However, the minority of Christians who had accepted the new theological formula were given the name of Monothelites (from *thelma*, meaning 'will'). In addition to these Christological controversies, there was persecution of the Palestinian Jews, who were accused of having collaborated with the Persians in 616 when the latter carried the Holy Cross* off to Ctesiphon. This added to the general strife in an already divided population. The unpopularity of the imperial government among not only the Copts in Egypt but also the Jacobites in

Syria made it unable to withstand the violent assault of the advancing Muslim armies.

The Holy Cross, believed to be the true Cross, was restored to Jerusalem in 630 by Emperor Heraclius (r. 610–41) after he had retaken it from the Persians.

Amr's Invasion of Egypt

Egypt was a rich country, owing to the fertile Nile valley. It also occupied a stategic position; its capital, Alexandria, was an important naval base of the Byzantines and a gateway to the rest of the north African corridor. Amr ibn al-As began his invasion of the country from Palestine in late 639, by making a swift raid on the Nile Delta. He then defeated the Roman troops at Heliopolis (five miles north-east of the modern city of Cairo) in the middle of 640 after luring them out of their secure fortress of Babylon, a great Byzantine citadel at the southern tip of the Nile Delta, into open battle.

c. 640

The Battle of Nihavand; The Capture of Persian Empire and Collapse of the Sasanid Dynasty

The Persians had been shattered at Qadisiya (Iraq) c. 637, and now, three years later, the Battle of Nihavand* (in western Persia) completed the conquest of the mighty Sasanids, and Persia was captured apart from a few of its eastern provinces.

The native Sasanid dynasty had ruled Persia since 226, when the Parthians were overthrown, and the capital, Ctesiphon, taken by Ardashir I (r. 226–40), the founder of the dynasty.** The Chosroes Yazdijird III fled to the eastern provinces but was later killed by a local miller in Merv (now in the USSR) in 651 after leading the life of a fugitive with a small group of faithful followers. A number of romantic legends about the life and sad end of this young king were to spring up later. The Parsis (meaning the inhabitants of Fars), a small group of Zoroastrians who left their Persian homeland to seek religious freedom in India, were to date their calendar from 16 June 632, the day on which Yazdijird III is said to have ascended the Persian throne.

In view of its importance, the Battle of Nihavand is referred to as the 'Victory of Victories' in Arab annals.
**It was under Ardashir I that the ancient Persian religion of Zarathustra (Zoroaster in the Greek form) was revived and made the state religion.*

641-2

The Fall of Palestine

The coastal town of Caesarea, which had a large Greek population, was receiving Byzantine assistance from the Egyptian port of Alexandria and had managed to defy the invaders. But in 641 it finally surrendered and the whole of Palestine fell into Muslim hands.

The Death of Emperor Heraclius; Arab Conquest of Egypt; Founding of Fustat

Amr ibn al-As had been continuing his campaign in Egypt after his victory at Heliopolis in July 640. Realising the danger, the Patriarch Cyrus—a strange character who became easily despondent in difficult circumstances and as cruel when he felt secure—quickly entered into peace negotiations and asked Emperor Heraclius for his approval, but instead the Emperor accused him of defeatism and treachery. However, Heraclius died in Feburary 641, and his son and successor, Constantine III, less than four months later. After considerable turmoil in the Imperial capital, Constans II (r. 641–68), the eleven-year-old son of Constantine III, was crowned but failed to command the loyalty of his subjects. In Egypt itself, Cyrus had already alienated a large number of Copts by the savagery of his religious persecution and they began to desert the Roman cause. Determined to resume negotiations, he hastily signed an agreement in November 641 surrendering the whole of Egypt to the Arabs. Almost a year had passed since Cyrus concluded with Amr the first peace treaty, which had been contemptously torn up by Heraclius. The terms of the new treaty were severe for the Byzantines, who were forced to leave this rich province with eleven months' grace, but the local Christians and the Jews received the same treatment which had previously been accorded to the 'People of the Book' in Syria, Palestine and Iraq.

The garrison of Babylon had already surrendered two months after the death of Heraclius, and six months later Amr started building a permanent military camp, named Fustat, near this fortress. This military colony later grew into a thriving metropolis and continued to be the Muslim capital of Egypt until 973, when the Fatimids (909–1171) made the new city of Cairo, founded near it (in 969), the seat of their government. Alexandria (capital of Hellenic Egypt), like the rest of the country, was evacuated by the Byzantine army in September 642 in accordance with the Cyrus-Amr peace treaty, and was occupied by the Arabs. Thus came to an abrupt end the Byzantine rule in Egypt, and the Copts viewed it with relief. Cyrus had died earlier, in March 642.

644

The Murder of Umar

Umar returned from the Pilgrimage he made to Mecca every year, and soon after his return was murdered, on 3 November, at the age of fifty three, in the mosque at Medina, by a Persian slave, one Abu Lulua, who had a personal grievance.

> The reigns of Abu Bakr and Umar brought internal harmony and external conquests. During the incredibly short period of twelve years, the Muslim empire had expanded to include Arabia, Iraq, western Persia, Syria, Palestine, northern Egypt and some parts of the north African coast. Internally, the foundations had been laid for the administration of the new empire, which were to be followed and built upon, with some modifications, by their successors, who did so competently without the benefit of having any previous personal experience or model from pre-Islamic days.

Uthman's Accession to the Caliphate

Umar was succeeded by nearly seventy-year-old Uthman ibn Affan (r. 644–56), the Prophet's son-in-law (through the marriage of Ruqayya) and a member of the aristrocratic Meccan clan, Umayya. Uthman, who was a wealthy merchant, became a Muslim quite early in the Prophet's mission. His conversion to Islam, as the first Muslim of high social standing, caused a sensation in Mecca and raised the morale of the early converts. However, being a man of easygoing nature, lacking drive and initiative, he had never played an active role in wars and politics. He is thought to have been elected not because he was the strongest and ablest candidate but because he offered the least opposition.

The early part of his twelve-year reign saw the continuation of the conquests started in the time of Umar, and there were noticeable military achievements. In the beginning, he was more popular than the stern Umar had been, for Uthman was genial and affectionate in his manner. It was initially a period of prosperity and good government but later general discontent arose and quickly gathered momentum. There were a number of reasons for this. The transition from being nomads of the Arabian desert to conquerors of a vast empire in less than twenty years had brought its own social tensions and problems. Also, as the conquest of new territories slowed down, the plunder from such territories started to dwindle, which made it difficult to meet the financial commitments to all those on the state Register of Pensions introduced by Caliph Umar. On the other hand, some leading Muslims had acquired a great deal of wealth from foreign conquests and were living in utmost luxury. This attracted denunciation from some ascetic quarters, who were concerned that all this wealth and luxury was undermining the values of the formerly hardy and frugal Arabs. Some early converts to Islam, in their puritan zeal, went so far as to denounce these riches as anti-Islamic and regarded them as something to be spent in charity and not to be hoarded in any way. Uthman's reaction to such criticism was tactless and inconsistent; he tried to suppress it in a heavy-handed manner which made the situation worse. The most serious charges directed against him personally were nepotism and favouritism in giving lucrative posts in the higher echelons of government to his kinsmen, all of whom belonged to the Umayya clan. But some did argue that these appointments could be justified on their own merits. This opened up the old rift between the Hashim and Umayya clans which had been just beneath the surface. Among the examples cited in support of these allegations was the replacement of the governors of Basra and Kufa by his two relatives. He also summarily dismissed Amr ibn al-As, the conqueror and governor of Egypt, and appointed his cousin and foster-brother, Abdullah ibn Sa'd, in his place, although the latter had at one time incurred the displeasure of the Prophet. Amr retired in Palestine and secretly encouraged dissident activity in Egypt. All these complex political, social and economic, as well as religious, factors were compounded resulting in profound discontent with the Caliph towards the end of his reign.

645

The Defeat of the Byzantine Naval Force off Alexandria

The Byzantines, supported by their fleet, attempted to recapture Egypt through Alexandria but were beaten off, bringing the Byzantine influence in Egypt permanently to an end.

647

The Arab Conquest of Tripolitania

Abdullah ibn Sa'd, the new governor of Egypt, led a strong attack on north Africa and destroyed the Byzantine army at Sbeitla (southern Tunisia) after several days of fighting. Gregory, the Byzantine governor, was killed and Tripoli was subjected to a large payment of tribute. However, Abdullah returned to Egypt without making any attempt to consolidate the conquest, and the Byzantines reoccupied the abandoned territories soon afterwards.

Caliph Uthman allowed Abdullah to keep an unduly large share of the booty, and mismanaged the rest by handing it over to Marwan ibn Hakam, his cousin and secretary, for disposal. This damaged the prestige of Uthman and added to the troubles which were still to come.

649

The Creation of a Navy by the Arabs

Muawiya ibn Abi Sufyan, governor of Syria, was one of the first to realize the full importance of having a navy; as long as the Byzantine fleet could sail the Mediterranean unopposed, the coastline of Syria, Palestine and Egypt would never be safe. He, together with Abdullah ibn Sa'd, governor of Egypt, successfully persuaded Caliph Uthman to give them permission to construct a fleet. As a result a large fleet was built in the dockyards of Egypt and Syria. While the fighting men were Arabs, the fleet was manned mostly by local Copts or Jacobites who, being Monophysite Christians, did not hesitate to serve against the Greeks. This achievement of building a naval force was of lasting importance for the Arabs, opening a new avenue of conquests.

Beginning of the Sea War Against the Byzantines; Conquest of Cyprus

A naval expedition was launched from the Syrian coast against Cyprus, an important Byzantine naval base, and the island was captured. A treaty was signed to the effect that the Cypriots would pay an annual tribute and remain neutral in the event of war between the Arabs and the Byzantines. This was the first maritime victory for the Muslims and the first island added to their empire.

650–2

The Compilation of the Quran

Caliph Uthman established a commission to prepare a text of the Quran from all available sources, including the compilation made during the reign of the first Caliph, Abu Bakr, and entrusted by him to Hafsa, one of the Prophet's widows and daughter of Caliph Umar ibn al-Khattab. Zayd ibn Thabit, one of the Prophet's former secretaries, played a leading role in this commission, as he had done in the previous compilation. During Muhammad's life time, Zayd, a native of Medina, used to write down Quranic passages for him as they were revealed; he also learnt Syriac in order to deal with correspondence in that language. Some time between 650 and 652, an official version of the Quran was compiled, copies of which were sent to various centres of the empire to be used as a reference.*

Uthman is best remembered for this important and fruitful achievement of his reign, and his edition of the Quran to this day remains the authoritative Word of God for Muslims all over the world.

The Quran (Arabic: Reading or Recitation) is regarded by Muslims as the infallible Word of God, a perfect transcript of eternal Tablet preserved in Heaven and hence pre-existent to the world and to man; it is, therefore, immutable in both form and content. The Quran was 'sent down' to the Prophet Muhammad through angel Gabriel in a series of Revelations over a period of approximately twenty-two years (610–32). Besides its extensive use in prayers as well as recitation for piety, it is the first text-book from which virtually every Muslim learns to read the Arabic language. This makes it the most widely read book ever written. The Quran is valued not only for its teaching but also as something sacred in itself. The sura 56:79, speaking of the Quran, says 'Only the purified shall touch it'. A good Muslim shall, therefore, be ritually purified before even touching a copy of the Quran.

The Quran is divided into 114 suras (or 'chapters') of unequal lengths. According to one enumeration, the whole text has 6,236 verses, 77,934 words and 323,621 letters; there are, however, other enumerations. The question whether the Quran, specifically revealed in Arabic, could be translated much exercised Muslim scholars in the past. Since it is God's 'uncreated' Word, its translation has traditionally been forbidden, for by its very nature translation is different from the original. Muslims throughout the world thus continue to recite its suras in Arabic, although they may not speak or even understand the language. All translations are looked upon as 'paraphrases' to facilitate understanding the sacred text, not translation that can be used for ritual purposes.

The Quran has been translated into all major languages of the world, some forty in all. The first translation into a foreign language was that in Latin (1143) by Robert of Ketton. After Peter the Venerable, Abbot of Cluny, visited Toledo, he commissioned a group of scholars to produce a series of works in an attempt to refute the beliefs of Islam, which was the great enemy, feared but also admired. The Latin translation was a part of this series and—not surprisingly—did not lead to any scholarly developments in Islamic studies. The first English translation was done, in 1649, by Alexander Ross, but it was based on an earlier French translation and not directly on the Arabic. George Sale's translation into English, in 1734, was the first such work based on the original Arabic. Since then, there have been numerous translations into English and many other languages, both by Muslim and non-Muslim scholars.

The Extension of the Arab Frontiers into Khurasan

During the year 650–2, Abdullah ibn Amir, governor of Basra, launched a series of successful attacks into the eastern provinces of Persia. He marched through Khurasan, overrunning Harat, Merv and Balkh. A column from his army crossed the Hindu Kush and captured Kabul while still another concentrated on the southern region capturing Makran. Thus the eastern boundries of the Muslim Empire were pushed as far as the River Oxus (modern Amu Darya, USSR/Afghanistan) reached the Indian border. This paved the way for future eastward conquests.

653

The Second Invasion of Cyprus

The Cypriots were accused of giving assistance to the Byzantine fleet, and Muawiya invaded the island for the second time, leaving behind a large garrison.

The Capture of Rhodes Island

The Arabs captured Rhodes island*, where, two years later, they sold to a Jewish merchant the remains of the Colossus (a 105-foot-high bronze statue of Helios, the sun god), one of the Seven Wonders of the ancient world. This shortest-lived of the Wonders once stood at the entrance to the harbour but collapsed in a severe earthquake in 224 or 223 BCE and had been left to lie in ruins for almost 900 years. It is an indication of the size of this massive structure that no less than 980 camels had to be employed to carry the scrap metal away.

Rhodes was raided more than once by the Arabs; later occupations were in 672 and 717.

655

Disastrous Defeat of Byzantines in a Naval Battle

The success of the Muslim navy in the Mediterranean provoked a Byzantine counter-attack and a decisive battle took place at Phoenix on the coast of Lycia (southern Turkey). After heavy fighting, the Byzantine navy of about 500 ships was severely defeated and its naval sumpemacy was destroyed. Emperor Constans II (r. 641–68), who was himself leading the battle, barely managed to escape alive.

This was the second major blow to Roman sea power, which was based on the naval command of the Mediterranean; the first had come as long ago as 427, when the Vandals crossed from Spain to north Africa. The reliance by the Romans on their navy was reflected in their preference for having provincial capitals and other strongholds in coastal cities, e.g., Caesarea, Alexandria and Carthage. The Arabs, on the other hand, used camels and horses as a means of conveyance and always relied on the desert in their strategic planning. They preferred, if the situation allowed, to move along the border of the desert, to which they could retreat for safety if the enemy proved to be too strong; the desert was impassable to the regular Roman armies. The Muslims had previously used the same strategy very effectively against the Persians.

Now the Arabs, too, became a formidable sea power. The major credit for the planning and construction of the Arab navy, and victory in battle, must go to Muawiya.

656

Spread of Unrest in the Muslim World; Death of Uthmanin a Revolt

Caliph Uthman was nearly eighty years old, his capacity to cope with the complex problems of the empire was decreasing and he had become impervious to helpful counsel. He had delegated considerable authority of his office (especially relating to the public treasury) to his controversial secretary and cousin, Marwan ibn Hakam, who, many years later, was to become a Caliph (684–5) of the Umayyad dynasty. The general body of the Arabs, always impatient of control, had been successfully kept under discipline with tact and firmness by the first two Caliphs. But they now began to chafe and sow the seeds of sedition in distant parts of the empire. Coupled with this was the increase in general malaise. Opposition to Uthman's rule became widespread, not only in Medina but also in the outlying provinces, particularly in Iraq and Egypt. The local mutineers in Kufa, Basra and Fustat were openly defying the central government. However, there was no trouble in Syria, which was well managed by Muawiya ibn Abi Sufyan. He was concerned with the Caliph's safety and advised him to move to Damascus, putting himself under the protection of the loyal Syrian army. But Uthman refused and also dismissed any suggestion of his abdication, insisting that the Caliphate had been bestowed upon him by God.

Although the Muslim Caliph was by now the ruler of a vast empire, he still lived a very simple life with no personal protection and was easily accessible to his subjects. Even after the murder of Umar (by a non-Muslim slave), it had not been felt necessary to appoint bodyguards for the Caliph's protection. No one ever thought of insurrection at home, so there were no soldiers in Medina or Mecca. The army was kept in the provinces and on the frontiers of the empire.

But the Caliph's life was now thought to be in so much danger that a few local young men were posted at Uthman's house to give him protection. But this measure was nowhere near enough to cope with a band of insurgents led by Muhammad, the son of the first Caliph, Abu Bakr, who marched on Medina from Egypt. The other leader of the rebellion was Malik al-Ashtar, an experienced soldier. The helpless old Caliph was besieged in his own house and was thus murdered on 17 June, while reading the Quran, which was spread over his lap. For the first time, Muslim blood was spilt by Muslims in the second holiest city and it turned out not to be the last. What followed was a period of schism and civil war.*

*The period between the uprising against Uthman and the death of Caliph Ali is usually referred to as the First Civil War in Islamic history, during which time Islam was divided into rival and feuding sects. For this reason, the historical records are quite confusing and contradictory, each depending on the doctrinal disposition of the historian and the time it was written.

The Accession of Ali to the Caliphate

Uthman was succeeded by Ali ibn Abi Talib (r. 656–61),the Prophet's cousin and a son-in-law (through the marriage of Fatima who died near the close of 632 or early 633), as the fourth and last of the Orthodox Caliphs. Abu Talib being poor, the Prophet took Ali into his care and brought him up in his household, as Abu Talib had done for him in his own childhood. Ali had become Muslim at the age of ten. He had also accompanied the Prophet in his migration in 622 from Mecca to Medina, the Hijra. In his youth, he had taken part in many famous battles such as Badr, Uhad and Khaybar, and had displayed rare courage. The Prophet had more than once given him the standard to carry in battle. He had, however, remained in Medina since the Prophet's death.

   Soon after the murder of Uthman, a reaction set in, for even those who had previously been hostile to the Caliph were horrified by the incident. The people only now realized the gravity and likely repercussions of what had happened. Ali, on becoming Caliph, was strongly and repeatedly urged by leading Muslims, including the Companions Talha ibn Abdullah and Zubair ibn al-Awwam, to punish the murderers of Uthman, but he took no steps to avenge the murder although professing deep lamentation over what had happened. For a time now, the authority of the state was completely undermined, and lawless elements roamed around unchecked. The assassination also once again opened up the old breach between the two rival clans, Umayya and Hashim; Uthman had belonged to the former whereas Ali came from the latter. In the short period of the five years of Ali's Caliphate, there was nothing but war and disaster. There was no territorial expansion in the empire; instead, thousands of Muslim lives were lost in internecine warfare.

The Battle of the Camel

Both Talha and Zubair, who were distinguished Meccans, quarrelled with Ali and renounced their allegiance, which deprived Ali of considerable support at the start of his Caliphate. Talha had the honour of saving the Prophet's life in the battle of Uhad (625), while Zubair was renowned for his reckless gallantry in scaling the Roman fortress of Babylon during the conquest of Egypt and was also a son-in-law of the first Caliph, Abu Bakr. The Prophet's widow, Aisha, had gone to Mecca for the Pilgrimage, where Talha and Zubair joined forces with her and then proceeded to Basra, where the 'Battle of the Camel' (so-called because the fiercest fighting was round the camel on which Aisha was mounted) took place near the town in the month of December. The battle ended in a victory for Ali, but there were a large number of casualties. Talha and Zubair were both killed, but Aisha was treated with due respect and escorted back to Medina where she retired from politics and lived for another twenty-two years before her death in 678. It was a new experience for the survivors to bury their dead, who had been killed in a battle not against the infidel, but of Muslims fighting against Muslims. The aged Muslims viewed the whole situation with utmost sadness and mourned the loss of their companions from the earlier days, who had done so much for the spread of Islam while it was still in its infancy.

657

The Move of the Capital to Kufa amid Continuing Unrest

After the Battle of the Camel, Caliph Ali spent a few days in Basra where he appointed his cousin Abdullah (d. 688), the son of Abbas, governor of the area. He then entered Kufa (January), a new town in Iraq which had grown out of a military camp established about twenty years earlier, and made it his new capital. Medina was never again the seat of government.

The battle did nothing to help Ali assert his authority and restore badly needed unity in the Muslim world. On the contrary, it damaged his reputation considerably, because the pious were inclined to blame him for the shedding of

Muslim blood in this battle, and troubles were simmering everywhere, particulary in Egypt and Syria.

The Battle of Siffin

Muawiya ibn Abi Sufyan, governor of Syria, being now head of the House of Umayya (to which the murdered Caliph belonged) was another powerful figure who demanded punishment of the assasins. When this was not forthcoming, he refused to pay allegiance to Ali, making his allegiance dependent upon retribution for the murder of Uthman. He kept himself neutral in the earlier battle between Ali and his opponents, and had been cleverly waiting for the right opportunity to challenge Ali's rule openly. In the meantime, however, he had been making propaganda and stirring up emotions against Ali by hanging the blood-stained shirt of Uthman from the pulpit of the Great Mosque of Damascus. The shirt and severed fingers of Naila, Uthman's wife, were smuggled out of Medina to Damascus soon after the tragic event of his assassination from which the Arab empire, and indeed Islam itself,was never to recover. This grotesque emblem was kept there in case the spirit of vengence began to subside.

Muawiya, a political genius, had governed Syria very successfully for nearly twenty years and built up a large and loyal army. He negotiated a truce with the Byzantines in return for payment of tribute so that he could be free to move his army into Iraq if and when the need arose. He had also by now a powerful and astute adviser in the person of Amr ibn al-As, the conqueror of Egypt, who had been deposed by Uthman but made friends with Muawiya. In the spring, Ali set out north-west through Iraq in an effort to vindicate his authority and engaged Muawiya's army along the Syrian frontier at Siffin, a ruined Roman site near the great bend of the Euphrates. The hostile forces faced one another for several months, engaging in no more than skirmishes. The horror of shedding the blood of fellow-Muslims yet again was felt on both sides and the will to fight was not very strong. However, prolonged negotiations for a peaceful settlement failed, and Muslims started fighting Muslims for the second time in their history in the month of July. As the battle was going in Ali's favour, the wily Amr suggested to Muawiya a ruse which brought the fighting to an inconclusive end. The soldiers of Muawiya's army fixed copies or leaves of the Quran on the points of their lances and raised them aloft as a symbol of their desire to settle the dispute by the Word of God—whatever that meant in practice. Ali, against his better judgement, was forced by the devout Muslims in his army into a ceasefire from a winning position. Thus the miraculous power of the Quran for the Believers brought the battle to an end forthwith, but the underlying dispute remained unresolved.

An agreement was reached to refer the matter to two arbitrators, one from each side, who would decide between the two parties on the basis of the

Quranic laws. Muawiya chose Amr as his representative while Ali's nominee was Abu Musa al-Ashari. Abu Musa was a veteran soldier and an acknowledged scholar of the Quran, but he had proved himself to be neutral in these civil wars by being earlier dismissed by Ali from the governorship of Kufa for refusing to fight in the Battle of the Camel (656). Thus, although Muawiya chose the best man to look after his interest in the arbitration, the supporters of Ali were so convinced that they were right that they insisted on choosing a neutral and pious man from their side. In the meantime, the two armies returned to their bases, Muawiya's to Damascus and Ali's to Kufa, and thus ended the Battle of Siffin without victory for either party. However, the rights and wrongs of the basic issues involved were to be debated for centuries to come. It caused a breach in Islam which was never to be healed.

658

Arbitration between Muawiya and Ali

The two arbitrators met at Adhruh*, about ten miles north-west of Maan in Jordan, in February 658**, seven months after the ceasefire at Siffin. Since the terms of reference were not very precise, arguments dragged on, sometimes at cross-purposes.

In the end, the arbitrators came to a curious decision. They announced that both Muawiya and Ali should step down and a new Caliph be elected. Ali and his supporters were stunned by this decision, which had lowered the Caliph in status to the same level as the rebellious Muawiya, whereas they were expecting the outcome to be merely a formal recognition of Ali's Caliphate. Ali was thus outwitted once again by Muawiya and his friend Amr. Ali refused to accept the verdict on the grounds that it was not in accordance with the Quran, and hence found himself technically in breach of his pledge to abide by the arbitration. This put Ali in a very weak position even among his own supporters, whereas Muawiya, on the other hand, started accepting the allegiance of his troops in Damascus. Ironically, the most vociferous opponents in Ali's camp were the very same people who had forced him into a ceasefire from the point of victory in the first place and then insisted on the choice of a neutral man like Abu Musa al-Ashari to represent them in the arbitration. The battle and arbitration farce settled nothing but instead increased bitterness between the two groups to such an extent that they resorted to cursing each other by name regularly in public prayers. Islam and the empire were both split.

*According to some historians, the meeting took place at Duma, the modern al-Jawf in Saudi Arabia.

**The year of 659 has also been suggested in some historical sources.

Formation of the Party of Kharijites

Although, in the excitement of the moment, the slogan 'Let God decide' had the immediate desired religious appeal to most of the people in the battlefield and stopped the fighting, it was so vague as to allow interpretation in different ways. It was only after the truce that the people started thinking of the full implications of what had been agreed. Even before the arbitrators met, Muawiya, by this device, had won a tacit victory in this dispute by indirectly getting himself recognized as a party equal in rank to the ruling Caliph, although he was, in fact, his subordinate and a rebel. The two central issues in the dispute were Ali's Caliphate and the punishment for Uthman's murderers. In the arbitration, Ali's supporters expected only the question of the Caliphate to be discussed without any reference to the regicide, but quite the opposite happened. When the deliberations were announced, Ali was clearly and openly the loser, because Muawiya had no Caliphate to be deposed from.

A group of puritan zealots among Ali's supporters were incensed with what had happened and felt that the whole concept of the Caliphate had been discredited by Ali's action. They revolted against him forming a separate party, known as the Kharijites (meaning 'seceders') under the slogan 'No decision (arbitration) but that of God'. In the month of July, Ali suppressed them temporarily in a bloody massacre in which nearly 2,000 of them were killed on the banks of the Nahrawan (in Iraq), but they were to reappear many times under various names in the history of Islam.

They formed the first sect to break away from the main stream of Islam. Being completely puritanical in outlook and with a strong dislike for political intrigue, they aspired to live in accordance with the literal interpretation of the Word of God. Because they believed that the basis of rule should be righteous character and piety alone, any Muslim irrespective of nationality and social standing could, in their view, become ruler provided he satisfied the condition of piety. They sought to enforce the 'Kingdom of God', and considered everyone but themselves as doomed to perdition. Moreover, because of its aggressive idealism, it attracted a large following in times of social or religious unrest and thus presented a dangerous threat to the consolidation of state authority at various periods of history till the Abbasid rule (750–1258). Although a fanatical religious movement, it gradually absorbed other rebel groups, some intolerant of almost any established political authority. This created internal conflict and disorder which eventually contributed to their virtual, though not complete, destruction.

Muawiya's Influence in Egypt

With Ali in such a weak position, alienated from the Kharijites, who had initially formed a large group of his followers, Muawiya was able to rule Syria completely independent of Kufa. He was keenly interested in gaining control of the rich province of Egypt, which was being badly governed by Muhammad ibn Abi Bakr, one of the mutineers involved in Uthman's murder and an appointee of Ali. Seeing that Ali was too busy dealing with the dissent in his own camp, he commisioned Amr (July) with 6,000 troops to regain the province which he had first conquered about eighteen years earlier. Muhammad, with no popular support, could raise only 2,000 men to fight with him and they were defeated and dispersed almost without a fight. After being caught, Muhammad was slain, and such was the hatred against him that his body was ignominiously burned in an ass's skin, to the delight of Muawiya's troops. The illustrious Amr (d. 663) thus once again became governor of Egypt, recognizing Muawiya as the legitimate Caliph.
29

660

Proclamation of Muawiya as Caliph in Defiance of Ali

Muawiya formally proclaimed himself Caliph (May) in Jerusalem, and received the oath of allegiance from the western provinces. Thus the world of Islam was split into two: Ali was in control, though not firmly, of Iraq and Persia, while Muawiya ruled Syria and Egypt.

661

Murder of Ali; Peaceful Abdication by Hasan of His Claim to the Caliphate

By now Caliph Ali had lost control of the western provinces of Syria and Egypt and even of Iraq, which had been a strong base of support at the time of his election; he was in a precarious position. The Kharijities had deserted him and fought against him, accusing him of the grave sin of submitting his claim to the Caliphate to arbitration and thus degrading the supreme office of the Muslim world. The rivalries of the Muslim leaders had become so abhorrent to these fanatics that they decided to rid Islam of Ali, Muawiya ibn Abi Sufyan and Amr ibn al-As by assasinating all three of them on the same day at public prayer. Their plot, however, did not work out as planned. Amr was unhurt in Fustat because he was, by chance, unwell on the day and his substitute was killed instead and Muawiya escaped with a slight injury in Damascus; but Ali was struck down by a fanatic Kharijite, Abdur Rahman ibn Muljam, on 20 January, at the door of the mosque in Kufa. Thus the fourth and last Orthodox or 'Rightly-guided' Caliph died from a mortal wound on his head at the age of just over sixty. He was interred at a spot six miles west of Kufa, where afterwards the town of Najaf was built.* It later became one of the great centres of pilgrimage in Islam, especially for the Shi'ites.

After the death of Ali, his elder son from Fatima, Hasan was declared in Kufa to be the legitimate successor to the Caliphate. Muawiya, who had proclaimed himself Caliph the year before, successfully persuaded Hasan to abdicate in return for a substantial pension for himself and the family of Ali. Hasan, increasingly unwilling to plunge the Muslim community into yet another civil war, accepted the terms offered by Muawiya and abdicated (July) after a shadowy rule of six months. He and his younger brother, Hussain, then left Kufa for Medina leaving the way open for Muawiya to enter Kufa with no serious contender for the Caliphate to challenge him. He thus became the *de facto* ruler of the Islamic world. From now on, Hasan lived in retirement for eight years in Medina where he died in 669 at the age of forty-five.

According to a Shi'ite tradition, this isolated site was chosen in accordance with the dying wish of Ali, who ordered that his corpse be put on a loose camel and buried wherever the camel knelt.

Establishment of the Umayyad Caliphate in Damascus

Thus began the Umayyad Caliphate (661–750), the first dynasty in the history of Islam, and Muawiya ibn Abi Sufyan became its first Caliph (661–80), establishing its capital at Damascus.* Once the disorder and the turbulence in various parts of the empire, especially in Iraq, which had bedevilled it for the last ten years, had been brought under control, often quite ruthlessly, the government was again centralized, but this time in Damascus, a metropolitan city with old cultural and administrative traditions. Syria also had the best-trained, best disciplined and most loyal army of all the provinces. Even in Mecca and Medina, there was unease about Muawiya becoming Caliph, because, like his father Abu Sufyan, he had remained a bitter opponent of the Prophet until the fall of Mecca in 630, when he became a Muslim. But the main source of dissension was Iraq and, in particular, the cities of Basra and Kufa. However, once order had been restored in the provinces, the second phase of expansion of the empire began. Under Umayyad rule, the Muslim empire expanded as far as the borders of India and China in the east, and to the Atlantic and the Pyrenees in the west. To say nothing of north Africa and Spain, this vast area was united under a single rule for the first time since the time of Alexander the Great (BCE 356–323).

The Arab history of early Islam which has come down to us was written by Arab historians and was developed mainly during the Umayyad's rival dynasty, the Abbasids (750–1258). It is, in general, hostile to the Umayyads, depicting them—with the sole exception of Umar II (r. 717–20)—as impious and worldly kings rather than true leaders of the Muslim community. They refuse the title of Caliphate to the reigns of Muawiya and his successors except for Umar II, who alone is granted the title of Caliph.

662

Granting of Governorships in Iraq to Mughira and Ziyad

Muawiya relied heavily on two of his lieutenants, Mughira ibn Shuba and Ziyad ibn Abihi, to suppress opposition to his rule from the Kharijites and supporters of the murdered Caliph Ali. Mughira, an unscrupulous opportunist, and Ziyad ibn Abihi (ibn Abihi meaning 'son of his father', i.e., of doubtful paternity) were both members of the Thaqif clan of the town of Taif. Mughira was given the governorship of Kufa and the task of making the local population submit to Muawiya's authority. Ziyad (d. 673), with his elequence, wisdom and ruthlessness, a most remarkable man. By his personal qualities, he had overcome the stigma of being the son of a vagrant slave girl, and had eventually been appointed governor of Basra by Caliph Ali.

After the murder of Ali, he refused to cooperate with Muawiya, but transferred his allegiance to him a year later, in 662. Muawiya, for his part, publicly acknowledged Ziyad as his half-brother through the extra-marital relations of his own father, Abu Sufyan, declaring him to be Ziyad ibn Abi Sufyan*. This was an extremely shrewd move on the part of Muawiya, since it gave Ziyad credibility and enormous satisfaction in a matter of personal pride, though Muawiya attracted considerable if short-lived criticism for this action. He was then given the most difficult job of the governorship of Basra, where he started his rule with an impromptu speech from the pulpit of the mosque, announcing the severest measures against the lack of restraint prevalent in the region. His proclamations did not turn out to be hollow threats; he adopted the most ruthless measures in restoring government authority, which had been totally undermined by rival religious and tribal factions. In order to minimize the tension between tribes and to keep a firm hold over the army, he divided it into four commands made up of different tribes, each with a leader chosen, not by them, but by the government. He thus abolished the old tribal basis of the Arab army, as had already been done by Muawiya himself in Syria.

No slur on Abu Sufyan was implied because all sins committed before becoming a Muslim were automatically pardoned on conversion to Islam.

668

The Raid on Sicily

An Arab fleet of 200 ships sailed from Alexandria and plundered Byzantine Sicily, which was thus overrun for the second time—the first having been in 652. This, however, did not lead to a permanent conquest of the island, which came much later, in 827, after many such raids.

670

Exodus of Many Iraqi Arabs to Khurasan

Mughira ibn Shuba died, and Ziyad ibn Abihi took over the vacant governorship of the turbulent Kufa. He settled some 50,000 Bedouins, with their families, in the eastern Persian province of Khurasan, and this eased off the turmoil in Iraq. He had now become the most powerful viceroy, and governed the entire eastern half of the empire from his magnificient court in Basra.

Conquest of North-West Africa by Uqba; Founding of Qairawan

When Amr ibn al-As was once more appointed governor of Egypt in 658 by Muawiya, Uqba ibn Nafi, his nephew and an impetuous soldier, started launching daring attacks into the Byzantine-held north African region west of Egypt. The army base he started from was in Fustat, nearly 1,500 miles away, and his supply line was thus overstretched. He, therefore, established (670) the garrison town of Qairawan (modern Tunisia), from which to consolidate his conquest, and set up a provincial government with its capital there. The new military base, like Basra, Kufa and Fustat before it, was later to develop into a famous city with the Great Mosque, founded by Uqba. The mosque became an important centre of learning, and the town a base for further expansion in north Africa later in the Umayyad period.

The mountain ranges of the Atlas, north of the Sahara Desert, had always been populated by a race known as Berbers, a tough and stubborn semi-nomadic people who had always offered savage resistance to an intruder. The Arabs were facing two enemies in the area from two different directions; the Berbers from the Atlas and the Byzantines from their coastal strongholds. Although Qairawan lay a few miles inland from the coastline to be safe from naval attacks from the Mediterranean, it was situated too close to the Berber territory. In the past, the Byzantines had kept control of the area from their regional capital, the ancient city of Carthage (first founded in the middle of the 9th century BCE by the Phoenicians, and situated ten miles to the north-east of Tunis) on the coast, but the Arabs, as always, preferred the inland and desert site of Qairawan.

The recklessly brave Uqba is depicted by tradition charging his horse into the Atlantic, stopped only by the furious oceanwaves, and calling God to witness that he had kept his oath to carry Islam to the extremities of the world. Nevertheless, he failed to exploit the political possibilities of the situation by playing off the Berbers against the Byzantines. Instead, he attacked both simultaneously, treating the Berbers with haughty contempt. On returning from his dashing adventure from the west, he was ambushed and killed in 683 near modern Biskra in Algeria, where his tomb has become a shrine. Soon after his death, the Berbers rose in revolt and nearly all his conquests were lost, including Qairawan; Cyrenaica (known to the Arabs as Barqa; in modern Libya), at the western border of Amr's rule in Egypt, became once again the Muslim frontier. But Uqba had prepared the ground, making the future conquest of north Africa inevitable.

Abortive Attack of the Arabs on Constantinople

Throughout his rule, Muawiya remained at war with the Byzantines. He took up the struggle even as the Syrian governor, first under Caliph Umar (r. 634–44) and then under his successor Caliph Uthman (r. 644–56), when he built a powerful fleet to engage them from both sea and land. The only time when there was a complete truce between the two opponents was when he was paying a tribute to Byzantium in return for being left free to face Caliph Ali in the Battle of Siffin (657), but as soon as he had united the empire, he resumed the conflict on an almost yearly basis. He regarded it as one of his most important tasks, both as a holy war against the unbelievers, which kept up the religious fervour of his subjects, and at the same time bolstered up his own religious prestige, and as a training ground for his Syrian troops to keep them disciplined and good fighting condition.

Muawiya now thought that the time had come for him to strike a great blow and, in 670, sent Yezid, his son and future nominee to succeed him, on the first of the three major expeditions sent during the Umayyad period to capture Constantinople.* This was the first military assignment of the Crown Prince Yezid, who had, up to then, been largely interested in pleasure-seeking activities. The imperial city, which was surrounded by water on three sides, was heavily fortified with walls and towers of immense height (up to 100 feet in places) and strength, which had, in the past, withstood the sophisticated military might of the Persian Chosroes. It also had a new and energetic emperor, Constantine IV (r. 668–85), the successor to Constans II (r. 642–68), who had resided in Sicily in an attempt to check the Arab advance in north Africa, but had been murdered in 668 in a conspiracy after being in power for seventeen years. Although the Arabs fought with tremendous courage and fortitude, they were unable to storm the city because they did not have the necessary skill and weapons to overcome the massive and complex system of protecting walls. The campaign was unsuccessful, and was given up after considerable losses.

Among the Arab army, brought for God's blessing, was the aged standard-bearer of the Prophet, Abu Ayyub al-Ansari, who died of illness and was buried by the walls. A legend grew up about this holy man, who had the honour of being a host to Muhammad in Medina at the time of the Hijra (622), and his tomb soon became a shrine for both Muslims and Christians; the Christians made pilgrimage to it in time of drought to pray for rain.

*There is uncertainty about the precise dates of these expeditions.

674

Arab Raid on Crete

The island of Crete was temporarily captured from the Byzantines by the Arabs.

The Byzantines' Use of 'Greek Fire'; Saving of Constantinople

Muslims again laid siege to Constantinople and this time the siege lasted for seven years. This second major confrontation to capture the imperial city was mainly between the two fleets, the Arabs having secured a naval base at Cyzicus, on the southern coast of the Sea of Marmara. The Byzantines used 'Greek Fire', a highly inflammable liquid mixture of sulphur, nitre and naphtha which was discharged from flame-throwing weapons. This not only greatly frightened the Arabs, who had never seen it before, but inflicted severe damage to their ships. The siege was abandoned, and the imperial capital was saved yet again.

678

The Death of Aisha

Aisha, widow of the Prophet Muhammad, died at the age of about sixty-five, having spent forty-six years in widowhood, and was interred at Medina. She had been living in retirement from politics since the Battle of the Camel (656), meeting pilgrims to the Prophet's tomb, which was in her apartment. She has always remained a revered personage to Muslims and is regarded as one of the most distinguished Traditionists.

679

The Declaration of Yezid as Heir-Apparent to the Caliphate

Muawiya nominated his son Yezid as his successor. Yezid's mother, Maysun, was a Jacobite Christian from the Kalb tribe and was a favourite wife of Muawiya. Muawiya thus introduced into the Caliphate, for the first time, the hereditary principle, whereby the reigning Caliph would proclaim one of his sons or even kinsmen as his successor and to whom allegiance would have to be sworn. It abolished the principle of seniority, which the Arabs had always favoured since the pre-Islamic days, and the elective system which had caused so much trouble in the past. This practice of hereditary succession was followed first by all the Umayyad Caliphs who came after Muawiya and then by the Abbasids (750–1258).

Maysun used to take young Yezid to her favourite open resort of Palmyrene in the Syrian desert to escape from the congested court life at Damascas. Yezid, in the company of her own Bedouin tribe, developed a taste for hunting, hard-riding, verse-making and other such pursuits. His playboy way of life and unpredictable behaviour was seemingly at odds with the sober Islamic code. The idea of hereditary succession was also new to the Arabs. Moreover Yezid's nomination, in particular, could not easily be justified. If his right to the Caliphate was based on heredity, the previous Caliph's son was entitled to it more than he was. If, on the other hand, the Caliphate should go to the most suitable person, then there were obviosly many candidates more competent for the post than Yezid. However, Muawiya, using his exceptional diplomatic skill, managed to persuade delegations from the provinces to recognize him as his heir to the throne.

680

Death of Muawiya and Succession of Yezid; Massacre of Hussain and His Party at Karbala

Muawiya died in April at the age of about seventy-five after a long and prosperous reign. His son and nominee, Yezid, was acclaimed in Damascus as Caliph (680–3). Most regions recognized Yezid but the opposition from the pro-Ali faction which his father had kept in check, rose against him. Yezid's main competitor for the Caliphate was Hussain, who, apart from being a son of the former Caliph Ali (r. 656–661), was also the surviving grandson of the Prophet. His elder brother, Hasan, had died in 669, and he himself had been living in retirement in Medina since 661, when Muawiya took power, but now refused to swear the oath of allegiance to Yezid. There were a number of followers of Ali's cause in Iraq who thought that the time was ripe to regain a leading role. They declared Hussain the legitimate Caliph after Ali and Hasan, and repeatedly invited Hussain to come to Kufa and assume the leadership in Iraq; after much reluctance, he yielded to the pressure. He first went to Mecca and then left for Kufa on the fatal adventure across the Arabian desert with a small group of his relatives and followers. In the meantime, Ubaidullah, son of Ziyad ibn Abihi and as ruthless as his father, had been appointed governor of Kufa by Yezid. Following in his father's footsteps, he arrested and executed a number of Hussain's supporters. On 10 October, Umar, son of the distinguished general and conqueror of Persia Sa'd ibn Abi Waqqas, in command of a large army, intercepted and surrounded Hussain's small convoy at Karbala, on the western bank of the Euphrates and about fifty miles north-west of Kufa. Ubaidullah insisted on an unconditional surrender from Hussain, and when he refused to do so, massacred him and his party in cold blood. 'The day of Karbala' later acquired a great and lasting religious significance with grave implications for the unity of Islam.

Thus died a grandson of the Prophet, and his head was sent to Yezid in Damascus. The head was given back to Hussain's sister and son Ali (Zainul Abidin)*, who had gone with it to Damascus, and was then buried with the body in Karbala. The tomb later became a great centre of pilgrimage for the Shi'ites**.

**His mother was the daughter of Yazdijird III, the last Sasanid king of Persia.*
***Almost immediately after the death of the Prophet Muhammad (632), a small group of Muslims had felt that Ali ibn Abi Talib, being the Prophet's son-in-law (through the*

marriage of Fatima) and cousin, was his only legitimate successor. They had also believed that the Caliphate belonged only to the decendants of the Prophet through the line of Ali and his first wife, Fatima. When Ali, who was about thirty years of age at the time, was passed over, they had formed a group which came to be known as the Shi'ites—from Shia, meaning 'the Party' (of Ali). Initially, the dispute had little to do with matters of doctrine as such but only with the question of succession. But as time went by it attracted non-Arab Muslims, largely of Persian origin, who resented their inferior status in the empire. It gradually broke away from the mainstream of Islam (the Sunnis) on both dynastic and doctrinal grounds and formed a separate sect. The blood of Hussain, even more than that of his father, Ali, provided the Shi'ite movement with a martyr and a rallying point. The tragedy at Karbala on 10 October CE 680 (10 Muharram AH 61) has never been forgotten, and even now, after more than thirteen hundred years, a scene to commemorate the event is enacted in a frenzy of sorrow and indignation every year by millions of Shi'ites.

682–3

The Uprising against Yezid in Mecca and Medina; Abdullah's Stubborn Fight against Umayyad Army; Death of Yezid

The elimination of Hussain did not bring peace for Yezid. Although Hussain was out of the way in his assertion to the Caliphate, the brutality of what had happened at Karbala had created an immense reaction against Yezid. Medina, which had cherished the Prophet and his descendants, openly revolted in the autumn of 682 against the Umayyad rule from Damascus. Feelings were running so high that Yezid sent a special governor to calm the situation. When this failed, Yezid sent an army of 12,000 in August 683 under Muslim (son of Uqba, first conqueror of north Africa) into Hijaz in order to quell the uprising. The Medinese, though brave and deeply committed to their cause, were no match for the trained Syrian army, and were defeated in a desperate battle at a place called Harrah, a lava field, just north of the city. The army then moved south to Mecca where Abdullah ibn Zubair, the son of a distinguished Companion who had fought against Ali and been slain in the 'Battle of the Camel' (656), had installed himself as Caliph, but Muslim died on the way. He was succeeded in command by Hussain ibn Numair, who besieged Mecca in September 683 from the surrounding hills. There was a great deal of fighting in the following two months and the Kaba itself was stoned. In the ensuing fire, the Kaba was badly damaged and the Black Stone was split into pieces. However, the death of Yezid in November, 683 made his army lift the seige and return to Damascus, leaving Arabia under the sway of the defiant Abdullah. Yezid was about thirty-eight years old at the time of his death. A complete rebuilding of the Kaba was undertaken by Abdullah, who tied the pieces of the Black Stone together and put it back in its place.

   It was just over fifty years since the Prophet Muhammad had died, but there were still some people in Medina who had been Companions of the Prophet.

There was also a strong tradition of puritan religious zeal in the city going back to the days of early Islam. The storming of the holy cities by the Damascus army was considered yet another act of sacrilege by the Umayyads. They had become unpopular in this part of the empire and were looked upon as impious by the self-righteous community. Given this widespread indignation, Abdullah (d. 692), with far less impressive credentials for the Caliphate than Hussain, proved to be a more dangerous adversary for the Umayyads in a bloody and protracted struggle.

Three Rival Claimants to the Caliphate

There was a period of anarchy lasting two years immediately following Yezid's death. Then suddenly, there were three rival aspirants to the Caliphate in different parts of the empire. Yezid had left behind as his heir a sickly boy of thirteen, who was acclaimed in Damascus as Muawiya II. Abdullah ibn Zubair was acknowledged as Caliph in Hijaz, and Ubaidullah in Basra where he had been viceroy of the eastern half of the empire, including Basra, Kufa and the whole of Persia, for two years. He had been promoted to this post by Yezid a few months after the massacre at Karbala in 680; his father Ziyad had held the same position a few years previously during the reign of Muawiya I.

When Abdullah tried to gather support for his cause outside Arabia and pressed his claim to the Caliphate in Basra, it led to civil strife, on tribal lines, between his supporters and those of Ubaidullah. At this juncture, Ubaidullah, who had become an object of hatred in Iraq for the brutal massacre of Hussain at Karbala and the severity with which he kept people in subjection, fled to the safety of Damascus.

684

Accession of Marwan as Caliph in Damascus

Out of the three contenders for the Caliphate, the child Muawiya II died in February and Ubaidullah ibn Ziyad had already been driven out of his base in Basra. With Muawiya II ended the rule of Abu Sufyan's desendants. For the moment, this left the field open for Abdullah ibn Zubair, whose support was increasing all the time. But he steadfastly refused to leave Mecca and march on Damascus, the real centre of power, in order to seize the opportunity created by the turmoil. In the meantime, the Umayyads gathered in Damascus and chose the oldest member of their clan, Marwan ibn Hakam, as Caliph in the month of June. The seventy-year-old Marwan had served Caliph Uthman (r. 644–56) as his secretary. The empire was plunged into civil war yet again between two rival contenders for the Caliphate of the Islamic world, but this time it had an added dimension.

The Battle of Marj Rahat; Consolidation of Marwan's Position

In pre-Islamic times, there had existed a keen and constant antagonism, verging on hatred, between the Himyarites and the Modharites—the most inexplicable of all reasons for Arabs to fight one another. However, this had been partly subdued by the Islamic teaching of religious brotherhood. But this conflict between the Arabs of the south and north broke out again when Yezid was accused by the Qais of favouring the southern tribe of Kalb. The supporters of the two rival claimants to the Caliphate were divided on tribal lines; the Kalb took Marwan's side, while the Qais in Syria declared their allegiance to Abdullah as the legitimate Caliph. A battle took place in July at Marj Rahat, a plain a few miles to the north-east of Damascus, in which the supporters of Abdullah were defeated, and Marwan was acknowledged as Caliph (684–5) by the whole of Syria, thereby establishing the Marwanid line of the eleven remaining Umayyad Caliphs, all of whom belonged to his family. He soon established his authority over Egypt too, but Abdullah held onto his real power base, which was in Arabia and Iraq. Thus the empire was once again split between two rivals from the opposing camps of Mecca; Abdullah belonging to the tribe of Hashim and Marwan to the Umayya.

Although the battle of Marj Rahat restored the rule of the Umayyads, it also opened up the disastrous feud between the Himyarites and the Modharites, which had been lying dormant for so many years. This hatred between the two groups of Arabs had flared up to such an extent that it was to remain alive for decades to come. Whereas Muawiya I had skilfully kept it in check in order to keep unity and give strength to his rule, some of the later less competent Umayyad rulers tended to rely on the support of one or the other faction in order to stay in power. The result was that, along with other factors, it slowly erroded the foundations of Umayyad power and contributed to its eventual downfall in 750. This polarization of the Muslim community into feuding factions did not remain confined to Syria but spread elsewhere in the empire, e.g., north Africa and Spain, where it was to continue under various names for centuries to come.

The Himyarites and the Modharites

At the time of the Prophet Muhammad's advent, the Arabian Peninsula had been inhabited by people of two different stocks, one claiming to be descendants of Qahtan (also identified as Joktan of the Old Testament) and the other of Ishmael (Arabic: Ismail), son of Abraham. In ancient times, the cradle of the former was Yemen; of the latter, Hijaz. The southerners living in and around Saba (biblical Sheba) under the Himyarite kings, formed the Azd tribe, the children of Azd, a descendant of Qahtan. They were collectively referred to by various names such as Yemenites, Qahtanites or Himyarites. But over the centuries, there had been considerable movement of population across the peninsula and the two groups had become geographically intermixed; some of the Himyarites had migrated to the north and, in the course of ages, had developed into further tribes bearing the names of descendants, such as, the Khuza near Mecca, the Aus and the Khazraj in Yathrib (Medina) and the Kalb in Syria. The last tribe had gained political importance with the Umayyads; the third Caliph Uthman's wife, Naila, came from this tribe, and so did Yezid's mother and wife. The Ishmaelite tribes of Arabia were also called the Maad, but more often the Modharites, from Modhar, the grandson of Maad. This northern branch of the Arab race was also scattered in different parts of the land and one of its tribes, the Qais, was settled in northern Syria. This tribe sometimes gave its name to the whole group.

Maad was the son of Adnan, a descendant of Ishmael, who is said to have assisted his father Abraham (Arabic: Ibrahim) in rebuilding the Kaba, a place of worship from the ancient times, after the Deluge. While engaged in its construction, he had received the sacred Black Stone from the angel Gabriel. Since then, the Kaba had been successively under the Modharites, the Jurhan and the Khuza before the Quraish took over. The Quraish claimed descendance from Maad and thus re-established the ancient link with Ishmael.

685

Accession of Abdul Malik; Feuding Factions in the Empire

Marwan ibn Hakam died and the Caliphate in the Umayyad dynasty passed to his extremely able son, Abdul Malik (r. 685–705). He took over a deeply divided empire which had suffered badly during the period of crisis and uncertainty following Yezid's death in 683. Only the western provinces acknowledged his Caliphate; Arabia, Iraq and Persia were openly on the side of his rival, Abdullah ibn Zubair. Iraq was particularly difficult to control because of strong opposition from both the Shi'ites and the puritan Kharijites. But before he could exert his authority in Iraq and consolidate his power, he had to concentrate his resources in northern Syria for nearly two years in order to rearguard his position from the Byzantines, who were likely to take advantage of the damaging strife which had engulfed the Muslim world in the previous five years. In the end he managed to conclude an armistice with them.

AbdulMalik was faced with the daunting task of reunification of the empire but applied himself with extraordinary ability and energy to achieving this goal. Apart from endless inter-tribal conflicts, especially between the Himyarites and the Modharites, the empire was torn among four mutually hostile groups who were at war with each other. First, there were the two rival Caliphs, Abdul Malik himself and Abdullah, fighting for the throne. The empire was divided roughly into two halves; the western regions supporting Abdul Malik, the eastern Abdullah. And then there were two further divisions based on religious sects, the Shi'ites and the Kharijites, who had risen in arms. Both of them were concentrated in Iraq, one of the provinces which, at least nominally, was under the influence of Abdullah. The Shi'ites, who were adherents of Ali ibn Abi Talib and his martyred son Hussain, believed that the Caliphate should run only in the line of succession of Ali and his first wife Fatima, the daughter of the Prophet Muhammad. The Kharijites were a fanatical religious group who abhorred the power struggle which had been going on in the Muslim world. They believed in the ideal of having a ruler who was the most pious Muslim selected—and quite often rejected—by them, irrespective of his social or national background. Thus both these groups rejected the claim of Abdullah to the Caliphate, who did not satisfy the aspirations of either of them.

Mukhtar's Revolt in Iraq

Ever since the massacre at Karbala in 680, there had been a large body of Shi'ites in Iraq, especially in Kufa, who were struck with remorse at their desertion of Hussain and his family on the fatal day. When, after Yezid's death, the government in Damascus lost control of the eastern provinces, they rose in arms under the banner of 'the Penitents', vowing vengeance against Hussain's murderers and others responsible.

Towards the end of Marwan's reign (684-5), they gathered at Karbala, 16,000 strong, round the grave of the martyred Hussain, in a highly charged atmosphere of religious revenge, and then started off with intense passion to avenge themselves on the Umayyads in Damascus. Although Iraq was one of the territories which accorded recognition to Abdullah in defiance of Damascus, there was not enough common ground between him and the Penitents to launch a united attack against Marwan, their common enemy. He was fighting for the Caliphate whereas they were longing for martyrdom to rid themselves of their guilt and to avenge the blood of Hussain. In spite of their tremendous devotion and gallantry in the battlefield, they badly lacked competent leadership to coordinate their efforts. Faced with an overwhelming and trained Syrian army, they were virtually exterminated at a place called Ain al-Warda along the Upper Euphrates, and their shattered remnants retreated to Kufa.

Subsequently, in the same year (685) they found a leader in the person of a political adventurer named Mukhtar ibn Abi Ubaid, a native of Taif. He rallied around him the surviving Shi'ites of Kufa, who, under his ingenius leadership and their battle slogan 'Vengeance for Hussain', suddenly rose in arms and quite unexpectedly took over the town, overthrowing its governor, who was an appointee of Abdullah. Although the Shi'ites were in a minority in Kufa, this dramatic turn of events gave Mukhtar an important and powerful base from which to strengthen his position. After his *coup d'etat*, he tried conciliation to win over the Kufans, but when this failed, his attitude changed completely; Mukhtar 'the Avenger' hunted down systematically the murderers of Hussain, who were still living in Kufa and killed them in a most revengeful manner to the satisfaction of the Shi'ites. He quickly assumed control of a large part of Iraq and northern Persia, hiving off territory previously under the influence of Abdullah, and thus splitting the empire three ways; Abdul Malik holding Syria and Egypt, Abdullah now controlling only Arabia and Basra, and the new contestant, Mukhtar. As for the Kharijites, they were no longer united and strong enough to pose any significant threat for some time to come and had been driven out of Basra.

Introduction of the Concept of the Mahdi *by Mukhtar*

Mukhtar initiated his revolts in the name of Muhammad ibn Hanafiya (named after the tribe of his mother), a son of Ali by a wife other than Fatima. Muhammad, not being Fatima's son, was not a descendant of the Prophet but he was the most prominent Alid who survived after the massacre at Karbala. Mukhtar's call to rise in arms had an immediate appeal to the deep-seated desires and emotions of many people, particularly the *Mawali* (the non-Arab Muslims) of Persian origin who resented their inferior status both social and economic (they had to pay a higher rate of taxes), in the Arab aristocratic system. They looked upon the Umayyad regime as a symbol of Arab domination and were attracted by the Shia, whose members showed a passionate enthusiasm to avenge the Umayyads for the blood of Hussain, and Mukhtar's eloquent promise of a just society. He was the first to introduce the concept of the *Mahdi* (meaning the 'rightly-guided one') similar to the biblical Messiah with which the *Mawali* were familiar from their Christian and Jewish backgrounds. The Persians were, of course, also used to the idea of sacred monarchy. He assured people of the arrival of the *Mahdi*, who would establish an ideal reign of absolute justice on earth. This gave them hope for their grievances to be settled and desires to come true in a distant future. Although his movement was crushed and he himself killed within less than two years, Mukhtar acquired a revolutionary significance; the idea of the *Mahdi* took a firm and lasting hold, the Shia was transformed from being a political party (based on the question of the

Caliphate after the Prophet's death) into a religious sect, and the *Mawali*, for the first time, were organized into a political force to demand equality with the Arab Muslims. All these developments were to leave a permanent mark on the future course of Islamic history.

Although in the Shi'ite creed the *Mahdi* became an essential figure, later identified with the 'Hidden Imam' who would reappear and rule by divine order, filling the world with righteousness, there also developed gradually a Sunni conception of the *Mahdi**. In later times, the idea often sustained Muslims when their community had fallen into an oppressed and impotent state, and many religious leaders have claimed the honour of being the *Mahdi* at various stages of Islamic history.

The most notable example of the Sunni Mahdi *in recent times was Mahdi Muhammad Ahmad, who set up a theocratic state in Sudan which survived from 1882 to 1898.*

686

Defeat of Damascus Army in Iraq

The pressure on Abdul Malik from the Byzantine front eased off and he attempted (in August), for the first time, to gain control of Iraq from Mukhtar ibn Abi Ubaid. But his venture ended in complete disaster for the Umayyad army, near Mosul, where their leader Ubaidullah ibn Ziyad, the former governor at the time of the massacre at Karbala and an object of hate in Iraq, was slain.

687

Death of Mukhtar in Siege of Kufa

Abdullah ibn Zubair was still based in Mecca, but his brother Musab tried to regain Iraq for him from the clutches of Mukhtar. The very preaching of racial equality which had helped Mukhtar to rise to power with the aid of the *Mawali* now turned the Arabs against him who feared the prospect of their privileged position being eroded. Musab exploited the situation to his advantage and organized a strong revolt of Bedouin warriors against Mukhtar. Kufa was besieged, and Mukhtar was killed in April at the age of about sixty-five; his rise and fall had both been swift. This now left just two contenders for the Caliphate—Abdul Malik and Abdullah.

691

Iraq under Abdul Malik's Control

Having bought a truce on the Byzantine frontiers in 689 and suppressed any opposition to his rule in Syria, Abdul Malik devoted his full attention to the reunification of the empire. Iraq had borne the brunt of the bloody civil wars while Abdullah ibn Zubair had remained in Mecca all this time, and Abdul Malik had watched with relief his enemies fighting one another in the territory belonging to his main rival. He now felt strong and secure enough to launch a military campaign in Iraq against Musab, who was holding it for his brother Abdullah. However, the Iraqis had grown weary of the ferocius convulsions of barbarism and religion which had been tearing their country apart; victory for one faction had led to more bloodshed and another victor who, in turn, had settled old scores with his opponents in a pitiless way, and so it went on. The two armies met at a place called Dair al-Jathalik on the west bank of the Tigris north of the spot where the city of Baghdad was to be founded later in 762. But this time Musab's army officers did not have enough conviction to fight yet another civil war with full vigour, and he was killed. The whole province of Iraq passed into the hands of Abdul Malik, leaving only Arabia out of his control and under the sway of Abdullah.

The Dome of the Rock (al-Aqsa)

Caliph Abdul Malik built in 691 the Dome of the Rock and, close by, al-Aqsa Mosque (meaning, the farthest mosque) in Jerusalem. Stylistically, it was a landmark in architectural history, being the first Islamic building with a dome; it is also the third holiest sanctuary.

> The site is traditionally identified with that mentioned in sura ('The Nocturnal Journey') 17:1 in the Quran. The splendid Dome was erected around the Holy Rock, about fifty-six feet long and forty-two feet wide but almost semicircular in shape and rising to a height of five feet above the ground, from where the Prophet Muhammad began his famous nocturnal journey to the Seventh Heaven. Although it has undergone a few alterations and repairs, it has retained its original form and is, therefore, the earliest Muslim monument still surviving and in use. The inscription in Kufic script round the dome is one of the oldest examples of Arabic writing extant and is thus a valuable source in the study of calligraphy. Al-Aqsa Mosque was rebuilt by the Abbasid Caliph, al-Mansur (r. 754–75), c. 770, after it had been destroyed in an earthquake.

In common usage, the term al-Aqsa is meant to include both the Dome and the Mosque, and other buildings around this sacred spot.

692

Siege of Mecca by Hajjaj; Death of Abdullah; End of Second Civil War

Having gained control of Iraq, Abdul Malik left it to his trusted and ruthless lieutenant Hajjaj ibn Yusuf to deal with his principal rival, Abdullah ibn Zubair, who was firmly established in Mecca. But the loss of Iraq had already constituted a severe blow to the latter's position. The holy city came under siege for the second time during the period of Abdullah's revolt against Umayyad rule, the first being in 683. Hajjaj disregarded its sanctity completely in his effort to put down the rebellion. A continous bombardment of rock missiles coming from catapults placed on the hills surrounding the holiest city of Islam spread havoc and ruin all around. After eight months of the blockade, the resistance crumbled. However, Abdullah refused to surrender and, with characteristic bravery, went down fighting (October) in this hopeless situation. The formidable Abdullah had defied Damascus and held the rival Caliphate for nine years. For this achievement of defeating Abdullah's anti-Umayyad movement, the former schoolmaster Hajjaj from Taif was given the governorship of Arabia at the young age of thirty. He continued exerting his authority, and in the next two years the region was pacified and brought under the complete control of Damascus.

This brought to an end the disastrous period of twelve years of the Second Civil War since the accession of Yezid in 680, the First having being of five years duration from the rising against Caliph Uthman in 656 to the death of Caliph Ali in 661. There were no more serious uprisings in the rest of Abdul Malik's reign, and he remained the undisputed ruler of the Muslim world. He later became known as 'Father of Kings', since four of his sons, al-Walid (r. 705–15), Sulaiman (r. 715–7), Yezid II (r. 720–4) and Hisham (r. 724–43) were called to the Caliphate.

695

Subjection of Iraq by Hajjaj

Having thoroughly cowed Arabia, Hajjaj ibn Yusuf was appointed, in January, governor of Iraq, which was the most turbulent part of the empire, where both the Shia and the Kharijites had been a continuous source of trouble for the Umayyads. After swiftly crossing six hundred miles of the Arabian desert from Medina with only twelve men, he arrived unexpectedly in the main mosque of Kufa in the disguise of a cameleer. Here, he took off his muffle and made a most threating speech from the pulpit, as Ziyad ibn Abihi had done (662) before him, promising the severest possible measures against anti-Umayyad elements from any quarter. And he, like Ziyad, was true to his word. His boundless loyalty to the Umayyad cause made him pursue his aim of restoring order in the province by every means, however ruthless. There was a strong similarity in this respect between him and his predecessor and fellow clansman Ziyad ibn Abihi from Taif*. And like Ziyad, he was made viceroy of the whole of the eastern half of the empire and given a free hand to run it. He continued receiving the same complete support and confidence from Abdul Malik's successor, al-Walid (r. 705–15), and remained in this post till his death in 714 at the age of about fifty-two.

The clan of Thaqif from the town of Taif produced four ruthless but competent soldiers, who left a deep mark on the history of Iraq under the early Umayyad rule: Mughira, Ziyad and Hajjaj on the side of Umayyads, and Mukhtar who fought against them.

696

Arabic as Official Language of the Empire; Introduction of Arabic Coinage

It had been the official policy of the Muslims to keep the old administrative machinery with its staff and proceedure intact in the conquered territories provided taxes were collected efficiently. For instance, even after sixty years of Arab rule, the public accounts were still kept in Greek in Syria, and Pahlavi in Persia and Iraq. Having consolidated the empire, Caliph Abdul Malik now turned his attention to streamlining civil administration.

The government in Damascus was organized on the basis of five *diwans*, or secretariats, dealing with land revenue and finance, the army, government correspondence, the postal service and chancery. The first three of these government departments had already existed—though not in a very developed form—since the days of the Orthodox Caliphs, particularly of Umar ibn al-Khattab (r. 634–44); the other two had been first established by Muawiya I (r. 661–80) but were now properly reorganized. In 696, Arabic was declared the official administrative language of the Muslim empire; Iraq was the first to adopt it, followed by Syria (700) and Egypt (705).

The Byzantines had used a gold coin, the *solidus*, as the basis their currency, while the Persians had employed the silver *dirham* in their monetary system.

Both these currencies continued to be legal tender under Muslim rule. A sporadic process to modify it by the superimposition of certain Quranic phrases had been started by Muawiya I, but it was followed with earnest in 696 by Abdul Malik. The new coins bore only Arabic and Islamic inscriptions; they were the gold *dinar* (about four grams in weight) and the silver *dirham*. A central mint was established (696) in Damascus, but it took a number of years before only Arabic coins were in circulation throughout the empire. In the time of Abdul Malik, the *dinar* was worth ten *dirhams*, later twelve or even more; the actual rate of exchange was, however, subject to market fluctuations, varing at diffirent times and palces.

Efficient machinery was set up to collect taxes and administer the revenue thus acquired. There were still the three main forms of taxes which had been introduced by the Prophet himself and later regulated by Caliph Umar (r. 634–44). They were

(i) The Poor Tax (*zakat*): paid by all Muslims owning a certain minimum amount of possessions, and distributed among the needy. It is one of the principal obligations of the Islamic faith.

(ii) The Land Tax: levied on all who cultivated land, though at a higher rate on non-Muslims than on Muslims.

(iii) The Poll Tax: collected from male adult non-Muslims of certain tolerated religions, e.g. Christians, Jews and Magians, in return for protection of themselves and their property and freedom of worship. Women, children, the aged, the sick, monks and slaves were exempt, except if any of them had an independent income.

Other sources of revenue for the government were the one-fifth of war booty, and payment of tributes by those districts which offered fight and were then conquered.

Suppression of Kharijites in Iraq

During the struggle between Abdul Malik and Abdullah ibn Zubair, the Kharijites gained strength and were once again threatening to tear Iraq apart. These intense fanatics, with the slogan 'No rule but that of God', had spread terror and devastation up and down the country, regarding everyone who was not in agreement with them as an infidel punishable by death. By now, there were a large number of people in their ranks who were nothing more than malcontents who were attracted by their extreme views. After long years of struggle, Hajjaj defeated them in 696, but only after an expeditionary force was sent by the Caliph from Syria. Their leader, Shabib, was defeated and drowned in the Dujail River (the modern River Karun, Persia) in 696 (or 697). It was mainly due to the energy and determination of Hajjaj that the Kharijites were suppressed and Iraq was spared of their brutality.

698

Recapture of Qairawan by the Arabs; Expulsion of Byzantines from North Africa; Foundation of Tunis

Uqba ibn Nafi had captured north Africa from the Byzantines in 670 and founded the town of Qairawan in order to use it as his base in the region west of Egypt. However, he had been unable to pacify the native population of Berbers and was eventually killed in 683; the Berbers had regained their land. Since then, there had been a number of attempts to recapture it, but the Arabs were up against a very hardy race of people, and victories had been costly and short-lived.

Now that Caliph Abdul Malik was at the height of his power, he diverted his resources to advance westward in that region. The Arabs, under the command of Hassan ibn Numan, recaptured the base at Qairawan after a series of daring operations carried out simultaneously against the Berbers in the Atlas and the Romans in their coastal fortresses. Hassan took Carthage, one of the greatest cities of the world, by storm, and razed it to the ground as the Romans had done earlier in the Third Punic War (BCE149–6) against the Carthaginians. With the fall of the capital, the remnant of the Roman army abandoned their fortresses and left the country. This was the final expulsion of the Byzantines from their African stronghold.

In 698, Hassan replaced the ancient city by developing a new town of Tunis on a site ten miles to the south-west, where it was less exposed to naval attacks by the Romans, who had a powerful fleet in the Mediterranean sea.

702

The Savagery of the Kahina in Berber Country

The Romans had been driven out of north Africa in 698 by an army under Hassan ibn Numan, and the Arabs were then confronted with only the original inhabitants, the Berbers. But the situation changed on both sides. A wild Berber tribe of the Atlas, the Zenata, acknowledged the leadership of a brave and heroic woman known as the Kahina, or prophetess. She was supposed to be gifted with supernatural attributes, and enjoyed the complete obedience of her people. The Arabs, on the other side, had been heavily reinforced by the Caliph with a powerful army, and placed again under the command of Hassan, a veteran campaigner in the area. At first, the Kahina had considerable success in driving the intruders out of her territory, but she found the new army much stronger to combat. In a desperate attempt to bar the progress of Hassan and deprive him of his main temptation in the wealth of the cities, she ordered that the entire country under her sway be laid to ruin. A decisive battle was fought at a coastal place called Tabarka, some eighty miles west of Carthage, in which she was defeated and slain. The destruction and savagery committed by the followers of this Berber Lioness proved of no avail; in fact, Hassan was hailed as a liberator by the inhabitants of the once-prosperous cities, who had suffered badly under her ruin-all policy. With skilful diplomacy, Hassan made an alliance with them against the remaining Greek resistance movement. Thus the Berbers were pacified at last after thirty years of alternating victory and defeat.

Consolidation by Hajjaj of Eastern Wing of the Empire

On the eastern side of the empire, Hajjaj ibn Yusuf had by now put down all the major uprisings and felt that the time had come to consolidate his rule. In 702 he built a new city called Wasit (meaning midway city) halfway between the two most turbulent cities of the empire, Kufa and Basra, and later used it as his base, controlling the whole of the eastern empire from this strategic location until his death in June, 714 at the age of only fifty-two.

He also turned his attention to improving civil matters in Iraq, which had once been a prosperous province but which had been devastated during the previous twenty years of civil wars. In the ensuing period, he undertook this task with characteristic vigour and was equally successful. He improved the irrigation system in this fertile country by digging a number of new canals and restoring the large one between the Euphrates and the Tigris. This network of canals, which flowed from the Euphrates into the Tigris, was also used for the transport of goods to and from Syria; in fact it opened up navigational routes linking different parts of Syria and Iraq with India through the Persian Gulf.

705

Incorporation of North-West Africa as a Full Province of the Empire

In north Africa, Hassan ibn Numan was replaced in around 705 by Musa ibn Nusair who combined the qualities of a good soldier and those of an equally good politician. The region was given the status of a full province of the empire—so far it had been a part of the province of Egypt—with its own capital at Qairawan, where Musa established his government. Previously, its governors had simply been envoys of the the governor of Egypt. With his conciliatory attitude, he succeeded in winning over the confidence of the local population, and in a short time the whole of the Berber nation was converted to

Islam. Having lost it in 683, north Africa once again came under Muslim rule as far as the Atlantic coast. The only exception was Ceuta, which was a Greek colony and was held by Count Julian under the king of Spain on behalf of the Roman Emperor, but the western islands of the Mediterranean were annexed to the Muslim world. Morocco was later used as a springboard to launch an attack into Europe in 711.

Thus came the turn of Arab influence in north Africa after a long succession of foreign invasions—Phoenician, Roman, Vandal and Roman again. The Romans had recaptured it in 553 from the Vandals, a barbarian tribe from north Europe, who had crossed from Spain to Africa in 427, taking its capital at Carthage in 439. However, during all this time, the Berbers of the interior had succeeded in remaining virtually independent in and around the Atlas Mountains. It was the first time that these pagan nomads had been not only subjugated by a foreign power but also converted to monotheism.* With the passage of time, this incredibly hardy race of people became more enthusiastic missionaries of Islam than the Arabs themselves and played a crucial role in many conquests in Africa and Spain.

Of all the races the Arabs conquered, the Berbers of north Africa had offered the most stubborn resistance. Even after becoming Muslim, they were not resigned to Arab domination.

Accession to the Caliphate of Abdul Malik's Son, al-Walid

Abdul Malik died in October at the age of sixty, and was succeeded as Caliph by his son al-Walid (r. 705–15) who reaped the benefit of the stability and prosperity already achieved. Al-Walid proved to be a worthy successor and continued to build on the achievements, both military and civil, of his brilliant father.   During his reign, the first European country—Spain—was conquered and annexed to the Muslim world. In Iraq, which was traditionally the most turbulent part of the empire, he retained the old faithful Hajjaj ibn Yusuf as governor and gave him his full suport, as his father had done before him. Hajjaj eventually gained complete control of the eastern half of the empire and maintained peace and order for his sovereign. In addition, there was considerable eastward expansion. India was invaded for the first time by the Arabs, and a small western part of it came under Muslim rule. The conquest of the region of Transoxiana which had started in 667, including Balkh, Bukhara, Samarqand, Khwarizm and Ferghana, was also completed, resulting in the Arab empire stretching from Samarqand to Toledo. With the eastern boundaries extended into Transoxiana, the Muslim world came into contact for the first time with a new culture and race of people—the Mongols. These barbarians later played a devastating role in the history of Islam.

Al-Walid's reign was one of peace and opulence, and witnessed the construction of many buildings of public welfare such as schools, poor-homes and hospitals, in addition to many beautiful places of worship. He appointed his cousin and the later Caliph, Umar ibn Abdul Aziz, as governor of Arabia under whom the Prophet's Mosque in Medina was enlarged and many improvements for the pilgrims were made in the holy cities of Mecca and Medina.

The Umayyad Mosque of Damascus

Al-Walid, a great patron of architecture, began the construction of the Great Mosque (later to be known as the Umayyad Mosque) of Damascus on the site of the Cathedral of Saint John the Baptist (which itself had previously replaced a pagan temple of Jupiter). When completed, it became not only a magnificent place of worship befitting the capital, but was also used for more formal audiences, held by the Caliph in a glorious chamber especially reserved for the purpose. It is regarded as the greatest of classical mosques of a new tradition.

711

Invasion of Spain by the Muslims

The year 711 saw the highest point of Arab power and expansion in both the west and the east. On the western side, a Muslim army of 12,000, consisting mostly of Berbers, under its Berber commander, Tariq ibn Ziyad, took the fateful step of crossing the sea from Tangier and landed in April at the foot of the incredibly steep rock of Gibraltar,* one of the most southerly points of Europe. Tariq was a freedman of Musa ibn Numair, the celebrated Arab governor of north Africa who had successfully driven out the remaining Byzantines from the coast west of Carthage and firmly established Islamic rule up to the Atlantic. Having properly fortified the Rock to serve as a base, he launched an attack into the mainland of Spain (known to the Arabs as Andalus**), which had been ruled by the Visigoths (West Goths—Germanic people) since 531. At the time, King Roderick was absent in the north of the country, which gave the invading army time to establish itself in the adjacent province of Algeciras. On hearing news of the landing, he marched south to confront the Muslims, but his army of 25,000 men was completely routed on the banks of the River Barbate (modern, Salado) and he himself was killed either in the battle itself or not long afterwards. This resulted in the complete collapse of organized resistance by the Gothic kingdom, which was already in a state of dynastic dispute, not to mention the discontent and misery among the subject population on a large scale. As had happened previously on two crucial occasions in the expansion of the Muslim empire—Yarmuk in Syria and Nihavand in Persia—the invaders now had only to deal with resistance from individual cities.

Encouraged by his momentous victory and having thrown the enemy into panic without its leader, Tariq exploited the situation to the full by not giving respite to the imperial army. He marched in haste with only 9,000 men—the rest of the tiny force was engaged to capture Cordova, Archidona and Elvira***—towards the Gothic capital, Toledo, some two hundred and fifty miles to the north across an unknown mountain terrain. Although his action was extremely daring, it proved justified in the end, for he found the city in total disarray and captured it without difficulty. From then on, town after town became an easy prey; Tariq had shattered an old kingdom in a matter of a few months.

A large part of the Iberian Peninsula was overrun in two years. The conquest led to Arab domination of a part of Europe for over seven centuries.

*The Rock of Gibraltar owes its name to Tariq, meaning Jabal Tariq or Tariq's mountain. It covers an area of just 2.5 square miles (after considerable land reclamation since Tariq's days) and rises abruptly to a height of some 1,400 feet.
**The name Andalusia is thought to be etymologically connected with 'Vandalicia', derived from the name of the Vandals—another Germanic tribe—who invaded Spain in 409 from France and crossed into north Africa twenty years later, finally establishing in 439 an African empire with its capital at Carthage; some of these people were still in the south of the peninsula. The Arabs applied the name of Andalus to the whole of the Iberian peninsula (modern Spain and Portugal), not only to the southern province of Spain now called Andalusia.
***Later to be known as Granada, with its famous Alhambra (al-Hamra meaning 'the red') palace perched on a steep hill and built in 1238 by Muhammad (I) al-Ghalib (r. 1232–1272), the first of the Nasrid kings, and finished by his successors. It is the finest example of Muslim art in Spain. This monumental complex was their last stronghold till 1492, when Granada was taken by the combined forces of Ferdinand II of Aragon (1452–1516) and Isabella of Castile (1451–1504), after their marriage in 1469, which had brought about the unification of Christian Spain under one crown.

Expansion of Muslims into Indus Valley

While Tariq was conquering Spain in the west, an overland expedition under the command of Muhammad ibn Qasim, a nephew and son-in-law of the Iraq governor, Hajjaj ibn Yusuf, advanced through southern Persia and Baluchistan (already in Muslim hands) and attacked the lower Indus Valley in 711. The seaport of Daibul(modern Karachi) and the city of Nirun (modern Hyderabad) fell into the hands of the invaders; both had old and rich Buddhist shrines. Qasim defeated and killed Dahir, the Brahman (Hindu) Raja of Sind, conquering Sind and reaching as far as Multan in southern Punjab two years later (713); the area now forms a part of Pakistan. The religion of Islam was thus implanted for the first time on the Indian subcontinent.

This conquest of the easternmost extremity of the Arab empire was not, however, followed up on any large scale by Muslims for another three hundred years, when the Ghaznavid Sultan Mahmud (r. 998–1030) started a fresh series of invasions from Afghanistan.

Assasination of Justinian II; Chaos in Byzantine Empire

The tyrant Emperor Justinian II (r. 705–11)* was assasinated which threw the Byzantine empire into chaos once again. There followed the quick succession of three rulers (Philippicus, Anastasius II and Theodosius III) to the imperial throne in the next five years, until Leo III the Isaurian seized power in 716 and brought back order and unity. During this period of turbulence, Caliph al-Walid was encouraged to commission his brother Maslama to make an attempt to break Byzantine power in Asia Minor. This eventually led to the famous siege of Constantinople in 716–7, which ended in failure.

*This was the second reign of Justinian II, the first being 685-95. The brutal emperor was nicknamed 'the Slit-nosed' by the Arabs because his nose had been amputated.

712–3

Musa's Campaign in Spain

When the news of the astonishing success of Tariq ibn Ziyad in Spain reached his chief, Musa ibn Nusair, in the capital, Qairawan, he decided to go to Spain himself. In June 712, he landed at Algeciras with 18,000 (according to some sources, 10,000) soldiers, this time mostly Arabs, and began his own campaign independently of Tariq. He followed a northward but more westerly route than Tariq's, concentrating mainly on those strongholds not attacked by Tariq, e.g., Medina Sidonia, Carmona, Alcala de Guadaira and Seville. Seville was the former Roman capital of Spain and a great intellectual centre, apart from being the largest city. It did stand up to the invaders but gave in eventually. The most stubborn resistance came from the ancient Roman colony of Merida, which was captured after several months of siege and great loss of life. He then proceeded to Toledo, completing a D-tour of the Muslim conquest in 713, where he met his lieutenant, Tariq, and rebuked him publically for exceeding his orders and continuing the campaign independently of his authority. However, in spite of this row, the conquest of Spain continued.

Traditionally, it is alleged by some historians that Musa's motive was no more than petty jealousy of the stupendous achievement of his former slave. However, it can be argued that he genuinely felt the need to provide military and political assistance, in view of what had happened earlier in his own region of north Africa. Uqba ibn Nafi, a brilliant and daring soldier, had flashed through the coastal planes for nearly fifteen hundred miles west of Egypt, demolishing all opposition which came in his way, till his horse was reputedly stopped north of Agadir only by 'the waves of the (Atlanic) ocean'. But since all this had been achieved with pure early Muslim enthusiasm without its being followed up with consolidation, the Arabs position had remained precarious in the area. When Uqba was ambushed and killed in 683, the invaders were thrown out soon after his death and the Arab frontier was pushed back to Barqa.

Arab Crossing of the Jaxartes and Raid on Khashgar; Spread of Islam to Boundary of China

On the eastern frontiers too, the Muslim conquests had been spectacular. Hajjaj ibn Yusuf, the powerful viceroy of Iraq, had Qutaiba ibn Muslim appointed governor of Khurasan in 704 with his base at Merv. Ever since his appointment, Qutaiba, an outstanding soldier and diplomat, had been making advances in this completely unknown territory in Central Asia. The core of his army was of Arab origin, from the tribes which had been removed in 670 from Iraq to this remote province. However, he also used the age-old animosity between the Persians, most of whom had adopted Islam, and the Turks; the River Oxus formed the traditional Iran/Turan boundary, i.e., between the Persian-speaking and the Turkish-speaking people. In this way, he managed to recruit into his army a significant number of *Mawali* (non-Arab Muslims) from the local Persian population.

Transoxiana was commercially an important region, having lucrative trade links with China, particularly in the import of Chinese silk. It was also fertile land. Qutaiba launched a series of successful campaigns and established a permanent Muslim foothold in 'the land beyond the river (Oxus)'; Balkh (705), Bukhara (706–9) and Samarqand and Khwarizm (modern Khiva, Uzbek SSR/ USSR) in (710–2).

Having gained control of Transoxiana, Qutaiba penetrated still further north-east. In 712 he occupied Ferghana, a fertile valley irrigated by the Jaxartes (modern Syr Darya), and crossed the river, capturing Shash (now Tashkent in USSR). The following year he even raided Kashgar, a frontier town of China, from where a delegation was sent to the Emperor of China to demand his submission which, of course, was turned down with philosophic good humour.

This was the climax of Umayyad expansion in the east and it looked as if the Muslims had reached limits set by geographical and ethnic factors. Unlike the comparatively easy conquest of Spain, the warfare in Central Asia had been long drawn-out and ruthless. But the achievement of spreading Islam in the area remained permanent. It brought the empire into contact with a new race of people and a new religion—the Mongols and Buddhism. The cities of Balkh, Bukhara and Samarqand had fire-temples as well as Buddhist monasteries, which were destroyed by the invaders. An increasing number of conversions to Islam followed among the Persion and Turkish inhabitants, particularly during the reign of Caliph Umar II (r. 717–20), when a fairer system of taxation for non-Arab Muslims was introduced.

A large number of these new converts joined the Arab army in Khurasan, and, through it, they were to play a significant role in both the overthrow of the Umayyads (750) and the subsequent history of Islam. Bukhara and Samarqand were destined to become great centres of Islamic intellectual and cultural life. Over the centuries to come, the religion of Islam was to spread even into China proper from this firm base. Even now China is estimated to have over ten million Muslims.

714-5

Dismissal in Disgrace of Musa and Tariq

In September 714, both Musa ibn Nusair and Tariq ibn Ziyad, while still campaigning hard in the northern mountainous region of Galicia in Spain, received peremptory orders from Caliph al-Walid in distant Damascus to report to him about the conquest. Musa, being a viceroy, was directly responsible to the Caliph and no body else. Ironically, he was charged with precisely the same offence for which he himself had harshly reprimanded his subordinate Tariq in the previous year—acting independently of his superior. Leaving his second son, Abdul Aziz, in charge of the newly acquired territory, he made a long overland journey via Africa, Egypt and Palestine, with Tariq and a long convoy of Berber chiefs, Gothic princes laden with crown jewellery, prisoners-of-war and slaves carrying enormous treasures of booty acquired in the ancient cities of Spain. When Musa, at the head of this triumphal procession, reached Syria in February 715, Caliph al-Walid was lying on his death bed. Soon al-Walid's harsh and vengeful brother Sulaiman (r. 715–7) took over the Caliphate and proved himself to be but a poor shadow of his brilliant father and brother. Instead of applauding the great achievements, he accorded humiliating treatment to the hero whom he regarded as too powerful and potentially dangerous. Musa had indeed grown too powerful, controlling an area nearly as large as that ruled by his master but there was no suggestion of him declaring independence from Damascus; in fact, he was credited with conceiving a grand but serious plan to conquer the whole of Christian Europe, involving France, Italy and Greece. However, while in Damascus, the two conquerors were dismissed in disgrace, and spent the rest of their days in proverty and obscurity.

Executions of Famous Generals

In the east, the mighty viceroy Hajjaj ibn Yusuf had died in 714, and Sulaiman's vengeance fell on his protegee Muhammad ibn Qasim, the first invader of India, and Qutaiba ibn Muslim, the conqueror of Transoxania. Muhammad was forced to resign his command, accused of various offences and was put to death. Qutaiba, anticipating hisdismissal, met the same fate indirectly by organizing an unsuccessful revolt from his base at Merv.

These simultaneous and senseless executions of the most prominent conquerors by the new Caliph had a damaging and subtle effect on the future course of the empire. The reason behind these actions was twofold: Sulaiman's fear of powerful men in his empire and his hatred of those who had supported his brother and predecessor al-Walid, whom he had disliked intensely. But this served as an ominous warning to Muslim generals and governors all over the empire of what could happen to them at the hands of a fearful and despotic Caliph. It thus created an air of mistrust and disloyalty between Damascus and outlying provinces in the vast empire.

716–7

Turmoil in Spain

Back in Spain, Abdul Aziz, from his seat of government in Seville, continued to consolidate the territory already conquered by his father and Tariq ibn Ziyad. Although the Muslims were now deprived of their two best captains, they launched a new offensive westward into (the modern state of) Portugal, eastern Spain taking Malaga, and northward to the Pyrenees. Like his father, his policy towards the conquered people was of tolerance and reconciliation. However, he did not survive for long. The despotic Caliph Sulaiman in Damascus became suspicious of his loyalty too and had him assasinated near Seville in March 716, in keeping with his characteristic fear of powerful subordinates.

The next forty years were a period of turbulance for Arab Spain till 756, when a fresh line of Umayyads was formed by Abdur Rahman. Violent discord developed first between the Arabs and the Berbers who had come with the two conquerors, and then among the Arabs themselves, on the lines of the ancient genealogical hostility between the southern and northern Arab tribes—the Himyarites and the Modharites.

Failure of Arab Siege of Constantinople; Accession of Umar II on Death of Sulaiman

The most notable military event in Sulaiman's brief reign of two and a half years was the third siege of Constantinople, which lasted for a whole year, 716–7.* The massive operation involved an army of 80,000 men accompanied by 1,800 ships under the command of Maslama ibn Abdul Malik, a brilliant soldier and a brother of the Caliph. But the imperial capital was too strongly fortified for the equipment available to the Arabs. Moreover, the Byzantine throne had now been seized by Leo III the Isaurian (r. 717–41, and founder of the Isaurian dynasty), a fearless general and a great organizer, who received full support from the Church too in beating off the infidel enemy. There were considerable losses for the Muslims, and while desperate fighting was going on in the exceptionally severe winter, Sulaiman died (717) in Damascus. The defensive genius of the Byzantines again saved the 'Second Rome'.

Although he left several brothers and sons, he had nominated as his successor his cousin, Umar (II) ibn Abdul Aziz (r. 717–20), who ordered the abandonment of the siege and the return of the army to Syria. This was the last major expedition of the Umayyads against the Byzantines, although minor skirmishes continued across the frontiers.

As with the first two, the precise date of this siege cannot be ascertained.

Umar's Endeavour to Reform the Unjust System of Taxation

In the early days of the conquests, subjects belonging to certain protected religions such as Christianity and Judaism (termed the *Dhimmis**) had been ordered to pay a poll tax, first instituted by Prophet Muhammad, in return for which their lives and property would be protected (*dhimma*, meaning protection). They had been allowed local autonomy under their own heads and religious laws. The religious heads had been responsible for paying the communities' taxes to the Muslim governor. But if they professed Islam, they ceased to be liable to the poll tax and paid only those taxes obligatory on all Muslims. This had worked well as long as the state administration was modest both in size and style.** But since then all this had changed. The Caliphs no longer lived like desert tribesmen, but had adopted the life style of emperors, with all the imperial trappings. A vast empire was to be administered and regular armies had to be maintained from the borders of India to the coast of the Atlantic. At the same time, many races, such as Persian, Egyptian and Berber, had been conquered and the number of non-Arab Muslims was rapidly growing all the time. This new class of Muslims, outnumbering the Arabs many times over, was known as the *Mawali* (singular, *Mawla*) because they had to become clients of the Arab tribes. This posed a serious problem with deep and lasting implications for the empire; should the converts be given exemption from the extra taxation in line with their new religious status, in which case government revenue would fall drastically causing economic breakdown, or should they be made to continue paying taxes at the old (and higher) rate, thus sowing the seeds of discontent among a very large section of an already diverse population. The government had decided on the latter option, with some exemptions granted. Moreover, although the *Mawali* were theoretically the equals of the Arabs, this equality was never conceded. The latter formed a ruling aristrocracy enjoying social superiority and a lower rate of taxation.

Exemption from the poll tax was, in fact, granted mainly to Arabs, but those who had rendered distinguished services to the State also received this concession. This caused a great deal of resentment among Muslims of non-Arab races. The *Mawali* had fought alongside the Arabs, especially in the provinces of Khurasan and north Africa, but had received less remuneration than their Arab fellow-soldiers. This division between Arab and non-Arab Muslims was both economic and social, with the former in a minority but forming a ruling class. Thus the main criterion for discrimination between subjects remained religion, but there was the additional question of whether they were Arabs or not. This was a major internal weakness of the Umayyad's frame of government and contributed to its ultimate downfall (750). There had already been considerable unrest in different parts of the empire because of the unjust system, and the *Mawali* had become a valuable recruitment asset for the opposition movement, mainly the Shia, which had been gathering momentum all the time.

Caliph Umar II, who had been born and brought up in the traditionally pious surroundings of Medina, realized the iniquitous nature of the fiscal system and the harm it was bound to do to the unity of the Muslim community in the long term. He also had the courage of his convictions, and in an effort to reconcile the *Mawali* began his rule by initiating reforms in taxation whereby non-Arab Muslims were taxed equally with Arab Muslims. As expected, the government was immediately in financial difficulties. At the same time, it encouraged many more non-Muslims to accept Islam, thereby causing a further drop in the revenue. He also gave more civil rights tó the non-Arab section of the population.

On another front, he took diplomatic steps to heal those wounds between the Shi'ites and the Umayyads which had plunged the empire into civil war so often in the past. He abolished the practice, introduced by Muawiya after the battle of Siffin and followed by other Umayyads since then, of cursing Ali ibn Abi Talib in the Friday sermon. Caliph Abu Bakr, on taking office in 632, had declared that all property belonging to the Prophet should be forfeit to the State. Since then, it had been a point of grievance with the Alids that the orchard of Fidak had not been allowed to be inherited by the Prophet's daughter, Fatima. Umar II restored it to the descendants of Ali. He also attended to another perennial problem—the conflict between the Modharite and the Himyarite Arabs. In an effort to allay internal disorder, he acted with impartiality between these two so-called northern and southern tribes of the Arabs.

All these measures had a unifying effect up to a point. However, he did not live long enough for his reforms to have a lasting influence on the growing discontent among the non-Arab converts, notably the Persians in the east and the Berbers in the west, which had become a serious problem threatening to break up the empire. In any case, all his reforms were forgotten soon after his death, and the administration reverted to what it had been before he took office. Umar II was a man of deep piety in the mould of the early Caliphs, but his motives could not be ascribed to his pious nature alone, for he also had a keen insight into public affairs. His short reign was remarkably free from sedition and civil strife.

Originally the status of Dhimmi *was confined only to the Christians and Jews—'People of the Book', as they were called. However, as the empire expanded, the privilege was extended to include the fire-worshiping Zoroastrians (mentioned, once only, in the Quran as* Majus) *in Persia, the Buddhists in Transoxiana, the Hindus in India and the pagan Berbers in north Africa; in fact, most of the religions in the conquered lands were gradually assimilated into this category. An exception was the pagan tribes of Arabia, but they had accepted Islam long before.*
**Caliph Umar (r. 634–44), the most powerful man of his time, used to walk around barefoot, dressed in rags, and lived in a mud shack.*

718

Crossing of Muslims into France

Although Spain was a part of the Muslim empire and came under the jurisdiction of the provincial governor in Qairawan, it had been left largely to its own devices for the previous four years since its conquerors, Tariq ibn Ziyad and Musa ibn Nusair, had been recalled to Damascus and disgraced. Spain now had Hurr ibn Abdur Rahman as its governor. The Muslims, both Berbers and Arabs, under his command, crossed into southern France for the first time, pushing their way through the eastern end of the Pyrenees. They occupied Narbonne, which was later used as a base to launch further raids as far as Burgundy and Aquitaine.

719

Cordova as the Centre of Muslim Government in Spain

The seat of the local government in Spain was moved from Seville to Cordova, which was destined to become for centuries a great centre of culture and learning in Europe. After 756, when a new line of the Umayyads started in Spain, Cordova became its capital and was adorned with beautiful buildings by successive Muslim rulers.

720

Death of Umar II and Accession of Yezid II; Empire under Internal Strains

Umar (II) ibn Abdul Aziz died in February at the age of thirty-nine after a reign of only two and a half years. He was followed by Yezid II (r. 720–4), another son of Abdul Malik and brother of two previous Caliphs, al-Walid and Sulaiman. He was also a grandson of Yezid I through the latter's daughter, Atika.

Yezid II was a weak and frivolous character, and there was no outstanding achievement during his reign; instead, things began to go seriously wrong for the empire and the Umayyads. All the measures introduced by his predecessor to remedy the situation were reversed. The undercurrents of discontent based on social, economic and religious divisions within the empire had been getting stronger, and were now challenging its very existence. What was worse, the old feud between the Himyarite and the Modharite Arabs had now spread to north Africa, Spain and even to the advanced bases of the operational forces in France.

721

Repulsion of Muslims from Toulouse

The Muslims began to meet tough resistance in France and were pushed back from Toulouse by Eudes, Duke of Aquitaine. This was the first defeat of the Muslims in France.

724

Death of Yezid II; Accession of Hisham

Yezid II died and was succeeded by his brother Hisham ibn Abdul Malik (r. 724–43), aged under forty, at a time when the empire was in turmoil. Hisham was the fourth son of the late Caliph Abdul Malik (r. 685–705) to ascend to the Caliphate. Although he was a competent and moderate man, the problems he faced were enormous and critical, threatening the very existence of the empire. He was later to be regarded by many historians as the last great statesman of the House of Umayyad.

Beginning of the Abbasid Movement

The internal dissensions were broadly based on sectarian as well as social divides. Ever since the civil war between Ali ibn Abi Talib and Muawiya ibn Abi Sufyan and the subsequent martyrdom of Ali's son Hussain, the Muslim world had been divided into opposing camps—the Shia and the Sunnis*. And then there was the fanatical puritan group of the Kharajites, who had been very successful in their missionary work in north Africa, where they were now firmly established. Originally from Iraq, they had spread their doctrine to various parts of Persia and Arabia. Social and related economic divisions also existed between the Arab and non-Arab Muslims, mainly the Persians in the east and the Berbers in the west. Moreover, the Arabs themselves were divided into tribal groupings of the Modharites and the Himyarites—the so-called northern and southern Arabs respectively.

To add to all this, a new anti-Umayyad movement had been gaining ground. The Prophet Muhammad had another uncle, Abbas, apart from Abu Talib, whose son was Ali. In this way, the two branches of the Hashim clan could claim to be equally related to the Prophet. But the descendants of Ali had the added advantage in that Ali had been married to the Prophet's daughter, Fatima, and, through her, they were the direct descendants of the Prophet. The descendants of Abbas had not played any role in public affairs so far, but now they had a certain Muhammad ibn Ali, the great-grandson of Abbas, as the head of the family, and he conceived the idea of capturing the Caliphate for himself. This man, who had been living in obscurity near Maan (in modern Jordan) seemed to possess a genius for political propaganda and orginization. He successfully spread a subversive underground network in the distant province of Khurasan, always jealous and resentful of Damascus, exploiting the grievances of the non-Arab Muslims in the area. The secret campaign was conducted by his emissaries in the name of 'The Family' — a vague term used by the Shi'ites to mean the descendants of Ali. In this way, he managed to win over the Shi'ites in his struggle for power and soon had a large following.

Sunni or Sunnite (from Arabic sunna, meaning 'custom' or 'habit', especially that of the Prophet Muhammad) is the name commonly given to the larger of the two divisions of Islam, the other being Shia. The Sunna is to be found in the *Hadith* (Traditions). Since all Muslims claim to follow Muhammad's way of life and the pious regard it as their ideal, the use of Sunni as a proper name for one party is not strictly correct, though time has sanctified the practice, mainly because the rest of the Muslim world has acquiesced to it. This has led some non-Muslims to believe that the Shia reject the Traditions; in fact, no section of Islam does that. The Sunnis acknowledge the first four Caliphs as the legitimate successors of Muhammad, receive the 'six genuine' books of Traditions (the Shia have their own collection of Traditions), and belong to one of the four schools of Islamic law founded respectively by Imams Hanifa, Shafi, Malik, and Hanbal.

728

Revolt of Persians against Arabs with Help from Turks

After the victories of Qutaiba ibn Muslim in Transoxiana during 712–3, there had been a large number of conversions to Islam among the Persian and Turkish inhabitants. A significant number of locally raised levies of the new converts had joined the Arab army. This process had been accelerated during the reign of Caliph Umar II (r. 717–20) because of the changes in taxation policy introduced by him to make it fairer for the non-Arab Muslims. However, all his reforming measures had been ignored soon after his death and the system was reverted to what it had been before he took office.

This produced bitter resentment among the converts, who were asked to restart paying the poll tax even after they had accepted the new Faith. They could not see why their Arab Muslim brethren—and they were theoretically equal to them—were exempt from this tax. For some, tax exemption had been an incentive to adopt Islam in the first place. Moreover, they had fought alongside the Arabs but received less remuneration. A number of them renounced the new Faith, but found themselves in a precarious position, for death was the penalty for recantation.

The Persian converts were so incensed that they were prepared to appeal for help to their traditional enemy, the Turks, against whom they had fought for the sake of Islam under Qutaiba only fifteen years earlier. A strong revolt against the Arabs broke out in Khurasan, and a powerful Turkish army from beyond the Jaxartes joined the rebels. The Arabs found themselves besieged in this extremely dangerous situation, having lost control of the whole of

Transoxiana to the rebels and their Turk allies under the Khaqan, or paramount Khan.

Death of Hasan al-Basri

Al-Hasan al-Basri (b. 624), a leading religious thinker, jurist and scholar died in Basra, where had lived for most of his life since about 657. This highly respected saintly man had turned his attention to some very fundamental and philosophical questions in the Islamic faith, and his thinking had left a strong influence in most of the religious movements.

730

Tough Resistance of Khazars

The Muslims suffered a disaster at the hands of the warlike Khazars in the mountainous region of the Caucasus; Azerbaijan was ravaged. It was only after two years of savage fighting that the area was brought under control, when the future Caliph Marwan II was appointed governor. But most of the next twelve years of Marwan's governorship were spent in warfare with the enemy during which time Georgia in the Caucasus was conquered by the Muslims.

732

The Battle of Tours

Exactly a century had passed since the Prophet's death. The Muslims in Spain, under its governor Abdur Rahman al-Ghafiqi, launched their last and biggest military expedition northward, through the western Pyrenes, into the heartland of France. Having defeated Duke Eudes of Aquitaine, they stormed Bordeau and ravaged it. Abdur Rahman then advanced northward in the direction of Tours, which was an important religious centre with its rich shrine of Saint Martin. Eudes appealed to Charles Martel, a brave soldier and Mayor of the Palace of the Frankish north, who halted the Arab advance at a place, 150 miles south of Paris, between Poitiers and Tours (later to be known both as the Battle of Poitiers and of Tours).

For the first seven days, the two armies stood facing each other anxiously in the cold month of October. Then Abdur Rahman took the offensive, but his light cavalry failed to make any impact on the human wall formed by the Frankish army and he suffered heavy casualties. Among the victims was Abdur

Rahman himself. The dissension between the Berbers and the Arabs had flared up again in the rear and there was not much hope of receiving reinforcements. In this situation, the Muslim army, deep in France, was further handicapped by over-extended communications; even the provincial base at Cordova was over 700 miles. When night fell, the two armies disengaged, and great was the amazement in the Frankish camp when it discovered at dawn on the following day that the Muslims had abandoned their camp and just vanished. Frankish losses were not light either, and Charles Martel did not follow the enemy. But he came off victorious—in fact, it was a defensive victory—even though the battle ended without a definite outcome.

Poitiers marked the north-western extremity of the Muslim Empire which had been built in just one hundred years by the desert-dwellers of Arabia and it now stood bigger than the Roman Empire around the year 100 when it was stretched to its greatest extent under Emperor Trajan (r. 98–117). But from its culminating point, the Umayyad Caliphate had already started declining, being torn apart by internal disputes, social and fiscal problems.

Poitiers was the furthest point Muslims ever reached in their conquest of Europe, and the battle later became famous for this reason rather than for any outstanding military exploits. However, after this serious setback, the Muslims were not completely thrown out but continued their raids in France for nearly two decades (e.g. Avignon in 734, Lyons in 743). They lost Narbonne, their last hold and strategic base, in 759.

The Muslims had been continuously fighting for one hundred years and had built an enormous empire starting from a tiny theocratic state centred in Medina. This expansion had brought its own problems, not least that of racial diversity, which, in the case of north Africa and Spain, had caused the strife between the Arabs and the Berbers, which had got worse and eventually burst out in all its primitive violence in 740, being crushed only after a bloody confrontation. Added to this was the old intertribal discord between the Modharite and Himyarite Arabs. But now the feud between the two groups of Arabs was taking on a religious complexion—the Modharites, on the whole, supported Sunni orthodoxy, whereas the Himyarites had adopted the Shi'ite posture. This part of the empire had also become a preaching ground for the Kharijite missionaries from the east, whose revolutionary egalitarianism had a deep emotional appeal to the disgruntled non-Arab races. This unending, multi-pronged dissention was destroying not only internal cohesion but also unanimity of feeling and purpose among the men fighting on the frontiers. The central authority over the Peninsula was eroded to such an extent that, on average, a governor of this land would last for no more than a year during the period between 732 and 755. The situation was aggravated by the long and difficult line of communication with Damascus, which always depended on the overland route through north Africa. The tide of Islam was already ebbing.

737

Defeat of Khazars in the Caucasus

The future Caliph Marwan II (r. 744–50) led a brilliant military campaign in the Caucasus and inflicted a severe blow on the Khazars of the lower Volga region, capturing their capital, Itil, at the mouth of the river.

738

End of Anti-Arab Alliance between Muslim Khurasanians and Pagan Turks

A serious revolt against Damascus by non-Arab Muslims in the north-eastern region of Transoxiana broke out in 728 as a result of the failure of the successors of Umar II (717–20) to continue his policy of taxation, which was fairer to the non-Arab Muslims. The Khurasani rebels found allies in the fierce Turkish tribes under the Khaqan from beyond the Jaxartes and took over the whole territory beyond the Oxus.

It had taken ten years of bitter fighting with great loss in this remote and harshly cold region to bring it under the Caliph's control. The hard struggle came to an abrupt end in 738 mainly because the Khaqan was killed by his own Turkish chief in his battle camp while preparing to march on Balkh. With his death, the alliance between the rebels and the Turks fell apart, and the Turkish hordes fled across the border only to engage in their previous pastime of fighting one another. It was the first time in the history of Islam that Muslims had made a confederation with infidels to fight fellow Muslims.

740–2

Berber Anti-Arab Revolt in North Africa

The Berbers were enraged, as had been the *Mawali* of Transoxiana in 728, that they had proved themselves to be good Muslims and zealous fighters in the cause of Islam, e.g., in north Africa and Spain, yet were required to pay higher taxes simply because of their non-Arabic origin. During the reign of Abdul

Malik (r. 685–705), the Kharijites were forcibly suppressed in the east, but after his death they began to infiltrate into north Africa. Here, they took full advantage of the Berbers' resentment and were very successful in spreading anti-Umayyad propaganda. Feelings flared up to such an extent that in 740 the Berbers rose *en masse* and a great revolt broke out from Morocco to Qairawan. After a continuous and bloody struggle, in which the Syrian expeditionary army was at one stage virtually exterminated, the revolt was finally crushed in 742 and Arab rule was re-established in north Africa. However, so much of their resources had to be diverted to the Berber revolt that the Arab advance in France, Sicily and Sardinia came to a halt.

Civil War in Spain

Inspired by all this, the Berbers of Spain also rose (741) in arms against the Arabs and a dangerous civil war followed, in which the governor, Abdul Malik, was killed. After Berber-Arab fighting had been brought under control, the Arabs started fighting among themselves on tribal lines. A period of general confusion ensued, during which several governors came and went till Yusuf ibn Abdur Rahman al-Fihri was made governor in 746, when order was restored. He turned out to be the last of the Umayyad governors of Spain before the Umayyad dynasty was overthrown (750) in Damascus.

Unsuccessful Bid for Power by Alids; Start of the Zaydi Sect

Independently of the Abbasid movement, a grandson of the martyred Hussain, Zayd ibn Ali* embarked on an uprising in Kufa against the Umayyads. As usual, the fickleminded Kufans did promise to give their full support, and, on that understanding, a day in the month of January 740 was fixed when a united rebellion was to take place. In the meantime, however, the local governor, Yusuf ibn Umar al-Thaqafi, got to know the plot and warned Zayd's supporters of the dire consequences if they took part in the planned revolt. It had the desired effect, and only a few hundred Kufans remained loyal to him when the actual time came. They were easily crushed in few days and Zayd himself was killed. His son, Yahya, a high-minded youth of seventeen, managed to escape to Persia, where he remained in hiding for several years before being put to death in the days of al-Walid II (r. 743–4). Thus ended in disaster the first attempt by a direct descendant of Ali ibn Abi Talib and Fatima, daughter of the Prophet, to seize the Caliphate by force.

The ill-prepared and politically inept rebellion of Zayd was an insignificant affair in itself but its impact was lasting. It deepened the alienation of the Iraqi Arabs from the Umayyads, which, in turn, helped the Abbasids in their propaganda. Indeed, the death of Zayd removed a possible Alid rival for the

Abbasids in their bid for power. They then turned the situation to their positive advantage; the Alids, who felt embittered, were made to think that the Abbasids were fighting for their cause. Thus the death of Zayd created more problems for the Umayyads in the long run than it solved. They might have had a divided and hence weak opposition to their rule, as had previously happened during the reign of Abdul Malik (r. 685–705), when the opposition had been divided three ways—the Kharijites, the Alids and the supporters of Abdullah ibn Zubair.

It also gave rise to the Zaydi sect** which was an offshoot of the Shia and the nearest to the Sunnis in its religious beliefs.

*This Ali, son of the martyred Hussain, is also known as Zainul Abidin. He was a survivor of the Karbala tragedy in 680 and one of the Imams of the Shia.
**A Zaydi state existed in Daylam on the southern shores of the Caspian Sea from c. 864 to 928; another was founded in 897 in Yemen. The Zaydis are scattered also in other Muslim countries.

743

Death of Hisham

Hisham died in the month of February at his residence in Rusafa (Syria), near Raqqa, on the upper Euphrates, after a reign of nearly twenty years, while still under sixty. With his death, not only did the golden age of the Umayyads come to a close, but a rapid decline also set in. By now the Muslim empire had reached its full extent on land. In the Mediterranean itself, the Muslims had become a formidable power, having gained temporary or long-term possession of many islands such as Cyprus, Rhodes, Crete, etc.

Accelerated Decline of the Umayyads; Accession of Marwan II

There was a quick succession of four Caliphs to the throne in the remaining seven years of the dynasty, of whom only the last Caliph, Marwan II (r. 744–50), showed any real dedication to his duties. The inexhaustible Marwan earned the nickname of Marwan the Ass.* He had already proved himself to be a brilliant commander in a campaign against the hardy Khazars during the twelve years preceding his Caliphate. But the intervening period between Hisham's death and Marwan's accession was marked by a violent power struggle within the House of Umayyad. It also saw three incompetent leaders—al-Walid II, Yezid III and Ibrahim—who helped to hasten the decline with their wasteful habits and love of pleasure. Added to this were sedition and bitter internal feuds of assorted kinds, which were spread throughout the empire and which were tearing it apart. So much political rot had set in that Marwan, who was more of a soldier than a politician, was unable to turn the tide.

To the Arabs, the ass was proverbial for its patient endurance and tenacity, and not for its stupidity.

The Abbasid Movement under the Leadership of Abu Muslim

Muhammad ibn Ali, the head of the Abbasid clan and brilliant originator of the Abbasid propaganda against the Umayyads, died (743), leaving the leadership of the movement to his son Ibrahim, who later appointed Abu Muslim to be in charge of the organizational side of the rebellion. Abu Muslim, a man of humble Persian origin (possibly an ex-slave), possessed rare qualities of leadership. He devoted himself with single-mindedness to creating a brilliant network of this secret anti-Umayyad movement and making it multi-faceted, so as to have a wide appeal to various groups of people with different grievances and aspirations. The propaganda turned out to be all things to all men. Also, the unending civil wars had created so much misery and chaos that the people were ready for any new regime which promised to create peace and justice in their land. And so successful was his campaign that they were lulled into believing that Abu Muslim was nothing less than their long-awaited saviour.

747

Irruption of Abbasid Rebellion in Khurasan

The secret Abbasid movement in the north-eastern region of the empire had been gathering momentum, and now the rebellion came out into the open, overthrowing the Umayyad governor of Khurasan. The slogan 'The Family' (of the Prophet) was used by the revolution which many of the Shi'ites took to mean that the Abbasids were working for the descendants of Ali and hence joined the campaign.

748

Takeover of Khurasan by Abu Muslim

In the month of March, Abu Muslim declared himself ruler of Khurasan, establishing his headquarters in Merv. Abu Muslim who had a large army and many able commanders, both Arab and Persian, was by then master of the whole of Khurasan. He started taking an oath of allegiance from the people in the name of the House of Hashim, the clan to which the Prophet Muhammad belonged. He thus broadened his appeal by avoiding the specific mention of the House of Abbas. The Umayyad authority completely vanished from the region; the Abbasid avalanche had become unstoppable. The black banners were proudly hoisted in public.*

The revolutionaries, whether Arabs, Persians or a mixture, had all one thing in common—they were the disgruntled groups of people who, among others, were the Persian *Mawali*, the Shi'ites and the Himyarite Arabs. The Kharijites did not join the movement as they had been consistent in their rejection of any prince claiming the Caliphate, but they staged an anti-government rebellion of their own in Iraq. The Modharite Arabs also did not ally themselves to the new movement, because they were being favoured by the current Caliph, Marwan II.

During all this time, no help was forthcoming from Damascus or the neighbouring Iraq, and the former Umayyad governor, Nasr ibn Sayyar, was left to fend for himself with the rebel army everwhere in hot pursuit.

Black and white were the respective colours of the Abbasids and the Umayyads. People showed their allegiance by wearing one of the two colours. Black, originally the standard of Muhammad, had been used previously by earlier opponents of the Umayyads.

Death of Wasil ibn Ata

Wasil ibn Ata, credited with being the founder of the famous school of rationalism called Mutazila, died in Basra. Wasil was connected with the circle of the famous thinker al-Hasan al-Basri (d. 728). This movement later attained great significance during the Abbasid period (750–1258), especially in the reign of al-Mamun (r. 813–33).

749

Increasing Momentum of the Abbasid Movement

Ibrahim ibn Muhammad, religious mentor of the Abbasid movement, had been keeping a low profile in his village near Maan and issuing secret instructions to his lieutenant, Abu Muslim, in distant Khurasan, who was in charge of the actual organization. Ibrahim was arrested by the Umayyad Caliph Marwan II and taken to northern Syria, where he was later executed in the month of August. But, in antipication of his arrest, he had already designated his brother Abul Abbas as his successor to the leadership of the movement.

Seizure of Iraq by Abul Abbas

After the defeat of a relief army from Syria, an Abbasid force captured Nihavand (May) in Persia and then Kufa (October) in Iraq. Although the Abbasid upheaval launched its final assault from the depths of Persia, it certainly also drew its considerable strength from the Iraqis, who had long been anti-Umayyad.

Soon after the Khurasan army took over Kufa, the new head of the Abbasid movement, Abul Abbas, who had recently come to the city from Maan, and had been in hiding, unexpectedly appeared in public and rode in triumph to the main mosque of Kufa, where he declared himself Caliph. From his inaugural speech, the Shi'ites, who had been among the enthusiastic supporters of the revolution, detected that the future course was likely to be run by the descendants of Abbas and not those of Ali, as they had hoped. They attempted to acclaim an Alid, but were ignored. The slogan 'The Family' (of the Prophet) had intentionally been left ambiguous during the whole campaign. However, the hated Umayyads had been thrown out, or were on the run, at least in the eastern provinces, and it was too early to predict with certainty the future events. So in the euphoria which followed, people flocked to swear their allegiance to Abul Abbas, but some disillusionment was already beginning to be felt in certain quarters.

750

The Battle of the Zab; Overthrow of the Umayyads by the Abbasids

At last, in January, Marwan (II) ibn Muhammad, the fourteenth and last Caliph of the Umayyad dynasty, came down to Mosul (Iraq) from Harran in Syria (he had always lived in Harran rather than Damascus) with an army, to take the field in person against the rebels. A battle took place near the River Zab, a tributary of the Tigris east of Mosul, in which Marwan was decisively defeated. This sealed the fate of the Umayyad Caliphate. Marwan himself fled to Egypt by way of Harran and the capital Damascus (which itself fell three months later), while the Abbasid forces took over the main cities of the Asian provinces without any difficulty. They reached Egypt within six months where Marwan was captured and put to death on 5 August at the age of over sixty. His head was cut off and sent to Abul Abbas, who had by then ascended the throne in an atmosphere of terror.

Massacre of Umayyad Family

In June 750, the Abbasids proceeded to exterminate the remnant of the fallen dynasty with savage thoroughness. This gruesome task was left to the new Caliph's uncle and victor in the Battle of the Zab, Abdullah ibn Ali, who had been rewarded with the governorship of Syria for his part in the revolution. Eighty or so Umayyad princes were invited to a banquet by Abdullah in Abu Futrus, a fortress on the River Awja (Syria). At a pre-arranged signal a band of executioners burst into the banquet hall and massacred the guests in cold blood. Scarcely was the carnage over than the banquet was served and indulged in to the accompaniment of the groans of the dying. Agents were sent all over the Muslim world to hunt down members of the deposed family; in particular, Abdullah's brother, Dawud, was given the job of governor of Mecca and Medina, and orders to extirpate the Umayyads in the holy cities. Such was the mad frenzy of the new rulers that they even went around desecrating the graves of the Umayyad Caliphs, with the exception of those of Muayiwa and Umar II.

Thus was shattered and came to an ignominious end the Umayyad Caliphate of Damascus after ninety years of glorius rule. This complete reversal was brought about not by external forces but by the disintegrating forces within the Muslim world.

The sole member of the family who dramatically escaped the massacre in Syria was Caliph Hisham's grandson, Abdur Rahman. He fled to Ceuta and eventually established a fresh line of Umayyads in Spain (756) and revived the old glory of his family in this distant province.

The Umayyad Government

The Umayyads had created a government out of feuding Bedouin tribes who were ready to engage in, and profit from, the wars of conquest of early Islam, but resented being subjected to central authority in any form. They jealously guarded their tribal independence and the freedom of the desert, being temperamentally averse to allegiance to a king or overloard. The very notion of a state on a national scale with power and authority centralized in one place was alien to them, their basic attachment being to the tribe or clan. They now formed the ruling class of the empire; the subject peoples were also of the most varied origins and religions. But the Umayyads with their administrative genius managed to develop a coherent Arabic culture with the religion of Islam and the Arabic language predominating everywhere throughout this vast empire.

There were various contributory factors to the success of the Umayyads. An important one was the transfer of its capital from Medina to Damascus and its reliance on Syria to provide the nucleus of its army and civil administration. Syria already had a high degree of civilization, and the Arabs who had migrated there in pre-Islamic days had consequently become more orderly and were more used to a centralized form of government than the people of Iraq, where the main rivals of the Umayyads, the Shi'ites, had established their base. The civil administration was also based on the well-tried Byzantine system which was first retained and later improved upon by availing the services of able advisers, both Muslim and non-Muslim.

The Prophet Muhammad himself had stated explicitly during his lifetime that each 'protected minority' should be allowed to practise its religion and govern itself in return for payment of tribute and poll tax. This policy had, on the whole, been continued. In its internal affairs, each protected minority was autonomous under its own religious head. Even in judicial matters of a civil and criminal nature, except where a Muslim was involved, these people were dealt with in accordance with their own laws and by their own religious head or his appointee. The relations between the Muslim and non-Muslim sections of the population were good. Syria, like many other parts of the empire, had remained largely Christian; Muawiya's wife (Yezid's mother, Maysun) was a Christian, and so was his poet and physician. The Muslims had been involved in frequent battles with the (Christian) Byzantines without being concerned with protecting their rear in Syria, which had a large Christian population of its own. The life span of Saint John of Damascus (c. 676–c. 754) had run parallel with that of the Umayyad dynasty. Saint John, the famous theologian and hymn writer of the Eastern Church, produced in Greek a lucid digest of Christian doctrines accompanied by tracts refuting Islam as an anti-Trinity heresy rather than a new religion—and he was allowed to do so, many times in open debates.

The Umayyads were also very careful to recruit their army from the more settled community of Syria rather than that of turbulent Iraq. In the ninety years of their reign, they doubled the size of the empire by their conquests in both the east and the west, carving out a domain nearly 4,500 miles across and stretching its wings in three continents.

Beginning of the Abbasid Dynasty

Abul Abbas was proclaimed the first Caliph (r. 750–4) of the new dynasty of Abbasids and took the well-earned title of al-Saffah (meaning 'Blood-shedder'). This turned out to be the longest lived dynasty in Islam (750–1258).

Most of his reign and that of his brother al-Mansur (r. 754–75) were taken up in suppressing a series of insurrections by various groups of discontented people. The general feelings of dissatisfaction which had grown in the later part of Umayyad rule among non-Arab Muslims, especially those of Persian origin, lay behind a number of these revolts. Many of these groups of people had given support to the Abbasid movement in their struggle to gain power but were disillusioned to see its achievements fall short of their expectations.

751

The Battle of Talas; Introduction of Paper-Making Industry in the Arab World

The Arabs defeated a Chinese army at Talas, in the high Pamirs (Central Asia), and captured some artisans, from whom they learned the technique of paper-making. They established this new industry in Baghdad (793) and it then gradually spread westward across the empire, reaching Egypt (c. 900 or earlier), Morocco (c. 1100) and Spain (c. 1150). This helped to reduce the need for making costly papyrus and thus fostered the growth of literature by enabling them to produce much cheaper books.

The Battle of Talas triggered off a civil war in China, where the splendid Tang dynasty (618–907) was already on the wane. This also marked the end of Chinese intervention in the region of Transoxiana. Tashkent was captured, and the supremacy of Islam in Central Asia was so firmly established that it was no longer challenged by the Chinese. This part of the empire was later to enjoy centuries of prosperity and produce a brilliant Muslim civilization of its own.

The manufacture of writing material akin to modern paper made from vegetable fibre, rags, etc., was invented by the Chinese around the year 100; of course, papyrus made from reeds found in the Nile swamps had been in use centuries before in ancient Egypt. Papyrus was made simply by laying side by side thin strips of the pith of the plant stems in two layers placed one above the other at right angles, compressing and then drying them into a taut sheet. However, it decayed in the damper, colder climate outside its native home of Egypt. The precious books, therefore, had to be written on parchment, but it was even more expensive than the papyrus. The introduction of paper—cheap, long-lasting and attractive—gave an impetus to learning as the invention of printing did in the fifteenth century.

The paper became available in western Europe in the twelfth century through factories established by the Arabs in Spain and Sicily, though the Europeans did not have their own paper mills until the fourteenth century. The first paper mill in England was built near Stevenage around 1490.

The oldest Arabic paper manuscript extant is dated Rabi I, ᴀʜ 252 (November 13—December 12, 866) and concernsTraditions (*Hadith*). It is preserved in the Leiden University Library.

<h1 style="text-align:center">753</h1>

Establishment of Abbasid Headquarters at Anbar

In 750, the Abbasids slashed their way through to power with the help of the Khurasan army under Abu Muslim and tried to eliminate the supporters of the previuos regime by fair means or foul. But these bloodthirsty tyrants did not feel secure enough to decide on a place safe enough to establish their permanent capital. The first Abbasid Caliph, al-Saffah (r. 749–54), therefore, started his reign from a castle near Kufa, both Damascus and Kufa being considered unsuitable to be made the capital of the new dynasty; and, of course, the Abbasids had no firm control over the provinces west of Egypt. Syria had been too long faithful to the newly toppled Umayyad regime, and the Kufans had proved themselves in the last hundred years to be tumultuous, and unreliable in their allegiance. In any case, Kufa was ruled out on another ground: a large section of the population was Shi'ite whose early aspirations had not materialized and who felt they had been let down by the Abbasids.

Al-Saffah decided in 753 to move his power base to Anbar, a town nearly hundred miles up the Euphrates. But the ultimate site for the capital still remained undecided.

<h1 style="text-align:center">754</h1>

Death of al-Saffah and Accession of al-Mansur

Al-Saffah died of smallpox (June) at the age of thirty-four. The site of his burial was kept secret for fear of reprisals being made for the vindictive frenzy he had meted out to the dead of the deposed Umayyad dynasty. It was much later, during the reign of al-Muntasir (r. 847–61), that his mausoleum was built.

Al-Saffah had already nominated his elder half-brother Abu Jaffar as his successor and his nephew Isa ibn Musa as his heir-presumptive. At the time of al-Saffah's death, Abu Jaffar was in Mecca on Pilgrimage, and Isa proclaimed him as Caliph in Kufa in his absence. On his return, Abu Jaffar, who was born of a Berber slave girl*, took up the Caliphate and assumed the title of al-Mansur, meaning the Victorious (rendered by God)**.

Al-Saffah's mother was an Arab from Yemen. All the Umayyad Caliphs, except Yezid III (whose mother was claimed to be a descendant of the last Persian Sasanid King, Yazdijird III), were born of Arab mothers, whereas, of all the thirty-seven Abbasids, only three Caliphs—al-Saffah, al-Mahdi and al-Amin—were of pure Arab blood. The rest had non-Arab slave mothers who were Berber, Persian, Turkish, Greek, Armenian, etc. Thus, although the Abbasid rulers were regarded as Arabs and the sole official language was Arabic, they rapidly started losing Arab racial identity after successive accession to the throne and by the mid-ninth century were genetically hardly Arabs at all.

**To bolster their own image, it became a common practice among the Abbasid Caliphs to bestow upon themselves, on taking office, throne-titles proclaiming divine support for their rule; other examples of such titles are al-Rashid, meaning 'the rightly-guided', al-Mutawakil ala'allah, meaning 'whose trust is in God', etc. It is generally believed that this religio-political idea was borrowed from pre-Islamic (Zoroastrian) Persia, where, although a king was not thought of as divine—like a Pharaoh in Egypt—he was nevertheless believed to have been chosen by Ahura Mazda ('The Wise Lord', the term used by Zoroastrians for God) for his righteous support of truth and his opposition to evil. In this way, the ancient Persian kings used to be surrounded by an aura of sacred glory.*

Unsuccessful Revolt by Abdullah ibn Ali

Immediately after al-Mansur's acession to the throne, his uncle, Abdullah ibn Ali, the governor of Syria who was responsible for the cold-blooded massacre of the Umayyad princes in 750, rose in revolt (754), claiming that the Caliphate should go to him. The rebellion was crushed with the help of the faithful Abu Muslim. Abdullah fled to Barsa where he lived in hiding with his brother, who was the governor there, but was killed eventually.

Murder of Abu Muslim

The same Abu Muslim who had also been the chief architect in the planning and execution of the Abbasid revolution, was now himself treacherously slain by al-Mansur, who feared that he would grow toopowerful and become a possible rival. Abu Muslim enjoyed unlimited power in Persia and unchalleged authority over the Khurasan army which had brought the Abbasids to power and was sustaining them. Such was the charisma of this man that a number of heretical sects (notably those led by al-Muqanna and Babak) arose after his death, inspired by his memory, denying that he was dead and claimimg that he would return to spread justice throughout the world.

755–6

Founding of Umayyad Dynasty in Spain by Abdur Rahman

In the general massacre of the Umayyad family by the Abbasid revolutionaries in 750, a young prince by the name of Abdur Rahman managed to escape. Disguised, penniless and accompanied by a faithful servant, he had been wondering since then across Palestine, Egypt and north Africa, where at last he was in the safety of his mother's Berber tribe. He eventually reached Ceuta in 755, from where he crossed into Spain and landed at Munecar, some forty miles east of Malaga. A man of exceptional audacity and steadfastness of purpose, he was determined to make a bid for power here in southern Spain (which was largely inhabited by Arabs from his homeland, Syria); he raised an army from among these Arabs, particularly from the Himyarite faction, who were traditionally loyal to the Umayyads.

The following year, he defeated the Abbasid governor, Yusuf al-Fihri (May), in a battle near Cordova on the bank of the Guadalquivir River and became the sole monarch of Muslim Spain as far as Barcelona and Saragossa for the next thirty-two years at the youthful age of twenty-six. He did not, however, succeed in dislodging Christian rule from the states of Leon and Navarre in the northern mountainous regions of the country. Helped by the impediment of overland communications (due to the Berber insurrection in north Africa during 740–61), he severed Spain for ever from the Abbasid Caliphate by founding, in 756, the Umayyad Amirate (later changed to Caliphate in 929)—from the word Amir, meaning commander, governor or prince—of Cordova, which ruled Spain till 1031, after which the country disintegrated into numerous small states in which local princes held power. The most important of these were the states of Badajoz, Toledo, Seville, Cordova, Granada, Valencia and Saragossa. With the fall of Granada, in January 1492, to the Christians, the last vestige of Muslim rule disappeared for ever from Spanish soil.

He later had to defend his realm against external attacks by armies sent from the north by the Frankish king Pepin and his son Charlemagne, and from the east by the Abbasid Caliph al-Mansur (r. 754–75). Internally, he had to face rebellions by diverse and often discontented elements of the population such as the Fihrites (the tribes of the former governor, Yusuf), Muslim Spaniards, Berbers, Christians, etc. But 'the Falcon of the Quraish', as he was later called by way of a compliment by his adversary Caliph al-Mansur of Baghdad, consolidated the state and maintained the power and unity of this vast territory.

Muslim Spain, with its capital, Cordova, enjoying a splendour rivalling Baghdad's, later became enormously important to Europe as a door to the learning and science of the East. Unlike some other parts of the Muslim world, such as Egypt, Persia and Iraq, the great mass of the subject population in Spain (as later in Sicily) remained loyal to their old respective religions of Christianity and Judaism. But under the tolerance shown by their new rulers in religious matters, they were able to keep their culture alive and live peacefully side by side with the Muslims, or Moors, the name given to the Muslim population of mixed Arab, Spanish, and Berber origins. Christian and Jewish communities were left unruffled to follow their faiths under their own religious laws and judges, whose jurisdiction did not, of course, include cases involving Muslims and offences against the religion of Islam. This amicable religio-cultural heterogeneity gave birth to a brilliant intellectual life, each group drawing upon the other's traditions and cooperation. The cities of the south, Toledo, Cordova, and Seville speedily became centres of the new culture and famed for their universities. Judged by its greatest men of learning, Arab culture (in the sense of Muslims of any racial origin writing their work in Arabic) reached its pinnacle in the ninth and tenth century in the East, and eleventh and twelfth century in Spain. This is the period so-called the Dark Ages, but dark only in Europe where science was dead and theology (then regarded 'queen of sciences') was the main preoccupation. The Arabs were, by and large, of practical bent, and this was reflected in their choice of subjects for study. Although Arabs' contribution in history and geography were impressive, their greatest achievements were in the field of natural sciences, mathematics, astronomy and medicine.

The quality of this culture can be judged by the number of translations of Arabic works into Latin in the later Middle Ages, and the tremendous repute which Arab scholars enjoyed in Europe. Much of this translated literature served as text books in Europe for centuries. For instance, the *Canon of Medicine* by Avicenna (Arabic: Ibn Sina d. 1037), which was translated into Latin (the language of the learned in Europe at that time and in succeeding centuries) by Gerard of Cremona (d. 1187) in the twelfth century, dominated the teaching of medical science until at least the end of sixteenth century. During 1470–1500 alone, it went through fifteen editions and one Hebrew. Of the works of al-Kindi (d. circa 873), one of the leading Muslim philosophers, more has survived in Latin than in Arabic. It is revealing that at the height of Arab civilization, this cultural transmission with the then backward Europe was almost one-way. Only one Latin text, it appears, was ever translated into Arabic; the Spanish Muslims regarded the civilization of the cold northern lands as meagre and not worth studying.

In addition to the intellectual achievements of the Arabs, the legacy of Greek culture and science also passed to Europe by way of Spain (and Sicily), largely in the form of Latin translations from Arabic versions of such works as those by Aristotle (BCE 384–322), Euclid (BCE 325–?), Ptolemy (c.75–?), Galen (c.130–c.200) and many others. The Arabs responded to, and were creatively stimulated by, the Greek literature. In turn, Arab science and philosophy made a large contribution to European thought, but strangely, their intellectual advancement did not continue; instead, it started declining from about the end of twelfth century, at a time when Europe was on the way to progress.

It also left behind architectural gems in Spain such as the renowned Mosque of Cordova, Medina al-Zahra and the magnificent Alhambra in Granada, to name but three.

Loss of Qairawan to the Berbers

The Berbers of north-west Africa had first been conquered by the Arabs about half a century earlier. The great majority of these pagans had accepted Islam and had become more zealous Muslims than the Arabs themselves; they took a very active and important part in the spread of Islam, both in Africa and in Spain. This, however, by no means made them resigned to Arab rule.

The Abbasids were too preoccupied in the East to spare time and resources for the distant provinces. Seizing the opportunity, the Berbers rose in revolt yet again in 755, sacked and then took over Qairawan. It was not until 761 that the rebels were defeated and Qairawan reoccupied.

758–60

Annexation of South Caspian Region to Muslim Empire

The inhabitants of the northern mountainous regions of Persia, namely Tabaristan and Daylam (south of the Caspian Sea), had never been fully converted to Islam, and they adhered to their old religion of Magian in these semi-independent principalities. Their attachment to the empire was no more than nominal. In 758, an army under the Caliph's brother, al-Mahdi, captured Tabaristan. Two years later, al-Mahdi marched on the neighbouring Daylam, which was similarly subdued and annexed to the empire.

The names of both Tabaristan and Daylam were later to leave imprints on Islamic history, the former by association with the most famous Arab historian, al-Tabari (838–923) and the latter for becoming, in 864, the first Zaydi (or Zaydite) state in Islam. Daylam was also the homeland of the Buwayhids.

762–3

Foundation of Baghdad

The Abbasids, who lived in constant fear of plots, had not had a proper capital since they had seized power in 750. Damascus was regarded as too precarious because of its long association with the Umayyad administration; Kufa was unsuitable because of its fickle-minded inhabitants and, in any case, many of them belonged to the Shia and, therefore, could not be relied upon. The only obviously safe site for the capital of the new incumbents was somewhere in Khurasan—the real power base of the Abbasids. But that would be too far removed towards one corner of the empire, which stretched westward to the Atlantic.

Al-Mansur, after carefully surveying the country, eventually decided on a suitable location for the permanent capital of the empire. In 762, he laid the foundations of Baghdad, a new city on a site well connected by a series of canals and on the west bank of Tigris, not far from the ancient cities of Babylon, Seleucia and Ctesiphon. But he had hardly finished laying the foundations when an Alid revolt was started, and so the construction of the new capital did not begin in earnest till 763, after the revolt had been suppressed. It took nearly five years and just under five million *dirhams* to build this city, which was based on an original design in town-planning. This completely circular city of some two miles in diameter with four gates was surrounded by the double walls with the Caliph's Golden Palace (so-called because of its gilded entrance) situated at its centre. The walled city was designed to be occupied primarily by the Caliph and his entourage. Al-Mansur took a keen personal interest in it, employing some 10,000 workers from different parts of the empire in the building of this new capital where he could live in splendour and isolation like the old Sasanid kings. The founding of Baghdad was destined to be the most famous action associated with the name of al-Mansur.

Its suburbs, which were inhabited by supporters of the Abbasid revolution from Khurasan and northern Persia, shortly outgrew its original boundary, and the right bank was also settled, with a boat bridge linking the two parts. By the tenth century, the city was among the world's largest capitals, rife with riches. It also shone as the main Islamic centre of learning in the East.

The New Outlook of the Muslim Empire

The Abbasid revolution transformed the purely semitic Arab empire into a multi-racial Muslim state; the official language did remain Arabic, the language of the Quran, which could not, must not, be translated, but the empire was no longer Arabian. The shifting of the capital to Baghdad changed the character of the empire in another way. An empire which had been westward-looking to the Mediterranean was henceforth to concentrate on Persia and the East. In a sense, the very centre of gravity of the empire was shifted.

Unsuccessful Alid Revolt

In anti-Umayyad propaganda leading up to the overthrow of the dynasty in 750, the Abbasids had kept the aims of the new movement deliberately general and vague in an attempt to appeal to the most diverse political and religious factions. They promised a reign of peace, justice and equality based on the Quranic laws. The slogan 'The Family' was extensively employed, which the Shia—the largest party in the anti-Umayyad coalition—took to mean the family of Ali, and anticipated that an Alid would be made Caliph if the revolution was successful. But once established in power, the Abbasids, after dallying with other possibilities, simply confirmed the Sunni orthodoxy of their predessors.

Now that their hopes of a peaceful society and Alid rule had been dashed, the Shi'ites felt cheated and let down. Two young men in Medina by the names of Muhammad and Ibrahim, who were direct descendants of Ali through his eldest son Hasan, started yet another ineffective and abortive uprising in 762. Denouncing al-Mansur as a tyrant who did not respect Islamic laws—the same charge which used to be levelled against the Umayyads by the Shi'ites—Muhammad (nicknamed 'the Pure Soul') quickly seized Medina, and his brother Ibrahim left for Basra intending to raise a revolt there. But the trained Khurasan army had no difficulty in quickly crushing the militarily inexperienced rebels in Medina, who dug a moat to protect themselves as had been done in the Prophet's time one hundred and thirty-five years earlier. Muhammad himself was killed, but the city itself, which did not pose any real threat to the government, was treated leniently; a general amnesty was declared. Ibrahim, however, made a much bigger impact with his revolt in Basra. He seized Ahwaz and even the Persian province of Fars, but failed to persuade the Kufans to turn against the ruling Caliph. Eventually, in February 863, the Abbasids regained control of the country, though only after some violent fighting at a place called Bahamra, south of Kufa, in which Ibrahim was killed. Thus came to a tragic end the latest in a series of attempts by the Shia to gain power. The rebellion displayed reckless heroism and political incompetence, both of which had become hallmark of an Alid uprising.

Breakaway of Spain from the Empire

In 763, Caliph al-Mansur sent an army to regain Spain from Abdur Rahman, a fugitive Umayyad prince who had defeated the local Abbasid governor and established there in 756 a new line of the Umayyads. The army was routed as a result of desperately heroic fighting by Abdur Rahman and his men. This put an end to any such further attempt by the Abbasids, and Spain remained for ever independent of Baghdad. Thus, after only thirteen years of the Abbasids being in power, the western wing of the empire started breaking away from the Caliphal control.

767

Death of Ibn Ishaq

Ibn Ishaq (full name: Muhammad ibn Ishaq), the first biographer of the Prophet, died in Baghdad. He was the grandson of a young Christian prisoner captured by Muslim troops in Iraq (633) and brought to Medina, where he was freed after accepting Islam. Born in about 704 at Medina, Ibn Ishaq studied in Alexandria and subsequently moved to Iraq, where he finally settled in Baghdad.

Ibn Ishaq's biography *Sirat Rasul Allah*, which is the main primary source on the Prophet Muhammad's life, has come down in history chiefly as an edited version by Ibn Hisham, who died some seventy years later in Cairo. But even after editing, the work is essentially that of Ibn Ishaq. The extensive biography fully covers the Prophet's life, starting with his genealogy and birth and concluding with his death.

Death of Imam Hanifa

The great intellectual and theologian Abu Hanifa (b. circa 700 in Kufa, and commonly known as Imam Hanifa), founder of the first of the four orthodox schools of jurisprudence in Islam, died in a Baghdad prison. He was thought to have been put in prison for his support to the Alid uprising of Muhammad 'the Pure Soul' in 762 in Basra. In order to preserve his freedom to speak authoritatively on all matters without compromise, he twice refused, and was then punished for assuming, the post of chief justice; he earned his living as a silk dealer in Kufa.

Abu Hanifa, grandson of a Persian freedman, spent nearly all his life in Kufa where he took an active part in theological discussions. He himself wrote no legal works, but he lectured to a number of brilliant disciples, especially Abu Yusuf (731–98) and al-Shaibani (749–c.804), who took it upon themselves to commit to writing and develop the celebrated logician's views. In spite of their own large contribution in expounding Abu Hanifa's teachings, they always faithfully regarded him as the founder of their school, which came to be known as Hanafi. Both Abu Yusaf and al-Shaibani were later appointed judges c.785 and 796 respectively.

The Four Schools of Jurisprudence

Quite early on, the Muslims started taking a keen interest in legal discussions to discover which course of action, in respect of the novel and complex issues (civil, criminal, financial, political, etc.) which were continually arising with the territorial expansion of the state, was in accordance with the Islamic principles. This led to an eleborate system of religious law called *Sharia* and jurisprudence called *Fiqh*. If the Quranic injunctions proved either inapplicable or insufficient Æof the total 6236 Quranic verses (see **650–2**, only about two hundred may be classified as strictly legislative and these are mainly, though not exclusively, from suras 2 and 4), the natural next step was to resort to the Traditions for an answer. The Traditions (usually written with a capital letter to indicate the technical Islamic sense of the word) are the acts and moral sayings of the Prophet Muhammad. In the event these two primary sources (the Quran and the Traditions) proved inconclusive, two supplementary sources, namely, consensus (*ijma*) of the community and analogical deduction (*qiyas*) were drawn upon. The consensus element gave the legal system a regional flexibility which allowed it to work and survive in the vast empire. There was thus a common concept of the nature of the jurisprudence and unity of Islamic law on the whole, but not on individual rulings. A legal decision in a particular case arrived at in Baghdad did not set a precedent for jurists in Tangier. The religious legal system was meant to cover and pronounce upon all aspects of Muslim life.

Originally, the study of law was started by the pious in Medina, when it was the capital of the empire to which novel problems were referred from the provinces for a directive. But Medina slowly gave way to Kufa and then to Baghdad when it became a great centre of learning with scholars in different fields and from different lands. Here, the study of Islamic law grew into a systematic and serious subject in its own right.

The need to apply the legal thought of Islam led to the rise of four schools of jurisprudence, each founded by and named after one of the four great commentators, usually called Imams (simply meaning, leaders; but not in the technical sense of the Shi'ite Imams). Roughly, the path followed by these four schools, which arose chiefly during the first Abbasid century but are still recognized as authoritative, was the same as that outlined above, although they might differ on emphasis and interpretation. The schools are, in chronological order: (1) The Hanafi School. Founded by Imam Abu Hanifa, this is the most speculative and tolerant of the four. It gained official recognition in the Ottoman Empire, and still has the largest number of followers in the Muslim world (nearly half), especially in Asia; (2) The Maliki School. Founded by Imam Malik ibn Anas (c.715–95), this attaches a special importance to the Traditions and is followed in the western and northern parts of Africa; (3) The Shafi School. Founded by Imam Muhammad ibn Idris ibn al-Shafi (767–820), this is prevalent in much of Egypt, East Africa, southern Arabia and the East Indies; (4) The Hanbal School. Founded by Imam Ahmad ibn Hanbal (780–855), this is the most conservative and uncompromising one, adhering to the letter of the Quran with asecondary reliance on the Traditions. But it now has no considerable following outside the puritanic reform movement of the Wahhabis, founded by Muhammad ibn Abdul Wahhab (1703–92), which is the official ideology of the Saudi Arabian kingdom.

All four Schools are Sunni Schools; the Shi'ites have their own body of law.

771

The Berber Revolt in North Africa

The Berbers in north-west Africa had by now adopted the puritan doctrine of the Kharijites, who sought to establish a true theocratic republic where no racial or social boundaries were to be recognized; everyone would be judged only by his moral qualities. In this turbulent land, yet another rebellion—the third in thirty years—broke out (771), and Qairawan was captured once again by the Berbers, who were this time fighting under the Kharijite banner.

Now that the Abbasids had established themselves firmly in power, Caliph al-Mansur went in person to Jerusalem to organize an army of 50,000 men to regain control over the province. It was only after a long year of savage fighting and a great deal of bloodshed that the Caliphal rule was re-established (772). But even then, no attempt was made to subdue the high Atlas region, which was still at large and where a number of independent Kharijite principalities were being set up by the Berbers.

775

Death of al-Mansur; Accession of al-Mahdi

Caliph al-Mansur died (October) at the age of sixty-four in his camp near Mecca, while on a pilgrimage. Al-Mansur's long reign of twenty-one years witnessed many fundamental changes in the way the empire was run. He was later to be regarded as the real founder of the Abbasid dynasty, laying down principles of government which were to be followed, with some amendments, by his successors. In the earliest phase of Muslim expansion, when the government was still in an embryonic stage, it was the guidelines of the second Orthodox Caliph, Umar ibn al-Khattab (r. 634–44), which set the pattern for the forthcoming administrations.

The following were some of the important changes in government brought about by al-Mansur, both in style and substance, which were to have a lasting effect on the future course of the Muslim empire.
(1) The Arabs lost the predominant position which they had hitherto enjoyed; leadership now passed to the Persians and Turks, instead. The new Caliphate was based on the support of the *Mawali*, especially those of Persian origin, who played an increasingly important role in both political and cultural life. This mistrust of their own nationals by the Abbasids was to contribute significantly to the eventual disintegration of the empire. The new class of trusted people, many of whom were freedmen of the Abbasid family itself, was given positions of trust and responsibility in every layer of local and central government. These freedmen—that is, former slaves— were, of course, always non-Arabs, since an Arab could not be a slave. According to the ideas of the time, they were under obligation of loyalty and service of their former masters, which gave the new rulers their badly needed sense of security. Expedient though this may have seemed, they were later to seize power for themselves when the Arabs had been sufficiently weakened by this shortsighted action of their own. The policy of employing Turkish former slaves in key positions such as palace guards proved to be particularly fatal, since it gave them an ideal opportunity to be active in court intrigues and plot against their patrons. They eventually became so powerful that Caliphal political authority slipped away into their hands.

How unimportant the Arabs had become with regard to the politics and government of the Abbasids can be gauged from the fact that the historians of the time rarely mention the Arab tribal feuds, which must have continued in their age-old way. In pre-Abbasid times, these conflicts, whenever they occured, had important political repercussions because of the central position which the Arabs held in the higher echelons of the administration, the army and the provinces.

(2) The administration was reorganized after the Sasanid (and to a lesser extent Byzantine) model. The Caliph, surrounded by court-ceremonials (and later by intrigues, too), lived like a glorious monarch, and became inaccessible to his subjects. The authority of the Caliphate was supported by the armed forces, and was exercised through a vast bureaucracy the pinnacle of which was the office of *vizier* or Chief Minister, answerable only to the Caliph—an important new development in the machinery and style of government.* It just so happened that the office was monopolized by just one Persian family—the Barmakids—until Caliph Harun al-Rashid (r. 786–809) wiped them out.

(3) There was a whole new eastwards orientation which was symbolized by the transfer of the Caliphal seat from Damascus to Baghdad. In fact, the Caliphate entered a new phase in its foreign policy; instead of focusing their efforts on the Mediterrean, north Africa and southern Europe—as the Umayyads had done during their time—the new rulers looked eastward and Persian influence, in particular, became strong. The new capital was central enough between Arabia, Egypt and Syria on one side and Persia, Khurasan and north-western India on the other. But the western parts were too distant to be controlled properly, and the political unity of the Caliphate started to dissolve when Baghdad showed a lack of firm commitment. Muslim Spain became independent of Baghdad after the new regime had been in power for only six years. Later still, a number of new local dynasties rose in north Africa; the Caliphal power became narrower and narrower. This affected the future of Europe also in that it was no more threatened by any possible Muslim invasion.

(4) The founding of Baghdad (which al-Mansur named the City of Peace) saw the full flowering of mediaeval Islamic civilization. Literature, theology, philosophy and natural sciences were developed here—and to a lesser extent in the twin cities of Kufa and Basra—mingling as it did Hellenistic, Christian, Jewish, Zoroastrian and Hindu ideas. The intense intellectual activity in the field of Islamic jurisprudence which started in Medina and Kufa during the Umayyad period continued for the first few decades, but then that, too, moved to the rising metropolitan Baghdad. In fact, Baghdad represented a complete antithesis of the way of life brought from the desert by the first Arab conquerors.

Caliph Al-Mansur was succeeded in the post by his thirty-three-year-old, son al-Mahdi (r. 775–85), born to an Arab Yemenite princess.

*Although the innovation of the office with this title is generally attributed to al-Mansur's successor, al-Mahdi, a general trend of the Caliph increasingly relying on an overall civil administrator had already been set; the first incumbent of this office under al-Mahdi was

the same Khalid the Barmakid who had held the influential post of chief collector of taxes
under al-Mansur.

776

Revolt of the Heretic al-Muqanna

A number of heresies had sprung up in the previous twenty years or so, in part
based on deep-rooted dissatisfaction, especially among the Persian peasantry.
Among the more serious of these was the one led by a follower of Abu Muslim,
the chief agent in bringing about the overthrow of the Umayyads, who called
himself al-Muqanna or 'the Veiled One', since he kept his face covered. He
combined extremist Shi'ite messianic ideas with older Persian currents of
thought and social protest. His followers wrere organized in a secret society
with grades of initiation; he taught the transmigration of the soul and claimed
to be a prophet in succession to Muhammad, Ali and Abu Muslim.

In 776, he conquered Khurasan and proved himself to be a tough leader
against the Arabs. Having successfully defied the armies sent against him, he
was eventually besieged in a castle (780) and, with no hope of escape or victory,
preferred to take his own life rather than fall into the hands of the Caliph's
army.

777

The Establishment of the Rustamid Dynasty

The Kharijites had been very active missionaries for their doctrine in north
Africa during the previous seventy years. By now, this egalitarian religo-
political sect had attracted a large following among the Berbers, who resented
the domination of their orthodox Arab masters. Moreover, the Kharijites took
on the whole a more moderate line in north Africa compared with their
savagely extremist brethren in Iraq (their country of origin) and, therefore,
commanded a wider appeal.

North Africa had been in chaos since the civil war broke out between the last
Umayyad Caliph, Marwan II, and the Abbasid revolutionaries. Neither
Marwan during his reign, nor the Abbasids after coming to power, had any
time or resources to spare for this distant province. This resulted in a number of
independent Berber Kharijite principalities being set up in the high Atlas
region. The most notable of these was the principality at Tahart (Modern
Tiaret in the Algerian Atlas) under the leadership of Abdur Rahman ibn
Rustam, who was of Persian descent, as his name suggests. He took on the

religious title of Imam and founded a new dynasty, the Rustamids (777–909). The subjects of this little mountain kingdom were keen Kharijites, observing the highest standards of puritan morality, many leading lives of asceticism.

Although the domain of Rustamid power was destined never to be large, it played an important role in the history of Islam in north Africa because of its location and foreign policy. Surrounded by enemies on both sides along the Mediterranean coast—the Shi'ite Idrisids on the west and the Sunni Aghlabids on the east—the Kharijite Rustamids shrewdly made an alliance with the Umayyads of Spain, and in this way played a political chess game in the region in which a large part eventually broke away from Baghdad. The Rustamid kingdom developed the trans-Saharan trade routes which brought prosperity to its capital Tahart, attracting a large number of emigrants and becoming a centre of learning. The tiny state came to an end in 909 with the capture of its capital by the Fatimids.

778

Charlemagne's Invasion of Spain; Death of Roland

Ever since the Umayyad Amir, Abdur Rahman, had come to power, twenty-two years before, Muslim Spain had been rent with strife by both Arabs and Berbers. During this period of anarchy and turmoil, a part of the country was lost to the Christians in the norh, who took full advantage of the situation. Now, the ambitious king of the Franks, Charlemagne (742–814), believed the opportunity was ripe to capture Spain from the Muslims, and crossed the Pyrenees with a vast army (778); he was also helped in by the local disaffected Arab chiefs, in particular the governor of Barcelona.

Having pushed his way through, he arrived under the walls of Saragossa, where he suffered a disastrous repulse. While retreating, Charlemagne, grandson of Charles Martel (c.688–741), was attacked and a large part of his army cut to pieces. Count Roland, his most celebrated paladin and nephew, was mortally wounded in the narrow pass of Roncesvalles, more than 3,000 feet high. His heroic defence was later to be immortalized in a brilliant French epic the *Chanson de Roland* (*Song of Roland*) of the eleventh or twelfth century.

The Byzantine Offensive

Throughout their reign, the Umayyads had tried to maintain military superiority over the Byzantines, particularly along the stategically important Taurus mountains separating the two empires, and raided their territory at opportune moments. But since the death of Caliph Hisham (743), the same vigilance had not been maintained, owing to the decline of the Umayyads followed by the civil war which brought the Abbasids to power. Seizing the opportunity, Emperor Constantine V (r. 741–75) turned the tables on the Muslims. He gained control of the Taurus passes, and the Muslim army was badly defeated (778) twenty-five miles east of the mountain range.

782

The Muslim Invasion of Asia Minor; Controversy about Icons

Determined to avenge the defeat of 778 in the Taurus and regain their fighting initiative, a massive Muslim army of ninety-five thousand men was prepared in the early part of 782. Caliph al-Mahdi gave its command to Harun, the future Caliph, who pursued the Byzantines across Asia Minor right up to the shores of the Bosphorus, immediately opposite Constantinople itself.

On the Byzantine side, the latest theological controversy was related to the use of images, or icons, in Christian worship. The Iconoclast (anti-icon) movement, initiated by Emperor Leo III (r. 717–41), reached its peak under his successor Constantine V (r. 741–75), when there was widespread and brutal persecution of those who defended icons. This religious convulsion was more marked in the capital than in the provinces, and always depended on imperial support, which changed sides. The present Byzantine ruler, Empress Irene (as Regent for her young son Constantine VI: 780–5 and in her own name: 797–802), was a passionate supporter of icons.* The empire being in such a turmoil and already weakened, Irene was compelled to accept a humiliating peace treaty from the Muslims, by which she was bound to pay an annual tribute of seventy thousand gold *dinars* to the Caliph.

This was the last time a Muslim army appeared before Constantinople until the Ottoman Turks (under Muhammad II the Conqueror, r. 1444–6 and 1451–81) finally captured it in 1453, and with this came to an end the Byzantine (or East Roman) empire. The great city (founded in 330), built on seven hills above the Bosphorus, then became commonly known as Istanbul, and flourished again as the capital of the Ottoman Empire (1342–1924) till 1923, when Mustafa Kemal Ataturk moved the capital to Ankara. The official change of its name from Constantinople to Istanbul took place as late as 1930.

The icons were finally restored in 843 on the first Sunday of Lent, a day still celebrated as a feast in the Eastern Orthodox Church.

785

Foundation of the Mosque of Cordova

Abdur Rahman I, Umayyad Amir of Spain, laid the foundations of the Great Mosque of Cordova near the Roman bridge on the Guadalquivir River (785). The site had once been occupied by a Visigothic cathedral. After a series of successive expansions in the reigns of Abdur Rahman II (r. 822–52) and al-Hakam II (r. 961–76), the mosque was finally completed shortly after 976 under the direction of al-Mansur, an all-powerful *Hajib* (meaning Chamberlain) in the days of Hisham II (r. 976–1009). Its importance lay in its being not only a magnificant place of worship but a symbol of Muslim domination of the intellectual life of Spain, and through it of Europe.

> The Mosque was transformed into a Christian cathedral after the fall of Cordova in 1236 and is used as such to the present day, but is still known by the popular name 'La Mezquita' (the mosque). Under the Muslim rule, this vast congregational mosque (570×425 feet) had twenty-one entrances, but some of these have been filled in or destroyed.

Escape of Idris to North Africa

In 785, yet another unsuccessful Shi'ite rebellion took place, this time in Hijaz. The insurrection was short-lived, but one of its leading participants, Idris ibn Abdullah* (d. 793), escaped first to Egypt and then to Morocco. Idris enjoyed the prestige of being a descendant of the Prophet (great-grandson of Ali's son Hasan) and managed to secure the support of the local Berber tribes, who, though already Muslim, were opposed to the government of Baghdad. Here he eventually established an independent principality and the Idrisid dynasty (789–926), with its capital at Fez**, which sought to introduce the doctrines of Shi'ism, though in a very mild form. This was the first Shi'ite dynasty.

Although the region had been, previously, under the influence of the egalitarian Kharijites, it had formed a part of the empire. In less than forty years of the Abbasid rule, this was the third break-away state. But the title of Caliph and Commander of Faithful was still left only for the Abbasid rulers in Baghdad.

*Idris was a brother of Muhammad 'the Pure Soul' who headed an abortive revolt in 762, after becoming disillusioned with the Abbasids.
**There is a slight uncertainty whether Idris himself, or his son, Moulay Idris, built the city of Fez on the site of the ancient Roman town of Volubilis (Walila, as known to the Arabs). According to some authorities, it was his son who founded it in 808. Soon afterwards, Fez acquired considerable importance in both the religious and intellectual

aspects of Islam. Its university/mosque reached the peak of its fame in the 14th century, and is still renowned for a collection of invaluable manuscripts on early Islam.

786

Accession of Harun

The brilliant and luxurious reign of the fifth Abbasid Caliph, Harun al-Rashid (r. 786–809), began in September, and under it the empire reached the peak of its fame, prosperity and culture. Twenty-two-year-old Harun succeeded his brother al-Hadi, both being sons of the same former slave mother, Khayzuran (d. 789), who was a strong personality and an influential figure in state affairs in the reigns of both her husband and her son.

Harun in his childhood was tutored by a Persian, called Yahya (d. 805) the Barmakid, and a strong bond of affinity had developed between the two. On becoming Caliph, Harun appointed his trusted man, who was also a loyal supporter of his mother, to the post of *vizier* (Chief Minister), giving him unlimited administrative powers while keeping himself very active visiting distant regions and overseeing state affairs. Yahya, whose grandfather was a Buddhist priest in Balkh, was a competent organizer and an ambitious man. He made full use of his position, and gradually became master of the administrative functions of the Caliph.

792

Raid of Muslims in Spain on Northern Frontiers

Ever since Muslim Spain had broken away from the central Abbasid authority and been left on its own, the Christian frontier tribes, on the instigation of Frankish rulers, had been raiding northern Spain incessantly, causing devastation and havoc in the area. Now that the second Ummayad ruler, Hisham I (r. 788–96), had put down rebellions within his own domains and restored peace, he turned his attention towards the north. With a punitive object in mind, he sent two columns of his army (792), both of which were equally successful. One recaptured Narbonne (which had been lost to the Franks in 759) and several other places, inflicting a severe defeat on the Count of Toulouse, while the other routed the Galacian tribesmen with massive slaughter, and made them submit.

795

Death of Imam Malik

Malik ibn Anas (commonly known as Imam Malik), Muslim jurist and founder of a school of law named after him, died in Medina, where he had spent most of his life. He had played a prominent role in the formulation of early Islamic legal doctrines and achieved considerable public esteem.

Although he did not take an active part in an Alid rising of 762 in Medina, he publically declared that the homage paid to the Caliph al-Mansur (r. 754–75) was not religiously binding since it was given under duress. When the rebellion failed, he received corporal punishment for his pronouncement but this only increased his prestige. In his later years, however, he regained favour with the central government, and was treated with respect by the Caliphs al-Mahdi (r. 775–85) and Harun al-Rashid (r. 786–809).

800

Foundation of the Aghlabid Dynasty

Caliph Harun al-Rashid, being preoccupied with the eastern part of the empire, showed diminishing interest in north Africa, where the Rustamids and the Idrisids had already carved out independent domains for themselves. A Khurasanian army officer, Ibrahim ibn Aghlab, offered the Caliph to restore order in Ifriqiya* and keep it under the control of Baghdad, provided governorship of the region with considerable autonomy was granted to him. His offer was accepted (800) in return for an annual payment of tribute of 40,000 *dinars*. In this sense, Ifriqiya was the first province to receive dominion status within the empire.

Being at a safe distance from Baghdad, Ibrahim, a man of exceptional ability and energy, established a new (Sunni) dynasty of rulers—the Aghlabids (r. 800–909)—and started exercising independent and hereditary rule from the capital at Qairawan in Tunisia, according only nominal recognition to the Caliph. From then onwards, the Abbasids exercised no authority beyond the western frontier of Egypt. Although some of Ibrahim's successors turned out to be debauched and more interested in their pursuit of pleasure than in their public duties, the century of the Aghlabid rule brought peace and prosperity to the area, which had been torn apart by endless Arab-Berber civil wars during the pre-800 years.

Although Ifriqiya was first conquered by the Muslims as early as 670, it was under the Aghlabids that its character was changed completely from being

Roman Africa to Muslim Ifriqiya. Latin, though mainly spoken in the big cities, was replaced by Arabic, and Islam not only took the place of Christianity but became a much more widely accepted religion. Their conquest of Sicily after a 50-year-long campaign had profound consequences for the future of western civilization. The Aghlabid rule finally became an easy first prey in 909 to the rapidly growing power of the Fatimids.

However, this set the pattern for a series of future local dynasties in north Africa and other peripheral provinces which ultimately reduced the sphere of the effective sovereignty of the Caliphate just to Iraq itself. In addition to the major dynasties, many less conspicuous examples were also later to be found within the Abbasid domain. These were petty semi-oligarchical states run by local governors, and the Caliphs were unable to reverse the trend.

In Roman times, the name Africa was applied only to the area centred around Carthage, which is roughly equivalent to modern Tunisia; Morocco was known as Mauritania. After their conquest of the land, the Arabs transformed the word Africa into Ifriqiya and applied it to a larger part of the central Mediterranean coast, which also included the eastern part of modern Algeria; Mauritania was changed to al-Maghrib which covered the part of the African coast further to the west. Neither the name Africa nor Ifriqiya was, however, applied to the continent south of the Sahara.

803

The Fall of the Barmakids

No sooner did Caliph Harun al-Rashid gain power in 786 than he appointed his former tutor and confidant, Yahya, the Barmakid, the Chief Minister. Later, Yahya's two sons joined their father forming a pivot in the administration of the empire. Being competent administrators and members of a highly cultured Persian family, the Barmakids grew immensely rich and powerful over the years. The name of the Barmakids, who were thought to have Shi'ite leanings, became synonymous with patronage, generosity and a sumptuous lifestyle. Consequently the Caliph felt dominated by them, and their exhalted position become irksome to him. He, therefore, decided in 803 to be rid of this powerful nucleus within the empire by ordering the instant confiscation of their vast wealth and the imprisonment of the whole family. Thus the most celebrated and powerful family in the government met its unexpected downfall after three generations of service to the Caliphate, never to rise again.

804-6

Harun's Campaign in Asia Minor.

In 802 Nicephorus I (r. 802–11) deposed and succeeded Empress Irene, under whom he had been minister of finance. One of the charges made against her was subservience to the Caliphate, in that she had agreed in 782 to the payment of a large tribute in return for peace on the eastern frontier. He tried to reverse the policy by writing a boastful letter to Caliph Harun al-Rashid not only repudiating the treaty unilaterly but also demanding repayment of the tribute alredy paid, to which the enraged Harun sent a brief but extremely contemptious reply, addressing the Emperor as a 'Roman dog', and simultaneously gathered a massive army under his personal command. In 804, he crossed into Byzantine territory, laid waste large a part of Asia Minor and slashed his way to the very coast of the Black Sea. Overwhelmed by all this and finding himself helpless in the face of a sweeping Muslim invasion, Nicephorus begged for peace, which was concluded on the humiliating condition of the continued payment of the annual tribute.

However, once the Muslims withdrew, the Emperor immediately rejected the new treaty, which invoked Harun's savage wrath; his army recrossed into Asia Minor with fire and sword. The Byzantine army was annihilated and the eastern part of the country was abandoned to the ravaging and plundering invaders. The Muslim army advanced as far into the enemy territory as Heraclea in 806, and once more the frightened Nicephorus pleaded for peace. This time the terms of the ensuing agreement were much more punitive and humiliating than previously; they included, in addition to the tribute, an ignominious tax on the emperor himself and each member of his household. Thousands of Christians were captured and later sold as slaves in the markets of Syria. On the sea, a naval task force landed in Cyprus in the flush of victory and quickly recaptured the island from the Byzantines.

Both the manner and scale of this invasion later proved to be the highest point in the military adventure of Harun's, and indeed of the Abbasid's period, beyond the frontiers of the empire.

808

The 'Day of the Ditch'

The city of Toledo, which was the former Visigothic capital of Spain, had been a continous source of trouble from native Christians for the Umayyad Amirate ever since the seat of government was moved to to Cordova. In 808, Amir al-

Hakam I (r. 796–822) decided to rid the city of all seditious elements in a most brutal way. He sent to Toledo his son, who invited all the leading men of the city to a banquet in the castle, where a ditch had been dug the night before. As each guest entered, he was beheaded in cold blood and his body was thrown into the ditch. Several hundred leaders were in this way slaughtered, and the people of Toledo—not surprisingly—abandoned all ideas of revolt. The day of this massacre later became known as the 'Day of the Ditch'.

809

The First Public Hospital

Earlier translation into Arabic of the medical texts of Galen (c. 130–201) and Hippocrates (d. circa BCE 485), celebrated physicians of the distant past, had created a lively interest in the science of medicine—the first Greek science to attract the Arab mind, partly because of its obvious practical importance and also partly because of the existence of old Persian tradition preserved in the great medical school-hospital at Jundishahpur or Gondeshapur (founded c. 555 by the great Sasanid ruler Anusharwan), a town not far from Baghdad. The foundation of the first free public hospital in the Islamic world was now laid (809) in Baghdad, and within a short space of time no major city of the empire was to be without one. They also functioned as teaching institutions, where medical students were trained and were awarded diplomas; no physician could practise without these government recognized qualifications. The pharmacists, too, had to pass a test.

Death of Harun and Accession of al-Amin

Although it had been an army of Khurasanians which had helped the Abbasids to rise to power in the first place, dissidence continued in the province as it had during the Umayyad days. This was because they had become disillusioned to see that the new rulers had not established the reign of mercy and justice which they had promised in their pre-revolutionary propaganda; in fact, to them, the Abbasids were no better, if not worse, than their predecessors.

In 807, a rebellion broke out in Khurasan, whose governor, Ali ibn Isa, had grown immensely rich and was a notorious tyrant during his ten years in the office. Gradually, the revolt spread in the province, and Caliph Harun decided to visit the area himself in the following year, when he installed his son al-Mamun (the future Caliph) at Merv as governor of Khurasan. Travelling from his principal residence at Raqqa on the Euphrates, he eventually reached Tus (near modern Meshed in Persia) in Khurasan, but his health was already declining rapidly. Soon after his arrival in the city, the Caliph died at the age of forty-five in March, 809 after twenty-three years of rule. He was followed in the Caliphal office consecutively by three of his sons, al-Amin, al-Mamun and al-Mutasim.

He had led a very active life travelling within the empire, invading the Byzantine territory on eight different occasions taking personal command of his armies, and going on the *Hajj* (Pilgrimage) no fewer than nine times, which involved long and monotonous camal journey through the desert. But still he lived a full life, denying himself no pleasure. During his reign, the Abbasid empire (though reduced in size) reached its pinnacle of fame, wealth and culture. The capital, Baghdad, was the richest city in the world, its only rival in luxury and refinement—but not a close one—being Constantinople. Industry, commerce and trade were flourishing both within the empire and with overseas countries. The Arabs built an extensive fleet of merchant ships which sailed regularly as far as Canton in China, trading on the way with India, Ceylon and Indonesia. There was a trading link with Russia and thence to Scandinavia (inhabited by pagans), but no trade with the rest of Europe.* This was partly due to the unending hostility between Islam and Christendom and partly due to the fact that the Mediterranean—the greatest highway of world trade—was now infested with battleships and pirates. Western Europe was thus cut off by this Muslim blockade of sea and land from trade with Asia, and was reduced to a purely agricultural economy, which contributed to its development as a feudal system with land-owning gentry instead of city merchants. It also restricted the spread of Christianity towards the East.** The international trade naturally required, and gave rise to, a banking system which was so highly developed that a cheque drawn at one end of the empire could be cashed at the other. But it was an age not only of opulence but also of refined manners, culture, literature and the arts. The preoccupation with conquering the world largely became a thing of the past. The educated classes grew in size, and among them public intellectual discussions largely replaced war-planning. None the less, neither the internal nor the external defence of the realm was compromised. Apart from the large scale military expedition in Asia Minor in 804, there was fighting—and plenty of it—to suppress internal revolts: in Daylam (792), Syria (c. 792–6), Egypt (794), Qairawan (798) and Samarqand (805).

However, in spite of regaining the military initiative over the Byzantines lost during the years of the Abbasid revolution, there was no permanent and significant territorial expansion. On the contrary, at the beginning of Harun's reign, the empire included all south-west Asia and the northern part of Africa, but by the end of his Caliphate the authority of Baghdad had completely disappeared west of Egypt. Harun showed a distinct lack of interest in the western wing of the empire.

Harun appears prominently in *The Thousand and One Nights* (also known as *The Arabian Nights*), a collection of fascinating stories of Indian, Persian, Arabic and Egyptian origin but of uncertain date and authorship, whose popular tales such as *Aladdin's Lamp*, *Ali Baba and the Forty Thieves* and *Sinbad the Sailor* have become a part of folklore. In the *Nights*—which have been translated into most of the main European and Asian languages— Harun and his court are idealized and romantacized fabulous descriptions. It is mainly through these fanciful tales that he has become the best known— particularly to Western readers—of all the Abassid Caliphs, if not of all the fifty-five Caliphs who ruled from the time of the Prophet Muhammad's death in 632 to the overthrow of the Islamic empire in 1258 by the Mongols.

A large number of Arab coins, found as far afield as Russia, Finland and Sweden, testify to the enormously wide commercial activities of the Muslims at this and later periods. Some of these coins are kept in the Helsinki museum.

**The situation changed when the rival Caliphate of the Fatimids was established in north Africa; they were more eager to replace the Abbasids than to fight the infidels. They opened diplomatic links with the Christians of Europe and the end of the long blockade was in sight.*

811–3

Fratricidal War between al-Amin and al-Mamun; Accession of al-Mamun

Even after nearly two centuries of Muslim rule, no formal principle regarding the Caliphate succession had been established and the same contention for power came up now and then as it had in the Umayyad days. In accordance with the wishes of the late Caliph Harun al-Rashid, his son by the famous Lady Zubaida, al-Amin, was proclaimed his successor in Baghdad in 809, while his other son, al-Mamun, had been governor of Khurasan since 808. But Harun's fear of civil war between these two came true within only a year of his death, although it now came to a head in 811 when the Khurasan army marched towards the capital, inflicting a severe defeat on the Caliph's army of some fifty thousand strong near Rayy (former city in Persia, not far south of Tehran). The rebel army laid a fearful siege to Baghdad in September, 812, which lasted for a whole year, during which time the beautiful city suffered severe damage. At last, the fateful happened; the thirty-seven-year-old Caliph al-Amin was killed and the capital city fell to al-Mamun's army. In spite of numerous turmoils, it was the first time that an Abbasid Caliph had been publicly killed since the dynasty had assumed power sixty-three years earlier. Al-Amin was also to be the last Caliph born of an Arab mother.

Thus Al-Mamun (r. 813–33), a great patron of art and science but politically not so apt, became Caliph after a damaging civil war. His reign was to rise to the same level of intellectual brilliance as his father's had risen to true splendour. He decided to keep his headquarters in Khurasan for a further six years before establishing himself in Baghdad in 819. The intervening period was marked with general chaos by a series of revolts headed by different Shi'ite groups in Mecca, Medina and Iraq itself.

814

The 'Suburb Affair'

In the first ninety years or so of Muslim rule in Spain, it was only the main stream of Islam which took root and was followed in the peninsula. But the situation changed somewhat around the year 800 when a Berber by the name of Yahya ibn Yahya (d. 847) and his associates introduced for the first time the Maliki doctrine of Islamic jurisprudence*, developed chiefly in Medina by Malik ibn Anas (c. 715–95), by way of a book containing specific questions of law and the answers to them. The movement gradually gave rise to a cohesive and influencial group of zealous religious teachers and jurists, most of whom were Spanish or Berber converts and had studied religion in Medina under leading theologians. These fanatics would accuse the ruler, Amir al-Hakam I (r. 796–822), of gross impiety at the slightest complaint, and implicitly provided the malcontents with a religious plank to oppose the government by any means they chose.

The climax came in 814 (according to some sources, 817), when there was a serious outbreak against the Amir in a southern suburb of Cordova which was dealt with the utmost severity. As a result, there was a complete exodus of the inhabitants of this quarter, which was raized to the ground on the orders of al-Hakam. The religio-political unrest was, however, confined mainly to the area around Cordova, a part of which was uncharacteristically going through an ascetic and puritanic spell. The episode later took its name as the 'Suburb Affair'. Although achieved by ruthless means, this brought badly needed peace and order to Spain during the remaining years of al-Hakam's reign.

The various racial mix of the population—Arabs, Berbers, Spaniards and Goths—had already become integrated into a relatively homogeneous nation acknowledging the Umayyad rule. Although a large proportion of the Spaniards and Goths had become Muslims (known as the *Muwalladun*), a substantial number still remained faithful to their old religion of Christianity (known as the *Mozarabs*), but the latter were treated with toleration and played their full role as Andalusians.** But in the north, the small Christian kingdoms of Leon and Navarre continued to be a source of trouble on the border, by way of giving support to any internal resistance movement.

The introduction of the Maliki school of thought was the chief intellectual activity in the field of religion which took place under the Umayyads in Spain. All the four schools of Islamic law were developed in the east.
**The Arab and Berber element in Muslim Spain was never more than a minority, though reliable population statistics for the time are not available.*

c. 815

Death of Geber

The celebrated Arab alchemist Geber (Arabic: Jabir ibn Hayyan), who flourished in Kufa at the height of Abbasid power, died at the age of about ninety-three. Born at Tus where his father was an active supporter of the Abbasid family in the pre-revolution days, Geber (as he was later to be known to the Europeans through the translation of his work into Latin) was the first of the important Arab alchemists and also the best. Inspired by the desire to discover the Elixir, or secret of life, and the 'philosopher's stone', which would transmute base metals (that is, metals which corrode or tarnish, such as lead, iron, tin and copper) into gold, he conducted a large number of experiments. His accurate and meticulous descriptions of valuable chemical experiments are contained in the numerous books he published, of which about twenty-two are extant in Arabic.

Although Geber published a large number of books, it is doubtful whether all the one hundred or so publications (both in Latin and in Arabic) bearing his name are realy his.

The mysterious substance called the Elixir (Arabic, *al-iksir*) was also supposed to be capable of prolonging life indefinitely and of acting as a panacea.

816

The Rebellion of Babak

In 780, the heretic rebel al-Muqanna in Khurasan was finally crushed after a desperate fight. But in the climate of general anarchy following the death of Caliph al-Amin (813), and while Caliph al-Mamun (r. 813–33) was still in Khurasan, there rose another popular and more serious revolt from the remnants of his followers. The new insurrection, under the leadership of a Persian by the name of Babak belonging to the Khurrami sect, was centred in Azerbaijan. His teachings were based on those of al-Muqanna, coupled with some communistic ideas advocated by the Mazdakism of the Sasanid time. Rejecting all the rules of morality imposed by any of the monotheist religions, his followers (Khurramites, meaning pleasure-seekers) terrorized the countryside surrounding their inaccessible mountain retreats in northern Persia, killing the men mercilessly and carrying away the women and children into savage captivity. Subsequently, sedition spread to large territories in Azerbaijan, Armenia and the northern regions of Persia, and, for over twenty years, the rebels successfully resisted the government armies sent against them. It was only during the reign of Caliph al-Mutasim, himself a keen soldier, that he was finally captured and executed in 838. Among all the Persian heretics, Babak proved to be the most menacing to the central authority because of the extent, duration, brutality, and cohesion of his leadership and power.

Such sects founded on the doctrines of such ancient Persian religions as Zoroastrianism, Manicheism and Mazdakism, coupled with mystery cults popular in pre-Islamic days, were a strain on the Caliphal resources and also sowed the seeds of separatist tendencies which contributed to the eventual breakaway of the Persian lands from Baghdad.

817–9

Nomination of Imam Ali al-Rida as Heir-Apparent; Entry of al-Mamun into Baghdad

During the previous year or so, the Shi'ites had intensified their campaign against the Abbasids, seizing the cities of Mecca, Medina, Wasit and Basra. There was a general wave of violence against the reigning family and their supporters.

Caliph al-Mamun developed a deep sympathy for the Shia, who had been involved for the last hundred and fifty years in a passionate but fruitless struggle for power which they believed was rightly theirs. He was still residing in Merv, kept ignorant by his Persian chief minister, Fadl ibn Sahl, about the extent of political chaos and civil disorder in Baghdad. During the Caliph's absence from the capital, it was Fadl who seemed to be in sole control.* In his effort to reconcile the Alids, al-Mamun took the unusual step of nominating, in 817, not one of his sons but none other than an Alid, Ali al-Rida** (d. 818), as heir-apparent to the Caliphate. He ordered that an oath of allegiance be taken to Ali. And to complete his move, he went as far as ordering that the black colour of the Abbasids be replaced with the green colour of the Shia as the government livery. The news of the proclamation, however, threw the House of Abbasid in Baghdad into a frenzy and added to the anarchy which already existed in the capital, while the Caliph remained largely unaware of it all in Merv. A few months later, the people of Baghdad decided to appoint al-Mamun's uncle, Ibrahim ibn al-Mahdi, to be a rival Caliph. But he proved to be a weak personality whose rule was confined to Baghdad only, and that, too, for only about two years, till al-Mamun decided to move his court from Merv to Baghdad in 819.

Al-Mamun took over the city without a fight, and Ibrahim fled. He remained in hiding for the next six years until 825, when he gave himself up (or was arrested) and was pardoned. Al-Mamun showed great leniency towards rebels and political opponents throughout his rule. In fact, his reign was remarkably free from the cruel tortures and mutilation so common in the past; he was said to take pleasure in forgiveness. He also wisely decided to give way to the popular demand for the national colour to be changed back to the Abbasid black from the Alid green; Ali al-Rida had, of course, already died in 818.

This seems to have foreshadowed the age of the puppet Caliphate which was to come, when the real power slipped into the hands of chief ministers or military commanders, the Caliphate being reduced to being a mere figure-head.

**The eighth Imam of the Imamis (Twelver Shi'ites). Ali al-Rida died and was buried at Tus (Persia), which was later renamed Meshed by the Shi'ites, the palace of martyrdom, since they accused al-Mamun of poisoning the Imam. It is the greatest Shi'ite place of pilgrimage in Persia.*

820

Appointment of Tahir as Governor of Khurasan

During the protracted fratricidal war between al-Amin and al-Mamun which followed Caliph Harun's death, a previously unknown Persian by the name of Tahir ibn Hussain distinguished himself by his energy, determination and military skil. The one-eyed Tahir (b.775) could use the sword in a battlefield so forcefully with either hand that his master al-Mamun gave him the nickname of Ambidextrous. He was one of the two generals responsible for al-Mamun's victory for the Caliphate over his half-brother (by a different mother) al-Amin, and was temporarily rewarded, before being moved to Raqqa on the Euphrates, with the governorship of Baghdad and northern Mesopotamia after the fall of the city (813) in whose defeat he had played the leading role.

In 820, he was sent to Khurasan to administer all the provinces east of Baghdad, which he did from his capital at Merv. As Caliph Harun had, only twenty years previously, allowed Ibrahim ibn Aghlab to set up an almost independent dynasty of Aghlabid in north Africa, a similar situation was developing in the east. Tahir became so powerful and autonomous in the very heart of the country which had given birth to Abbasid power that, just before his death in 822, he discontinued mentioning the name of the reigning Caliph al-Mamun in the Friday sermon, which was tantamount to a declaration of independence. But this was quietly tolerated, and when he died the vacant governorship was passed to his son, Talha. By then, the family had grown too resourceful and strong to be dislodged easily. Talha's brother, Abdullah, held the powerful position of commander-in-chief of the Caliph's army and, in fact, succeeded the former in Khurasan (828) after serving the Caliph in Egypt and distinguishing himself the previous year by ending an occupation of Alexandria by Muslim refugees from Spain. Besides, the Babak rebellion was still raging in Azerbaijan; under the circumstances, the Caliph took the prudent course of accepting the situation, and in this way the Tahirid dynasty—the first family to gain an effectively autonomous state in the east (apart from minor border districts)—was established *de facto* and ruled from its capital at Nishapur, virtually independent of Baghdad but making regular payment of tribute to the Caliphate. But while the principal line of the family ruled Khurasan, its other members continued holding many senior appointments in the empire, such as those of governor of Baghdad and of Egypt. The dynasty, with a strong Sunni leaning, lasted for just over half a century, when it was overthrown in 873 by the founder of the rival Saffarids.

Establishment of Petty Dynasties

Although it was a conveient way out of difficult regional problems for the centre to 'rent out' the distant provinces, thereby receiving tribute without the trouble of administering them, in the long run it proved to be an important contributory factor in the break-up of the Caliphate. Moreover, the revenue collected by way of tribute and 'donations' was much less than that previously drawn from taxation, which itself created problems for the central government. These governors were under the umbrella of Baghdad but only nominally, and by the middle of the tenth century they had grown numerous and so autonomous that the Caliph lost all his secular authority. The influence of the central government (which itself came under increasing control by the powerful Turkish palace guards from the middle of the ninth century) became secondary to that of the petty dynasties which sprang up in various parts of the empire. However, all this was a decline in the Abbasid power but not an end of the empire itself, which, though transformed in

character, remained strongly Islamic in nature. It became a collection of
separate governments,professing the same religion and sharing the
particular customs that it had inspired and imposed on the Muslim
community in its entirety.

The Death of Imam Shafi

Muhammad ibn Idris al-Shafi (commonly known as Imam Shafi), the founder
of the Shafi school of law in Islam, died in Fustat. He was born in Ghaza in 767,
but brought up and educated in Mecca till the age of twenty, when he moved to
Medina to continue his studies under Imam Malik. He went to Egypt in about
814, where he spent the remainder of his life.

Before Shafi's time, the teachings of the great jurists such as Imam Hanifa
and Imam Malik had dominated current legal opinion, but it was in the
absence of any systematic treatment of the bases on which the laws had stood
or the methods by which they had been derived. Imam Shafi, gifted with
extraordinary talents for religious literature, rose to the task. His greatest
contribution in the field of law was the establishment of a new discipline, the
study of *usul al-fiqh* (the fundamentals of jurisprudence). Although he
started writing his legal theories only during the last sixteen years or so of his
life, he produced an unrivalled amount of work, most of which is still held in
high esteem by Muslim scholars. Among his principal pupils was Imam
Hanbal (780–855), who afterwards founded a new legal school, known by his
own name.
   Shafi's tomb in Cairo is a shrine, attracting a large number of faithful
devotees.

821

Ribats

As early as the eighth century, the Muslim Empire had entrusted the protection
of its frontiers, especially the remote ones in Central Asia, to pious individuals
(the *ghazis*) who desired to win merit by fighting for the faith. A remarkable
product of this spirit was the special forts, known as *ribats**, where they lived
permanently or temporarily devoting all their time, under intense religious
feelings, in military excercises, prayer and meditation. The garrisons of the

ribats were, however, not vowed to a life of religion but consisted of ordinary Muslims who went through a religious retreat.

The Aghlabids built a large number of these religio-military outposts, of distinctly Islamic architectural design, along the Mediterranean coast, forming an efficient alarm system, since *ribats* also served as watchtowers and carried . beaconfires. The most important in the chain of these *ribats* was founded in 821 at Sousse (Susa)** on the sea coast sixty miles SSE of Tunis; it is from Sousse that a successful attack was launched (827) into Sicily to capture the island. This early-warning system served primarily as a protection from naval attacks.

The town of Rabat in Morocco was originally founded in the twelfth century as a ribat.
**It is mainly in Tunisia that *ribats* have been preserved to this day.

823

The Death of al-Waqidi

Al-Waqidi (full name: Muhammad ibn Umar al-Waqidi), the well-known historian, died in Baghdad. Born in 747 at Medina, he collected a large amount of material about various aspects of the Prophet Muhammad's career and about the early conquests of Islam, and published, under the title *Kitab al-Maghazi*, a monumental chronology. This proved to be a useful source for later historians to draw upon. He wrote another twenty books, largely historical.

827

The Capture of Crete

Some of the Muslim refugees thrown out of Spain in 814 took shelter in Fez, but about 15,000 of them went to the sea port of Alexandria, which they managed to hold against the Abbasid governors until 827, when they were overcome by governor Abdullah (son of Tahir, the founder of Tahirid dynasty in the east) and were forced to flee. Thereupon they proceeded to conquer Crete, the fourth largest island in the Mediterranean, where they established their own government, which lasted for nearly a century and a half until the island was regained by the Byzantines in 961. This second Muslim conquest of Crete—the first having been in 674 and of short duration—gave them a commanding position over the Aegean sea.

The Muslim Invasion of Sicily

While this was going on near the Egyptian end of the Mediterranean coast, the Aghlabids (800–909), who were in power further to the west, were busy equipping themselves with a strong naval force and started, in about 827, a series of campaigns, lasting about half a century, to capture Sicily, the largest island in the Mediterranean, from the Byzantines. The first firm foothold of the Arabs in the island was Palermo, which was captured and made the capital in 831.* Using Sicily as a naval base, the Aghlabid fleet, which was supreme in the central Mediterranean, later conquered Sardinia in the north and Malta in the south.

The conquest of Sicily later proved to be the most brilliant feat of the Aghlabids when it became a great seat of Arabic culture in the West and a channel, second only to Spain, for Europe to inherit Arab intellectual riches.**
At a time when the Arab empire was under going brutal destruction by hordes of Tatars and Turks in the east, the Arab skill, learning and science—nurtured in the east—fortunately started penetrating and enriching Europe. The island remained under Muslim rule, first under the Aghlabids and from 909 onward under the Fatimids, until the Norman conquest (1060–91), forming a centre for the diffusion of Islamic culture to Christian Europe.

In Sicily itself, the Muslims promoted agriculture, commerce and the arts and sciences, turning the island into a prosperous and thriving place.

A number of sporadic plundering raids into Sicily had been made from the middle of the seventh century, but the Aghlabid's attempt was the first seriously planned policy to capture the island.
**But unlike Spain, today Sicily does not retain any significant traces of the Islamic influence of the past.*

830–3

The House of Wisdom

The interest of the Abbasid Caliphs in Greek science had begun soon after the founding of their dynasty in 750. For instance, the first Arabic translations of the medical works of Galen and Hippocrates had been made under the patronage of the second Abbasid Caliph, al-Mansur (r. 754–5), by his official translator, Abu Yahya ibn al-Batriq (d. between 796 and 806).

Now, eighty years afterwards, Caliph al-Mamun, himself devoted to learned pursuits, harnessed and fostered this eagerness for knowledge by establishing in 830 the famous Bayt al-Hikma (House of Wisdom) in the cosmopolitan city of Baghdad, which had become a meeting place for Indians, Persians, Sogdians (from Transoxiana), Turks, Arabs, Greeks, Copts, Berbers and even Chinese. The place was rife with the cross-fertilization of ideas.

The House of Wisdom consisted of a rich library, an academy, a translation bureau and several astronomical observatories. In this powerhouse of intellect, staffed with salaried Christian and Muslim scholars from different parts of the empire, a well-organized effort was made for the meticulous translation of original Greek texts (entirely on philosophy and science, not poetry, drama or history) into Arabic. The translation was done in two stages: first from Greek into Syriac and then into Arabic. The reason for this was that the Christian communities, whose language was Syriac, tended to know Greek but not Arabic, while Muslim scholars found it easier to learn Syriac, which is closely related to Arabic, than they did to gain a knowledge of Greek. Where no Arabic equivalent existed, the Greek terms were simply transliterated, which brought many new words into the language, such as *falsafah* (philosophy), *asturlab* (astrolabe), *jumatriya* (geometry) and *jughrafiyah* (geography). Emissaries were sent to the Byzantine Emperor himself in Constantinople requesting Greek manuscripts, as had been done previously by Caliph al-Mansur, who received a number of Greek books, in particuler the most famous work of Euclid (fl. circa 300 BCE), the *Elements*.* The head of the team of translators was a very well-versed Nestorian Christian from Hira by the name of Hunayn ibn Ishaq (809–73) who himself was a practising physician of high repute and who had also studied Greek. Later, some younger members of his family also joined his staff. In addition to the new translations, early translations of important works were revised or redone. The translation of the Greek books was one factor in the intellectual activities of the Muslim world of the ninth century, and it continued in some measure until the twelfth. There were indeed other translations, particulaly Indian books, some of which had previously been translated into Pahlavi. The wave of translation extended roughly over the first century of the Abbasid rule (750–850).

A large number of these works were later to be retranslated—for the most part in Spain and Sicily—mainly into Latin but some in Hebrew, too, and thus became known to mediaeval Europe. The Arabs were, in the first instance, pupils of the Greeks; however, once they had assimilated what was to be learnt from the Greeks, they went on to make important advances of their own in the field of science and philosophy. Of course, many of the translators such as Hunayn, Yuhanna ibn Masawayh (777–857), Thabit ibn Qurrah (c.836–901) and Qusta ibn Luqa (d. circa 922) were simultaneously original contributors. Ibn Masawayh's treatise on ophthalmology is the oldest extant in Arabic.**

This was a time when the tradition of intellectual activities was well established in Spain, too; in the city of Cordova alone, there are no less than seventy libraries.

Euclid's Elements *is probably better known than any other mathematical book and, with extensive modifications, is still widely used as a textbook of geometry; because of this, his own name has become synonymous with geometry. The first printed edition of Euclid was a translation from Arabic into Latin in 1482.*
**One copy is kept in Taymur Pasha Library, Cairo, another in Leningrad.*

The Inquisition of al-Mamun

The highly cultivated and intellectually active Caliph al-Mamun, who took a keen interest in philosophical and religious discussions, in 827 openly gave his support to the doctrine of the created Quran and issued a proclamation to this effect. This official recognition of the Mutazilite teachings was later imposed on people towards the end of his reign, in about 833, by causing a great majority of the leading theologians and judges to subscribe to the view publicly. Those who did not conform but adhered to the orthodox doctrine were purged; this is known as the *Minha* (Inquisition). The most notable victim of the Inquisition was the famous religious scholar and Traditionist, Ahmad ibn Hanbal (780–855), the founder of the Hanbal school of religious law, who was flogged and put into prison. The Mutazilite teachings, coupled with the persecution of the orthodox, continued for the next fifteen years to be the official doctrine of the state until it was repudiated by Caliph al-Mutawakkil (r. 847–61), when the Quran was declared to be uncreated, a commonly held belief in the Islamic community. The interference by the Caliph in religious controversy turned out to be a damaging political move which, coupled with other factors, undermined the authority of the Caliphate and the unity of the empire. In fact, it was the first time that oppression had taken place, with official blessing, on theological grounds in Islam—a phenomenon so common in Christianity and a cause of its weakness.

The Mutazilites

As the Muslims became increasingly acquainted with Greek logic and philosophy, they started looking at the religion also in an attempt to seek a more rational basis of their belief. The Greeks, who were very fond of subtle arguments and of expressing them in technical terms, had done the same with regard to Christianity more than three hundred years earlier, which had led to a number of schisms in the Church. In contrast to the unquestioning simplicity of the early Arabs of central Arabia, the latter Muslims addressed themselves to some basic questions: the Nature and Attributes of God, the meaning and scope of Revelation, and the question of free-will and predestination.

There was a group of religious thinkers who were, in general, rationalistic in their outlook and took the stand that predestination was dangerous to religion. They came to be known as the Mutazilites and became associated with a particular theological controversy: whether the Quran was created or uncreated. They asserted, in opposition to the generally held view, that the Quran was created, i.e., it was a Work but not the Word of God. The Word of God, being eternal, cannot be fully encompassed in a Revelation which is limited by time. If the Quran is uncreated, this implies its eternal nature and, therefore, it cannot be changed, whereas if it is created, its injunctions can be understood by reason and modified by the decision of a divinely inspired person to suit the changing circumstances. On the face of it, this appears to be a hair-splitting argument, but the implications were very grave with regard to the changeable nature of the Quran. When the doctrine was given official recognition by Caliph al-Mamun, it stirred a violent reaction among the Muslim community, which believed (and still believes) in the Quran being a transcript of the Tablet preserved in Heaven. In essence, the Mutazilites maintained that there was no eternal law for mankind, and the Revelation was subject to reason.

From the theological viewpoint, Mutazilism arose nearly a century earlier from an attempt to define the religious position of the Muslim who committed a grave sin. The Kharijites' verdict on such a person was that he had become an outright infidel, while others, such as the liberal and tolerant Murji'ites, claimed that he was, tentatively at least, still a Muslim, leaving to the Last Judgement, that is, to God, the fixing of his final status. Only God can judge who is a true Muslim and who is not. The Mutazilites advocated a compromise: he was in an 'intermediate state' of belief and unbelief, in a state, so to speak, from which he could redeem himself by repentance. As time went on, their doctrines developed, and by al-Mamun's time, they had acquired the doctrine of the createdness of the Quran. They asserted their rational freedom in most matters of Faith, for which they were bitterly attacked by their orthodox critics.

The Death of al-Mamun

There had been no Arab invasions of Byzantine territory since Harun's expedition of 804–6. Caliph al-Mamun and his son Abbas launched successful raids in Asia Minor in the summer of 830, capturing several towns but

withdrawing in the following autumn. The same pattern of military campaign
was repeated annually for the next three years, but it was more in the form of
traditional Arab raids rather than a serious attempt to make permanent inroads
into Byzantine territory.

The Caliph, while engaged in one such campaign, suddenly fell ill and died in
his camp near Taurus in August 833 at the age of forty-seven. He was
succeeded by his brother al-Mutasim (r. 833–42), whom he himself had
nominated for the post. Al-Mutasim—Harun's third son to become Caliph—
was a man of imposing physique and great personal courage, but devoid of
cultural interests and education, the complete opposite of al-Mamun in this
respect.

834

The Death of Ibn Hisham

The Muslim historian Ibn Hisham, who edited and enlarged the first
fundamental work on the life of the Prophet Muhammad by Ibn Ishaq (d. 767),
died in Cairo.

The Jat Revolt

In the marshes of lower Iraq, between Basra and Wasit, an Indian people called
the Jat (Zutt, in Arabic) had been living for centuries since the days of the
Sasanids (the exact time and reason of their migration into Iraq is unknown).
For some years now they had taken to highway robbery, disrupting traffic and
plundering urban areas. Gradually, the situation became so dangerous, and
communications between Baghdad and the sea so obstructed that Caliph al-
Mutasim (r. 833–42) in 834 was forced to dispatch an army to put down the
rebellion. Nearly seventeen thousand of them were captured and settled on the
border with the Byzantines in Asia Minor.

> Some authorities believe that gypsies, dark Causasian people leading a
> migratory way of life, are descendants of the Jat who were captured in later
> wars with the Bayzantines and sold in Europe. Often persecuted by civil and
> religious authorities, they moved from country to country and by the
> beginning of sixteenth century, had spread to every part of Europe.

836

The Transfer of the Capital to Samarra

Traditionally, the Abbasids, afraid of their Quraish rivals, had relied on the Persians and Khurasanis—instead of the Arabs—for their support. But there was a gradual shift to the Turks as the former recruiting ground was lost to the Tahirids. Caliph al-Mutasim (r. 833–42), himself a son of Harun by a Turkish slave, intensified the practice of recruiting regiments from these Turkish mercenaries, a non-semitic people of Central Asiatic origin, to such a level that they formed the main strength of the army. His personal bodyguard alone included no less than ten thousand of them. These valorous fighters and superb horsemen, whom the Caliph bought as slaves from the barbarian tribes of Transoxiana (which was under the Samanid rule), had grown arrogant and misused the royal favour to such an extent that they were bitterly hated by the local population.

Fearing a serious civil disorder, al-Mutasim in 836 moved the capital from Baghdad to Samarra, some seventy miles further up the Tigris. But the change in the seat of the empire did not make any difference to the state of affairs. The new and beautiful city of Samarra remained the capital during the reigns of eight successive Caliphs for the next fifty-six years, after which Baghdad resumed its status in 892.

> Al-Mutasim's infatuation with the Turkish mercenaries later proved to be a disaster for the Caliphal authority. Many of these men, who were prized for their steppe hardiness, could not speak Arabic and were not even Muslim, while some had accepted the Faith less from conviction than from expediency. They were thus bound to the empire by no strong emotional or spiritual commitment but were eventually to become real masters of it. They came to wield so much power that the Caliphs became mere puppets in their hands whom they could crown or depose (or even murder) at their will. Their loyalty was all too often directed toward their commanders of similar ethnic origins instead of to 'foreigners' in positions of authority.

846

Harassment by the Muslims of Southern Italy

The Muslims started the conquest of Sicily in 827 under the Aghlabid flag, but progress was slow owing to the lack of any dynamic leadership from Qairawan and to tough opposition on the island. However, without waiting to complete the conquest, they started using the part of the island under their control to fan out into the Mediterranean with their raiding expeditions.

They attacked, in 846, the mainland of southern Italy, capturing Ostia and thence appearing before the walls of Rome itself. They withdrew from the city, but not before sacking the Shrine of Saint Peter. The capital city was threatened, but not captured, again in 849. Although the Muslims never managed to gain a permanent control of any part of southern Italy, they remained a continuous source of harassment and incursion in the ninth and tenth century. Unlike Sicily itself, which is separated from the mainland by only the few-miles-wide Strait of Messina, Arabo-Islamic civilization did not leave any imprints in Italy.

The Muslims had already effectively replaced the once supreme Byzantine sea power in the Mediterranean, but in the next century or so they established their unchallenged dominance of the sea. In the east too, the Muslims had become a strong seafaring nation, sailing regularly as far as China.

847–50

The Death of al-Wathiq and Accession of al-Mutawakkil

Caliph al-Wathiq (r. 842–7) died without having made a nomination for the succession. His twenty-seven-year-old brother, Jafar, was made Caliph in preference to al-Wathiq's son by a group of Turkish military officers who had by now gained considerable influence and were very active in court intrigues. Al-Mutawakkil (r. 847–61), the throne-name which Jafar chose for himself, turned out to be a cruel and vindictive ruler, given to debauchery, who spent most of his time in semi-isolation in Samarra, surrounded by his Turkish guards and other hangers-on.

The early part of his fifteen-year-reign was marked by a bland reversal of the policies of his predecessors in respect of the Mutazilite doctrine, the Shia, and non-Muslims. As a young man, he held no political or military position of any importance, and his belligerence was thought to be a sharp reaction to the unfavourable treatment he had received at the hands of his predecessor and his entourage. No sooner did he assume power than he began to dismiss, imprison and, in some cases, torture the ministers of the previous government.

In about 849, the main contentious issue in the Mutazilite dogma, which had received official support by the previous three Caliphs, was denounced and the 'uncreatedness' or eternity of the Quran was upheld once again. In fact, the situation was completely reversed: now it was the turn of Mutazilite leaders, such as the chief judge, Ibn Abi Duad, to be declared heretical and persecuted (he died in prison). Orthodoxy was restored to royal favour with the same vigour as it had been suppressed during the previous twenty years.

Likewise, the pro-Shia policy of the previous thirty-five years was reversed into insensitive hostility towards the Alids, to the extent that the tomb of Hussain at Karbala was destroyed (850) on his orders and the ground ploughed up. Furthermore, pilgrimage to the Shi'ite sacred site was forbidden under threat of heavy penalties. The Alid property at Fidak from the days of the Prophet Muhammad was also confiscated. At the same time, there was a concerted effort to revive Sunni policies and bring them to the fore.

Al-Mutawakkil was intolerant also of the Christians and the Jews (many of whom until then had occupied high government offices), against whom he introduced new, or enforced vigorously the old, discriminating laws. They were forbidden to work in the civil service, forced to wear special clothing and subjected to general vexation.

Despite all this, there were no serious wars or open rebellions during his reign. The empire continued under its own momentum from its heyday; the economy flourished and learning was widspread.

The Death of al-Khwarizmi

Al-Khwarizmi (full nmae: Muhammad ibn Musa al-Khwarizmi), an outstanding Muslim mathematician, died in about 850. Born c. 780 in Khwarizm (modern Khiva in USSR), he worked in the famous centre of intellectual activities in Baghdad, the House of Wisdom, in the first Golden Age of Islamic science. His book in Arabic entitled *Hisab al-jabr wa'l-muqabalah* (Mathematics of Transposition and Cancellation) laid the foundation of algebra. It was the Latin transliteration of the the title word *al-jabr* (meaning, transposition) which originated the term 'algebra'. The book is a compilation of rules for arithmetical solutions of linear and quadratic equations, for elementry geometry, and for inheritance problems concerning the distribution of money according to proportions. After being rendered into Latin in the twelfth century by the eminent Toledan translator Gerard of Cremona (c. 1114–1187),* it introduced the subect of algebra into Europe and became its main textbook until the sixteenth century.

Another of his profoundly important contributions was that he drew on the ancient Hindu sources on mathematics, which had been developed entirely independently of the influence of Greek mathematics, and fused the two together. He introduced the Hindu (or Indian) numerals, including the zero, which revolutionized mathematical manipulation and developed it into a method of calculation as we know it today.

He also compiled a set of astronomical tables, based largely on the *Sindhind*, an Arabic version of the Sanskrit work *Brahma-Sinddhanta*. This treatise on astronomy was brought to Baghdad in about 771 by an Indian traveller, and was translated into Arabic by Muhammad ibn Ibrahim al-Fazari (d. circa 800) on the order of Caliph al-Mansur (r. 754–75). He called his tables of future planetary and stellar positions *Zij al-Sindhind*, to indicate their link with the Indian work.

The Arabic Numerals

When his work on numerals was first translated into Latin in the twelfth century by Adelard of Bath (c. 1090–c. 1150) from England, these numerals were mistakenly labelled 'Arabic numerals', although al-Khawarizmi had called them Hindi numerals to indicate their Indian origin. Christian Europe was very slow to adopt the new system of calculation. It was only after a great deal of persuasion by the Italian mathematician Leonardo Fibonacci (c. 1170–c. 1230), who himself had been taught by a Muslim and had travelled widely in Muslim north Africa, and the appearance of his book *Liber Abaci* (Book of the Abacus) in 1202 that the new symbols and arithmatic system were adopted in Italy in preference to the old and clumsy system employing letters of the alphabet which the Greek and Romans had used. Fibonacci was a native of Pisa, and Italy was the first European country where the Indian numerals, including the zero, took root. The new method of calculation led to a tremendous advancement in mathematics, astronomy and physics, since it simplified mathematical manipulations enormously. The word 'cypher' signifying 'nothing', or 'zero', is derived from the Arabic word *sifr* with the same meaning.

In the Latin translation of his work on numerals, his own name was transliterated as *Al-goritimi*, from which the European word 'algorism' (the old term for arithmetic) was derived.

The western Crusade against the Muslims in Spain resulted in the fall of Toledo in 1085, which marked the beginning of the translation into Latin of the Greek-Muslim scientific works from Arabic. Spain was the most important centre of contact between the Europeans and the Muslims because of its bilingual Christian and Muslim inhabitants, as well as a large number of Jews, some of whom were trilingual. The most active period of translation began with the establishment in Toledo of a regular school of translation at the initiative of Archbishop Raymond I (1126–52), which attracted many famous scholars from various parts of Europe to study Muslim learning. It was here that the first Latin translation of the Quran was made, in 1143, by an Englishman, Robert of Ketton (Latin: Robertus Retenensis). The most important translator was Gerard of Cremona, who came from Italy and spent much of his life in Toledo working under the auspices of the Church. When he died, his pupils drew up a list of seventy-one of his translations of Arabic works—and it was not exhaustive—covering nearly all fields of Muslim learning.

852

Seizure of Damietta by Byzantines

The Byzantines took advantage of the unrest at the Caliphal centre in Iraq coupled with the government neglect of the Mediterranean to capture the prosperous industrial town of Damietta in the Nile Delta.

Foundation of Toledo as Semi-Independent Republic

The city of Toledo had always been a hotbed of sedition and a continual centre of rebellion against the government of Cordova. It was now separated from the main body of Muslim Spain, forming its own semi-independent republic, which survived for the next eighty years, when Abdur Rahman III (r. 912–61) established his authority over it.

855

The Death of Imam Hanbal

Ahmad ibn Hanbal (commonly known as Imam Hanbal), founder of the Hanbal school of Muslim law, died in his native town of Baghdad at the age of seventy-five. He belonged first and foremost to the Traditionist movement, taking the position that the only 'roots of law' are the Quran and the Sunna, and that the divine law is not in any respect dependent on human reasoning. He spearheaded the opposition to all unorthodox thinkers such as the Mutazilites, the Shi'ite and others. He was a victim of the Inquisition held c. 833 by Caliph al-Mamun (r. 813–33) for leading the campaign asserting the eternal nature of the Quran, which was then contrary to the official dogma. After that, he became a symbol of the masses' opposition to their rulers; his steadfastness in the face of torture won him high esteem and devotion among the people in Iraq, where his teaching—despite its appearance of being anti-intellectual—continued to be followed by the majority until the Hanafi school was introduced under the influence of the Seljuq Turks.

861

The Murder of al-Mutawakkil

Caliph al-Mutawakkil (r. 847–61) was particularly attached to a Greek slave concubine by whom he had a son, al-Mutazz. Under her persuasion, he revoked his previous nomination and designated al-Mutazz for succession to the Caliphate, which caused his eldest son and heir-apparent, al-Muntasir, to conspire with the Turkish palace guards, who were by now no less powerful and designing at the court than the household troops of the Roman Emperors (the Praetorian Guard) had been at one time. There was a similarity with the Roman armies, too, in that they had incorporated western barbarians who fought for hire. Headed by the Turkish commander and Caliph's confidant, Bugha the Junior, a group of half a dozen soldiers entered al-Mutawakkil's private quarters one night in December and murdered him. Bugha had been a slave and the palace butler until promoted to the high rank. Next morning, al-Muntasir was installed as Caliph in Samarra and al-Mutazz was thrown into prison. But the new twenty-five-year-old Caliph soon fell foul of his fellow conspirators and was found dead six months later. Bugha's career provides an interesting illustration of what pluck, talent and ambition could accomplish in a Muslim state.

As later events would show, this was not just a local palace feud but a fateful event which was the culmination of the unabated growth of power of the Turks in Caliphal affairs; worse still, they now became fully aware of their own strength and of their sovereign's weakness. The death of al-Mutawakkil marked the rapid decline of the once mighty Abbasid rulers, who had been in power for just over a century. They were later reduced to being mere figureheads, made and unmade by their own slave guards and kept in idle impotence. Their duties were virtually confined to presiding over ceremonies, conferring honorary titles and receiving religious deputations, all of which the Turks were quite happy to leave to them. There was, however, no conflict between them on doctrinal grounds because the Turks, too, were Sunnis.

The assassination of al-Mutawakkil precipitated a period of struggle between short-lived Caliphs and their Turkish guards; in the next nine years, no less than four Caliphs succeeded one another, all being murdered. A new factor contributing to the chaos and instability was the growing influence of the woman courtiers through these slaves in political affairs.

864

Establishment of the Zaydi Principality in Daylam

In 791, some descendants of Zayd ibn Ali (a grandson of Hussain), who, in 740, had revolted against the Umayyads at Kufa in the name of fellow Alids, took refuge in the small, remote, pagan kingdom of Daylam on the south-west coast of the Caspian Sea. Here, they set up, in 864, a new state of the Zaydis, which they started ruling as Imams, but it collapsed in 928 when they were driven out by the Sunni Samanids (819–1005). Although the Zaydi reign was short and turbulent, it did leave behind an enduring mark in Islamic history in that the Caspian region became a centre of the Shi'ite ideology—though ultimately of a different form (that of the Twelvers)—in Persia.

865

The Siege of Baghdad; the Murder of al-Mustain

A quarrel developed between some senior Turkish generals at the court, and Caliph al-Mustain (r. 862–6) fled with one faction of the leaders supporting him, from Samarra to Baghdad, where Arab soldiers were still predominant. Meanwhile al-Mutazz, the second son of al-Mutawakkil (r. 847–61), was released from prison and declared Caliph in Samarra. When in Baghdad, al-Mustain took some pro-Alid measures with the hope of gaining popular support, but the main body of Turks in Samarra pursued him, laid siege to the beautiful city for nine months, and forced him to abdicate in January 866. Al-Mustain was murdered soon afterwards.

867

Establishment of Saffarid Dynasty

Like Iraq, eastern Persia had been going through turmoil during the previous five years. After the enlightened and comparatively prosperous rule of his two predecessors, it was the turn of Muhammad, fifth in line of the Tahirid family, to take over in 862 on the death of his father. A weak and frivolous character, he was not up to the job. To make the matter worse, his elevation to power coincided with the meteoric rise of a rival power further south in the province of Sijistan (or Sistan).

In 861, the year in which Caliph al-Mutawakkil was murdered by his own mercenary troops, a twenty-seven-year-old tradesman by the the name of Yaqub ibn Layth (d. 879), known as al-Saffar (the coppersmith), rose in rebellion in his native province of Sijistan without any pretensions to a religious or social cause to justify his campaign. A common bandit but born leader of fighting men, he had organized a large army, absorbing many caliph-rejecting fugitive Kharijites and various other malcontents of the area into its ranks. His well-disciplined army was fashioned on a new style, that of being loyal to its leader rather than to any religious or doctrinal concept. He soon won a measure of respect by expanding eastward and conquering the pagan land of Afghanistan, where he began to act as an independent ruler.

In 867, he moved westward, encroaching on the Tahirid land, capturing Herat (867), Kirman (869) and then the agriculturally rich province of Fars. Finally, the capital, Nishapur, fell into his hands (873), and the pro-Abbasid Tahirid state was overthrown. Yaqub thus founded a dynasty of rulers, the Saffarids (867–c.1495), whose empire at its greatest extent included Khurasan, Isfahan, Fars, Kirman, Sijistan and the Kabul valley. However, in 900, the family suffered disastrous defeat at the hands of the Samanids (819–1005), after which their lands passed under Samanid control, though, remarkably, their influence (in a subordinate capacity) lingered on until the end of the fifteenth century, but only in Sijistan.

868

The Death of al-Jahiz

Al-Jahiz (full name: Abu Uthman Amr ibn Bahr, but better known by the nickname of al-Jahiz, 'the goggle-eyed'), theologian, intellectual and a famous prose-writer, died in Basra, where he had been born c.776. Although from a modest social background, he gained acceptance in literary circles and in high society by his sheer intellect and wit. During the reign of Caliph al-Mamun (r. 813–33), he moved to Baghdad, and later to Samarra when the capital was moved to there, though he never held an official position at court, always supporting himself with donations from rich and powerful functionaries in return for dedicating his books to them; he received 5,000 gold *dinars* from the official to whom he dedicated his most famous work *Kitab al-Hayawan*(*Book of Animals*).

According to a legend he was crushed to death by a collapsing pile of books in his study. Legendry though it may be, the story does portray the world in which al-Jahiz spent his long life of ninety-two years. His omnivorous curiosity was evident from the nearly two hundred works he composed, in Arabic, of varying length and on an extraordinary range of topics, which inluded treatises on theology (from the Mutazilite standpoint), misers, food, civil servants, donkeys and thieves. But his masterpiece was undoubtedly the seven-volume *Book of Animals*, which, strangely, has little to do with zoology but is a mine of information about proverbs, jokes, anecdotes, traditions, superstitions and the like. Taking his writings together, he, in effect, provided a comprehensive education in the humanities of his time, all of which later scholars have been able to draw upon to get a picture of the various strata of society during the ninth century.

Appointment of Ahmad ibn Tulun as Governor of Egypt

It became a normal practice for the governor of Egypt to remain at the Caliphal court in Baghdad or Samarra in order to safeguard his own interests, while the day-to-day administration was left to a deputy. In 868, a thirty-three-year-old Turkish soldier by the name of Ahmad ibn Tulun was sent out to Egypt to serve as deputy governor, but within a year he managed to gain his own military and financial foothold in the province, thus establishing the first local dynasty, the Tulunids (868–905), of Egypt, and later jointly of Egypt, Palestine and Syria.

During the rule of this enterprising soldier-politician, agriculture, commerce and industry were promoted, government finances reorganized and a large-scale public building programme undertaken. The Zanj revolt of 869 in southern Iraq helped Tulun in two ways: it preoccupied the central government, and at the same time diverted the oriental trade to the Red Sea route which increased the prosperity of Egypt. In 879, he built the famous mosque bearing his name in the capital, Fustat. Tulun also built up a large and powerful army of Greek, Turk and Nubian (now called Sudanese) slaves in addition to a strong navy, by which he kept a hold on Syria, which he had captured in 878. After his death in 884, the subsequent four Tulunid rulers turned out to be ineffectual, and the Abbasids regained control over Egypt in 905, only to loose it again permanently thirty years later, initially to another dynasty, the Ikhshidids (935–69).

The easily governable nature of this rich province can be seen from the fact that al-Mamun had been the first Caliph ever to have felt the need to visit it, which he did in 832 when he quelled a disturbance by the Arab refugees from Spain and established a Khurasanian army there; the Caliph was in Syria at the time. The Copts, with a long history of foreign domination, did not seem to have developed any strong national feelings which would sustain their separate identity, as in the case of the Persians in the east. The occasional Coptic risings against their rulers were concerned with no more than local grievances against taxation rather than any general religious movement or national revival. Egypt, in fact, remained the least troublesome—though financially and strategically important—province in the whole of the Muslim world.

Under the Tulunids, Egypt became a soveriegn state for the first time since the end of Ptolemaic rule (30 BCE) in the country.

869–70

The Accession of al-Muhtadi

The Caliphate had been so downgraded and treated with so much contempt by the Turkish soldiery that the latter now rioted on the streets in the capital, Samarra, demanding arrears of pay. When this was not forthcoming to their satisfaction, they first beat up treasury officials and then the Caliph al-Mutazz himself was thrown into a dungeon (869), where he died. Meanwhile, the Turks had chosen al-Muhtadi, a son of al-Wathiq (r. 842–7), but he unexpectedly turned out to be a firm, couragous and deeply religious person, who would have made a great Caliph in different circumstances. But this was not to be; when he tried to stand up to the Turkish commanders for their political excesses and their plundering the treasury, he too was captured and killed in 870 after a brief reign of less than a year.

Then, another son of al-Mutawakkil (r. 847–61) was proclaimed Caliph with the title of al-Mutamid (r. 870–92). The new Caliph was a feeble personality, but his reign, in contrast to those of his four predecessors, lasted over twenty years, notably because of his much more capable brother, al-Muwaffaq (d. 891), who gradually took over effective power in the name of the Caliph. The situation at court, too, underwent a change in the ensuing period which unexpectedly brought comparative peace and prosperity. The Turkish guards who had held power for so long had grown old and were themselves replaced by a younger Arabicized generation and, more important, did not form an exclusive clique any more but were divided into factions.

In fact, by the end of 892, many fundamental changes had taken place which altered the very nature of the empire. Not only its power over the military, but the semi-religious aura of the Caliphate, on which the whole structure of the Muslim world had stood for so long, disappeared. Realizing that the Caliph was a politically helpless prisoner in his own palace and that government was being excercised by a group of illiterate barbarian soldiers, some provinces both in the west and the east gradually fell away, leaving the Empire fragmented.

The Outbreak of the Zanj Rebellion

Although slavery, which had been common in Arabia in pre-Islamic days, was accepted by the Prophet as an institution, he strongly enjoined that kindness be shown to slaves; liberation of them was to be regarded as a pious act; the Quran, too, orders humane treatment for slaves in passages such as Suras 4:36 and 24:33. Currently, there were a large number of slaves of many nationalities in the empire, most of them having been prisoners-of-war or purchased in time of peace. Some were negroes, others were Turks and still others white. The white slaves were mainly Greeks and Slavs, Armenians and Berbers. After every campaign, many thousands, sometimes tens of thousands, of captives from hostile territory were sold as slaves. But they did not form the main basis of production, as in the Roman Empire. The deployment of slaves on public works and plantation was the exception; instead, they were mostly employed in households for domestic duties, or put in military service and were treated well.

One of the rare projects involving gang slavery was in progress in which a large number of negro slaves from east Africa were being employed in southern Iraq in harsh conditions to drain the salt marshes east of Basra. A certain Persian by the name of Ali ibn Muhammad, claiming to be descended from Ali through his wife Fatima (the Prophet's daughter), organized the negroes (known as the Zanj, akin to Zanzibar, in Arabic) into a strong and rapidly growing revolt by promising them freedom and wealth. His call became even more attractive when he later adopted the rebellious stance of the Kharijites: anyone, 'even a black slave', whose only qualification was piety, could be elected Caliph, and all dissidents, even Muslims, were infidels to be waged a holy war against. In 869, they defeated the Caliphal army in Basra and the following year gained control of southern Iraq by capturing a port on the Persian Gulf and severing the sea link to Basra and thence to Baghdad itself, thereby badly disrupting trade. The rebellion spread dangerously; for the next fourteen years, southern Iraq was plagued with their ravages, which the badly jolted government (it had to defend simultaneously against inroads by the Saffarids in Persia) was unable to stamp out. They sacked Basra (871), captured Wasit (878) and even threatened Baghdad itself.

The Death of al-Bukhari

Al-Bukhari(full name: Muhammad ibn Ismail al-Jufi al-Bukhari), Arabic scholar and Muslim saint born in Bukhara, died near Samarqand at the age of sixty. The Traditions being a source of law second only to the Quran, the accuracy of those in circulation was vital, since fabrication and dubious reports had been attempted to justify particular sectarian or political points of view. The mammoth task of verification of these Traditions was undertaken by al-Bukhari with the single-mindedness which befitted the daunting challenge. For sixteen years, he travelled widely over the Muslim world in his unflagging effort to collect trustworthy Traditions. He sifted through and critically evaluated no less than 600,000 Traditions (undoubtedly containing many duplications and overlappings) and diligently reduced the immense corpus to a compilation of just over 7,000. He took the task with so much solemnity and responsibility that he would perform the ceremonial ablution and prayer before committing a Tradition to writing. His collection was honoured with the title *al-Sahih* (meaning 'the genuine' or 'authentic') and is still regarded as the commentary *par excellence*. It is not only given complete credence but is highly revered, and constitutes the foundation of all later works on Islam.

Al-Bukhari's tomb is situated near Samarqand (USSR).

The authenticity and value of a Tradition was judged by its *isnad* (chain of transmitters) stretching back to the Prophet himself, each of whom had to be scrutinized for credibility. Each Tradition was then declared 'genuine', 'fair' or 'weak'. Of the six 'genuine' collections, al-Bukhari's is the foremost and is acclaimed by Muslims as being next only to the Quran in authority. The *Sahih* of Muslim ibn al-Hajjaj (d. 875) ranks next, close to that of al-Bukhari. The remaining four are the compilations made by Ibn Maja (d. 886), Abu Dawud (d. 888), al-Tirmidhi (d. 892), al-Nasai (d. 916). These six books are followed by the Sunnis.

The Shi'ites examined Traditions from their own standpoint and considered trustworthy only those which were based on the authority of Ali and his followers. They therefore have their own body of Traditions, and hold the five collections written respectively by Muhammad ibn Yaqub al-Kulini (d. 939), Ali ibn Babuya al-Kummi (d. 991), two by Muhammad al-Tusi (d. 1067), and Ali ibn Tahir al-Sharif al-Murtada (d. 1044) in particularly high esteem.

These books are referred to by some European scholars as 'canonical', but this is incorrect, since there is no body in Islam capable of legislating on religious matters, as did the ecumenical councils in Christianity.

873

The Death of Hunyan ibn Ishaq

Hunayn ibn Ishaq (b. 809), head of the team of translators in the renowned House of Wisdom, died in Baghdad. A Christian and native of Hira, Hunayn was trained as a physician but also mastered the Greek language. Under the patronage of the Abbasid Caliphs, this leading intellectual figure made a tremendous contribution in the field of learning both as a prolific author and as a translator. In an effort to produce reliable and scholarly translations of Greek treatises, he would travel far and wide to collate and check the authenticity of manuscripts before embarking on a translation. Hunayn, together with his team, produced translations into Arabic of many monumental Greek works such as those by Hippocrates, Aristotle, Dioscorides and Galen, as well as commentaries, and revisions of earlier translations. His main achievement in the field of translation was making available in Arabic almost the whole of the immense corpus of Galen's medical writings, as well as Plato's *Republic* and the *Materia Medica* of Dioscorides.

Hunayn was later to be remembered also for his own at least twenty-nine original contributions in the field of the life sciences. In particular, his ten treatises on the eye—the first systemic textbook with ophthalmological diagrams—were to have a profound influence on the development of the subject for several centuries to come. He was honoured by being appointed the personal physician of Caliph al-Mutawakkil (r. 847–61). Much of his own work, as well as his translations, later appeared in Latin in Europe.

The Death of al-Kindi

Al-Kindi (full name: Abu Yusuf Yaqub ibn Ishaq al-Kindi), the first outstanding Muslim philosopher, known as 'the philosopher of the Arabs', died c.873 in Baghdad at the age of about seventy. Born of a noble Arab descent through the tribe of Kinda, he enjoyed the favour of the Caliphs al-Mamun (r. 813–33) and al-Mutasim (r. 833–42). He studied at Basra and Baghdad and was noted for being the one of the earliest scholars in the eastern Caliphate who became thoroughly versed in the writings of Aristotle (384–322 BCE) and whose logic he sought to support essential dogmas of Islam. He emphasized the righteousness as well as unity of God and considered that the Creator revealing Himself in Prophecy was a reasonable truth and the highest form of Knowledge. Al-Kindi concerned himself not only with those philosophical questions which had previously been treated by the Aristotelian Neoplatonists of Alexandria but with an astonishing range of subjects such as astrology, medicine, arithmetic, music, astronomy, the manufacture of swords, cooking and many others. Besides his translations and commentaries on Aristotle's work, he is credited with having written over 250 treatises on a great variety of subjects, but very few are extant. Of these, more have survived in their Latin translations than in their original Arabic form. His chief work on optics, in its Latin translation, influenced Roger Bacon (c. 1214–92).

878

Annexation of Syria to Egypt

In 868, the rise of an autonomous Tulunid centre in Egypt had opened a new phase in the history of Syria which henceforth became a disputed territory between the rulers of Cairo and Baghdad. While al-Muwaffaq (brother of Caliph al-Mutamid but virtual ruler) was fully occupied with the Zanj rebellion in Iraq, Ahmad ibn Tulun (r. 868–84) took advantage of the death of the governor of Syria by promptly capturing the province and annexing it to his territory (878). This precedent was to be followed in later times by almost every independent ruler of Egypt; while some would attempt to control the whole of Syria, others would remaincontent with a bridgehead in Palestine, leaving the rest to Baghdad or to local petty dynasties.

Thus only ten years after his appointment as governor, Ibn Tulun became the most powerful of all provincial rulers and shared a frontier with the Byzantines, whom he was to defeat (883) near Tarsus in a border clash.

882–3

The Final Defeat of the Zanj

In 882, the Caliphal army entrusted to al-Muwaffaq launched a major offensive against the fourteen-year-old-rebellion by the Zanj slaves and expelled them from all the land that they had conquered. But they were not finally crushed for another year, when their leader Ali ibn Muhammad was killed (883).

890

The Outbreak of the Qarmatian Revolt

A heretical and subversive movement had grown out of the Ismaili sect (of the Shia) and its members were known as Qarmatians, after its leader, a certain Hamdan Qarmat. Hamdan came to Kufa at the time when the Zanj rebellion was still strong in southern Iraq and tried to join them, but failed to come to an agreement. However, the aftermath of the insurrection, coupled with the political disorder and social unrest which the Abbasid society was going through, created a favourable atmosphere for the new movement.

Feelings of discontent were fermenting among the under-privileged because of the polarization of both wealth and political power. The Caliphs were caught in a vicious circle; their own subjects were alienated, and they were obliged to depend on mercenaries to deal with several unruly provincial governors. The use of mercenaries made it roughly true that the more money was spent the more military strength the Caliph acquired. This, in turn, meant a heavy burden of taxation on the backs of the peasantry and inevitable resentment against the government. The other source of income was trade, which depended on security, but security too could be maintained only with troops, so much so that even the efficient collection of taxes needed military backing. Later, during the reign of al-Muqtadir (r. 908–32), the right to collect taxes would be 'farmed out' to the leaders of these mercenaries, or governors, who would pay their troops from local state funds and not from the depleted Caliphal treasury. But this was to create new examples of oppression.

The zealous Hamdan, who was an Iraqi tribesman, managed to gather a large number of followers from the masses of his own people with his efficient propaganda offering to cure the social ills. In 890, he built the headquarters (which he called *Dar al-Hijra*, meaning the house of refuge) east of Kufa of the new movement, which was based on a system of communism (although slave labour was used) and financed from a common fund supported by contributions. The real doctrines of this intensely egalitarian community were kept secret and were only revealed to adepts who had to pass through several grades of initiation. They showed nothing but contempt for the outward forms of Islam; and their own activities were regarded as blasphemous in the extreme by the orthodox. Their extreme ideas were matched equally by their terrorism, subversion and ruthlessness. They would massacre their enemies, even Muslims who opposed them, without mercy.

Soon the Qarmatian movement grew in strength and its ravages continued to terrorize Islam for a century before they were finally crushed. Taking advantage of the disorder left behind in lower Iraq after the Zanj revolt, they gained considerable strength in Bahrain, where they succeeded in establishing a strong and independent state (899) with al-Ahsa as its capital. Bahrain then became a base for their propaganda as well as their military campaigns, keeping the realm in constant turmoil. The movement became a stubborn source of insurrection, and it was only after a long campaign that they were suppressed in Syria (903) and Iraq (906), but the government was unable to dislodge them from Bahrain.

The Shia

It had been the political and dynastic question regarding the leadership of the Muslim community after the Prophet's death (632) which had originally given rise to the Shia (a collective term meaning party) of Ali in the very early days of Islam. The partisans had maintained that only the descendants of the Prophet Muhammad through Ali and his wife Fatima could be the legitimate successors (or Caliphs) of the Prophet, with Ali being the first in the line; they, therefore, regarded the first three Caliphs, Abu Bakr, Umar and Uthman as usurpers. However, over the years, the Shia, which makes up about ten per cent of all Muslims, gradually developed into a religious movement with distinct doctrines. Although Mukhtar's short-lived revolt of 685–7 had given it a definite twist in the new direction, it was the frustration of repeated political defeats and prolonged persecutions which eventually moulded it into a separate religious sect with its own theology and body of law antagonistic to that of the orthodox Sunnis. At the core of their belief was the idea of the Imam (Arabic: leader, pattern), who was not only of true descent from Muhammad through the Ali-Fatima line but who also possessed special qualities. While some extreme adherents of the Shi'ite cause claimed the Imam to have no less than divine attributes, a generally accepted view which was more moderate and with which Shi'ism is now associated was that the hereditary Imam is sinless, gifted with supernatural knowledge and power and capable of knowing the true and hidden (esoteric) meaning of the Quran, for the Imam alone is infallible. To this was added another belief, that of the *Mahdi* (or 'Hidden Imam'), the expected founder of a new order of justice and peace on earth. The Mahdi, until his return at the end of the age, guides mankind through chosen representatives in each generation and thus the Imamate does not come to an end. Different sections of the Shia believe in varying degrees of divinity for the Imam. Thus the Shi'ite Imam differed fundamentally from the Sunni Caliph, who was a leader of the Muslim community only in temporal matters.

The disputes over the vital question of who was the rightful Imam sharply divided Shi'ism into three separate main persuasions: the Zaydis, the Ismailis and the Imamis. The Zaydis acknowledge the first five Imams, the Ismailis seven and the Imamis twelve. They are hence designated as 'Fivers', 'Seveners' and 'Twelvers' respectively. These main divisions have their own numerous sub-divisions totalling, according to some sources, no fewer than thirty-two (or even more).

The Zaydi sect differs from the others in professing to acknowledge Zayd ibn Ali (martyred in 740 fighting against the Umayyads) as their fifth Imam instead of his brother, Muhammad al-Baqir (d. 731/3), who is the fifth Imam of the other sects. They demand that the Imam shall be the descendant of Fatima and Ali, without any distinction between the Hasanid and Hussainid lines, i.e., not succession by inheritance, but having the ability to assert his rule by force of arms if necessary; the idea of a 'Hidden Imam' is, therefore, rejected and likewise a child cannot be considered. Their Imam is rightly-guided but not divine. Of all the Shi'ite sects, they are closest to the Sunnis in belief and most moderate in politics. Unlike other Shi'ite groups, they do not consider the first two Orthodox Caliphs, Abu Bakr and Umar, to have been usurpers.

The Ismailis with their sub-divisions have been politically the most active in the history of Islam, representing the most radical Shi'ite belief. They derive their name from the eldest son (Ismail) of the sixth Imam, Jafar al-Sadiq. Ismail had died in 760 within the lifetime of his father, who had disinherited him after being told of his intemperance. After Jafar's death (765), the main body of the Shia had accepted his second son, Musa al-Kazim, as the seventh Imam, but some Shi'ites branched off into recognizing Ismail as the seventh Imam. They argued that Ismail being, the Imam-designate was sinless, and hence the charges against him could not have been true. In their fervent belief, they declared that he was not dead but had withdrawn into concealment to excercise his indisputable authority as a 'Hidden Imam' and would return as the Mahdi, although there were some who acknowledged that he did die, but left a son, Muhammad, who fled to India from the persecution of Harun al-Rashid, where he 'disappeared', and it was he who was the expected Mahdi. Later, the Ismailis absorbed the most extreme elements and hetrodox ideas, all disposed to rebellion, and divided themselves into various branches. The most notable of them were the Qarmatians of Iraq, Syria and Arabia, the Fatimids of north Africa and Egypt, the Assasins (or Hashishin) of Alamut mountain in northern Persia, and the Druzes of southern Lebanon. The present-day main stream of the Ismailis (or Seveners) are much more moderate in their views than their ancestors were at the start of the sect, when Ismail was declared to be the very incarnation of God Himself.

The Imamis (Twelvers) form the main body of the Shi'ites. They get their name from reckoning Muhammad al-Mahdi as the twelfth Imam who is said to have 'withdrawn' or to have 'gone into concealment' when a child in 878, but who will return as the Mahdi to fill the world with truth and justice. Since then the *Mujtahids* (the Shi'ite divines) have been able to pronounce upon legal and doctrinal matters under the guidance of the 'hidden Imam', so their decisions have the same status among the Shi'ites as *ijma* and *qiyas* do among the Sunnis.

Despite many rulers having been of Shia persuasion, Shi'ism remained almost everywhere a minority faith until 1502, when Imamism was made—and has continued to be—the state religion in Persia by the Safavid dynasty (1501–1732). The followers of the dynasty were colloquially known as the Kizil-bash (in Turkish meaning 'red heads') because of the red caps they used to wear.

892

Restoration of Baghdad as Capital

The Abbasid capital was moved from Samarra back to Baghdad after Samarra had been the seat of government for fifty-six years stretching over the reigns of eight consecutive Caliphs. Samarra was abandoned gradually to fall into ruins.

The Death of al-Mutamid and Accession of al-Mutadid

The weak Caliph al-Mutamid (r. 870–92) died and was succeeded by his capable and energetic nephew, al-Mutadid (r. 892–902), who set himself the task of restoring the power and prestige of the Caliphate, which had, since 861, been a mere shadow in Samarra under the powerful Turkish military commanders. He was largely successful, except that the revolt by the Qarmatians around 900 brought the state once more to the verge of dissolution.

894

Outbreak of Rebellion in Spain by Ibn Hafsan

The reign of Amir Abdur Rahman II (which ended in 852) had been followed by a period of crisis in Spain which was to last for sixty years. During the weak and incompetent leadership from Cordova, a number of ambitious individuals in the provinces had found support among the discontented who had grievances for one reason or another.

Perhaps the most stubborn and prolonged of these rebellions against the central goverment was the one which broke out in 894. It was led by Umar ibn Hafsan (a Muslim of Spanish stock) and his sons, who consolidated their position in the mountains near Malaga. This anti-government stronghold became a constant source of trouble for the authority in Cordova during the next thirty-four years.

897

The Establishment of the Zaydi State

In 864, a Zaydi state was set up in the south-west coastland of the Caspian Sea. In 897, another descendant of Zayd established a principality in Yemen with its centre at Sada and later at Sana.* In order to protect their domain, the Imams (as the rulers claimed to be) of Yemen had to hold out in countless struggles against the local Kharijites, Qarmatians and other opponents, as well as against the rulers of Egypt and the Caliphs. Subsequently, the Zaydi faith gained a permanent hold in Yemen.

*There is considerable uncertainty about the date.
   The Zaydi Imams of Yemen, under the dynastic name of Rassids, ruled the country, with some interuptions, until 1962, when an army coup lead to the proclamation of a republic.

900

Samanid Rule

In the first half of the eighth century, a certain Saman Khuda, who was a landowner in the province of Balkh and who had become a Muslim, had established a friendship with the Umayyad viceroy of Khurasan and had helped him to defeat a Turkish invasion in 737. Ever since, the Persian family had remained loyal to its Arab connection; his son Asad had served the early Abbasids. A century later, it gained influence and a foothold in the region through four sons of Asad being appointed provincial governors of Samarqand, Ferghana, Shash, and Herat, under both the Tahirids and the Abbasids.

   In 873, the rapidly growing power of Yaqub al-Saffar, whose followers included many bandits and heterodox people posed a serious threat when it put an end to the Tahirid state and thus annexed Khurasan. In 875, Yaqub ventured to march against Baghdad itself and came within fifty miles of the capital before being defeated and repulsed in the following year. The Samanid family had steadily grown so important that in an attempt to check the Saffarids' expansionist ambitions, the Caliph al-Mutamid (r. 870–92) appointed Nasr ibn Ahmad (875), son of one of Saman's four grandsons, governor of the whole of Transoxiana, a post which he kept until his death in 892, and the family thence acquired an independent status.

   Like the Tahirids, the Samanids, too, were loyal supporters of the Abbasids, professing the Sunni orthodox stance (with the possible exception of Nasr II, r.914–43) and representing the social *status quo*. But, except for the investiture insignia received from Baghdad, they were autonomous. Although these investitures did not mean any actual increase in territory here or elsewhere, for that had to be won by the sword, none the less a patent from the Caliph gave local rulers a legitimacy which loomed large in the eyes of many people, and therefore was a powerful instrument for securing and maintaining authority. The Samanids created a strong basis for their rule by firmly securing thenorthern frontiers of the state against raids by pagan Turkish tribes of the steppes and by creating a good internal government in this fertile and rich province.

Both Yaqub and Nasr were succeeded by their respective brothers, Amr and Ismail. In 900, Ismail crossed the Oxus with his strong army, and virtually annihilated the Saffarids, capturing their leader, Amr, who was sent to the Caliph in Baghdad where he later died in captivity. The Saffarid empire thus collapsed and from then on the family was reduced to the status of local and subordinate rulers of Sijistan, where the shadowy dynasty maintained its existance for six more centuries successively under Samanids, Ghaznavids, Seljuqs and Mongols.

The Samanids—the third native Persian dynasty—reached the pinnacle of its power under Nasr II, the greatest ruler of his house, when it reigned over the whole of east Persia (touching the Indian border in the east), Transoxiana and Tabaristan. Under their wise and energetic rule, expanding industry and commerce brought prosperity to the region, which was centrally placed on caravan trade routes connecting Persia with China, Iraq, eastern Europe and Scandinavia. The Samanids were also great patrons of art, literature and science, and made their capital Bukhara, along with Samarqand, a brilliant centre of Muslim civilizatin, where the fusion of Arab and Persian thought produced intellectual attainment rivalling Baghdad. At the court of Bukhara flourished many men of great learning, such as Firdawsi (c. 934–1020), one of the greatest Persian poets, who composed his early works during this period, Rudaki (d. 940), the first poet of note to write poems in the 'New Persian'*, Balami, who completed his Persian translation (963) of an abridged version of the mammoth world history by his fellow-countyman al-Tabari (839–923), Rhazes (c. 865–925), who produced a large part of his works on medicine and the celebrated physician-scientist Avicenna (980–1037), all of whom worked in the great library of Bukhara. The language in the scientific fields remained Arabic, but the Samanids, who claimed descent from a noble Sasanid family and were ardent admirers of Persian culture, also encouraged the revival of the Persian language and literature after it being eclipsed by Arabic for two and a half centuries. This was also a period in which the Persian national spirit was aroused and re-established.

Two other features of the century-long Samanid rule were the conversion of the pagan Turks to Islam and the subsidiary slave trade, which reached its peak during that time. The Samanid role in both these activities proved to be of great importance in world history in the following centuries. It was mainly through their efforts that Islam became the religion of virtually all the Turkish peoples. And because of the close association of the Samanids with Sunni Islam, most of the Turks, too, became followers of this branch of the religion. Moreover, the Turkish slaves from the steppes, who were in high demand in Baghdad and elsewhere for military service, were brought back after raids into the border towns, and then exported.

Once recruited into the Muslim army, a slave might rise to the highest command, and some did so, even founding their own dynasties. Like the Abbasids, the Samanids, too, made the mistake of employing the Turkish slaves in large numbers as officials and soldiers who gradually became as powerful, if not more, as their masters. Ironically, it was the Islamicized Qarakhanids (or Ilek Khans), Turkish chiefs advancing from Central Asia, who occupied Bukhara itself in 999, without meeting any sustained resistance, since enough support could not be gathered to wage a holy war (*jihad*) against these Sunni Muslims. Six years later, the last of the Samanids, Ismail II (r. 1000–5), pressed by the Qarakhanids from the east and the Ghaznavids (slave-soldiers in origin) from the south, lost his life in battle. This was the time when the Ghaznavids were expanding their territory at a phenomenal rate under their famous leader, Mahmud of Ghazna (r. 998–1030). After the Samanid rule came to an end, their land was divided between the Qarakhanids and Mahmud, the former annexing Transoxiana and the latter Khurasan, with the Oxus forming the frontier.

The 'Old Persian', spoken until about the third century BCE, was written in cuneiform. The 'Middle Persian' (or Pahlavi), spoken from the third century BCE to the ninth century CE, was written in Aramaic ideographic script; this was the language in which, apart from a varied literature, most texts of the Zoroastrian and Manichaean religious traditions were written. The language then gradually began to approach the final, much simpler form of 'Modern Persian' (or Farsi), written with the Arabic alphabet and with many words adapted from Arabic. It was under the Samanids that Moderm Persian became established as a literary language, and it has changed very little since then.

901

The Death of Thabit ibn Qurrah

Thabit ibn Qurrah, a mathematician, philosopher and representative of the flourishing Arab-Islamic culture of the ninth century, died. Born c. 836 of a prominent family settled in Harran (modern Turkey), a city noted as the seat of an enduring Hellenistic astronomical cult and a school of philosophy and medicine, he had led a group of translators, drawn mainly from his co-religionists, the Sabians (star-worshippers). He, together with his team at the Harranian school, is credited with having translated, or retranslated, a large part of the Greek mathematical and astronomical works, including those of Archimedes (d. 212 BCE). Among the earlier translations he improved upon, was that of Euclid and Ptolemy's *Almagest**, both by Hunayn ibn Ishaq (809–73), head of the Nestorian Christian group of translators in Baghdad. Another of his retranslations, which was to be invaluable to future scholars, was that of Ptolemy's *Geography*, which had, among other information, a catalogue of places, with their latitudes and longitudes. Following Ptolemy, later Muslim geographers, in general, measured longitude from the prime meridian, that of the islands now known as the Canaries. In addition to his useful translations, Thabit wrote more than seventy original works in varied fields such as mathematics, astronomy, astrology, medicine, physics, philosophy, ethics and music. Being star-worshippers, the Sabians had always been interested in astronomy and the closely related subject of mathematics. He enjoyed the patronage and friendship of Caliph al-Mutadid (r. 892–902). Thabit was succeeded in his great work by his sons who formed a dynasty of translators and original scientists.

It was the Arabic version of this important work on astronomy which was later translated into Latin in 1175, and which dominated the field throughout the Renaissance. The Almagest (from the Greek word megiste, meaning greatest) was the final refinement of Greek knowledge of astronomy.

903–5

Reconquest of Syria and Egypt; End of the Tulunid Dynasty

A major preoccupation of the new Caliph, al-Muktafi (r. 902–8), was the growing insurrections caused by the Qarmatians which he had inherited from his father and predecessor, al-Mutadid. Having established their base in Bahrain (899) and threatened the neighbourhood of Basra and Kufa, in 903 they appeared in Syria (which was under Tulunid rule), capturing some cities, including Damascus. This provided al-Muktafi with the pretext for direct intervention. In summer 903, he sent an army to help the Tulunid governor of Syria to fight against the Qarmatians, who were then badly beaten, though they remained still active in parts of Iraq, and Bahrain.

After gaining control of Syria, in 905, the victorious expeditionary force launched a combined sea and land attack on Egypt to regain it from the Tulunid line, whose recent members had been incompetent rulers, and the country was rent with clashes over succession. The Abbasid army had no difficulty in capturing the Egyptian capital, Fustat, after the Tulunid ruler had been assasinated by his own men. Thus the Tulunid dynasty came to an abrupt end after a short life of thirty-seven years.

908

The Death of al-Muktafi

Although the reign of al-Muktafi, from 902 to 908, was taken up largely with the Qarmatian problem, he upheld the prestige of the Caliphal office, which had been recovered earlier by his father al-Mutadid (r. 892–902). It was, in fact, increased with the recapture of Egypt and Syria from the Tulunids. But after that he died at the early age of thirty-two, his twelve-year-old brother, al-Muqtadir (r.908–32), was put up to succeed him, and the realm was thrown into chaos once again. Baghdad witnessed successive outbreaks of rioting and *coups d'etat*.

909

The Emergence of the Fatimids in North Africa; the End of the Aghlabid Dynasty

For nearly a century after the disappearance of their last Imam, the Ismailis remained an insignificant outgrowth of the Shia with no poliical aspirations. This, however, all changed in 873, when a man named Abdullah ibn Maimun al-Qaddah (d. circa 875) appeared on the scene and assumed the leadership of the sect, claiming for himself and his successors the position of a chosen legate of the *Mahdi*. He professed to be inspired and had the power to perform miracles. Being a man of far-reaching political vision, he soon established a vast network of secret but active organizations in various parts of the empire preaching a doctrine of revolution against the Sunni order and the Abbasid Caliphate. In 893, a certain Abu Abdullah was sent out to Tunisia from such a mission in Yemen (according to some sources, Salamiya in Syria) with the task of propagating the Ismaili faith and inspiring the Berbers to rebel against their Sunni Aghlabid rulers. In 902 and then 904, there were uprisings in Syria, too, where a claimant to the Imamate, Sa'id ibn Ahmad, who had assumed the name of Ubaidullah, was living near Hims, but these were quickly suppressed. He later travelled to north Africa to join Abdullah but was captured and imprisoned in Sijilmassa by the Rustamids, who, being Kharijite, refused to acknowledge any hereditary claim to power.

Meanwhile, the Fatimid *da'i* (propagandist), Abu Abdullah, had been very active in the missionary work, and his promise of the imminent arrival of the Mahdi (for which he was 'preparing' the people) to inaugurate a reign of peace and justice on earth fired religious enthusiasm among the simple Berbers, who were eager to escape the tyranny of the last Aghlabid ruler, Ziyadat Allah III (r.903–9). Having firmly established himself, he overthrew the century-old Aghlabid dynasty in 909 with the help of his converts from the Kitama Berber tribe and captured Qairawan. Six months later, he rescued Ubaidullah from Sijilmassa, overrunning and putting an end to the small principality of the Rustamids. Ubaidullah, who claimed to be a lineal descendant (through a line of 'Hidden Imams') from Muhammad, son of Ismail, was installed in Qairawan and assumed the titles of both Mahdi and Caliph.* There were now two rival Caliphs in the Muslim world, each head of his own government.

Once the first Fatimid ruler, Ubaidullah (r. 909–34), was in the saddle, a rift developed between him and Abu Abdullah, who had ceaselessly worked for Ubaidullah's elevation and also enjoyed an unquestioned loyalty among the Kitama Berbers. Abdullah's execution in 911 by his master led to revolts among the Kitama and the Kharijites of the Atlas, but these were eventually suppressed after two years of heavy fighting. This left the Fatimid rule well established both in Ifriqiya and Sicily, which paved the way for their further expansion.

The emergence of the Fatimids was a major event in Islamic history. They— being heads of a rival religious movement—regarded themselves to be the only legitimate authority in Islam, and set up a Caliphate (909–1171) of their own with its fortress capital at the new coastal city of Mahdia (built around 916, some thirty miles east of Qairawan), politically and ideologically hostile to Baghdad. Before the Fatimids, the provincial rulers both in the east and in the west, though virtually independent, acknowledged at least a token suzerainty of the Abbasid Caliph as head of the Muslim community; this was true even in the case of the Kharijite Rustamids. But that was all changed with the advent of the anti-Abbasid Fatimids, who claimed to be descendants of Fatima (hence the dynastic name), daughter of the Prophet Muhammad and wife of his cousin Ali ibn Abi Talib. This gave them the status of Imam and hence the rightful Caliph, both by descent and by divine choice custodians of the true Faith. Being Imams, they were the embodiment of God's infallible Guidance to mankind, so they combined the duties of an emperor and a religious leader. At its peak, the Fatimid empire included north Africa, Sicily, the Red Sea coast of Africa, Hijaz (including Mecca and Medina), Yemen, Palestine and Syria. In particular, the control over the holy cities of Mecca and Medina gave them enormous religious prestige and political leverage.

*Ubaidullah's claim to have Ali-Fatima descent (by way of having Ismail as his ancestor six generations back) was accepted by Arab historians such as Ibn al-Athir, al-Maqrizi and Ibn Khaldun. This claim was, however, suspected or disputed by contemporary Sunni opponents, who denied the Fatimid's Alid connection.

912–8

Accession of Abdur Rahman III in Spain

In 912, twenty-three-year-old Abdur Rahman III ascended the throne in succession to his grandfather, Abdullah (r.888–912), at a time when the Spanish Umayyad Amirate was on the decline, beset with internal warfare and threatened from the north by the warlike King of Leon, Ordono II. The Berber tribes of the highlands devastated the fertile coastal regions. The newly converted population revolted, and so did the Christians, incited by some zealot priests in quest of martyrdom. Even in north Africa, a new and aggressive power, that of the Fatimids, had arisen, determined to conquer both Morocco and Spain. Surrounded by dangers from all sides, the gallant and wise young prince set about restoring the authority of the Amirate (which, effectively, had shrunk to within a few miles of Cordova itself) in the southern part of the peninsula. But, while he was thus engaged, Ordono II made use of the opportunity and marched down in 914 as far as Merida (a hundred miles north of Cordova) and laid waste the ancient town. Abdur Rahman reacted with a raid into the king's own territory, thus recovering Merida, but the Muslim army was defeated near San Estevan in the north.

By 918, however, most of the rebellious domains in the south had been brought under control, and the pressure on Abdur Rahman abated, in particular with the death of Umar ibn Hafsun (917), who had defied Cordova and held power in the mountains near Malaga for the previous twenty-four years; but it was to be another ten years before Ibn Hafsun's stronghold was captured and destroyed. In 918, he turned the tables on the Christian kings of Leon and Navarre and himslf initiated a successful military campaign against them. But it took a concerted campaign of six years to secure his northern frontiers (in which he was partly helped by the civil wars among the Christians), and about the same time (924) the rebel strong-holds in Valencia and the Ebro valley were subdued; only the old Visigothic capital of Toledo, which was finally to succumb in 932, remained defiant.

921

Capture of Morocco by the Fatimids

The city of Fez was captured by a Fatimid army, and its Idrisid ruler, Yahya IV (r. 905–22), was forced to acknowledge the suzerainty of the Fatimid Caliph Ubaidullah (r.909–34). The following year, Yahya, who, like the Fatimids, claimed descent from Ali and Fatima, was driven out of the city, and the Idrisid rule in Morocco effectively crumbled.

From then on, Morocco, too, came under Fatimid control, making them masters of north Africa (west of Egypt) and Sicily in just twelve years. They had wiped out three evenly balanced local dynasties (the Aghlabids, Rustamids and Idrisids), creating an imbalance of power in the area and thus posing a threat to Muslim Spain.

922

The Death of al-Hallaj

Al-Hallaj (full name: Abu al-Mughith al-Hussain ibn Mansur al-Hallaj), the celebrated but controversial Muslim mystic—Sufi—was crucified and brutally tortured to death in Baghdad for his views.

Born of a Zoroastrian grandfather around the year 858 in the Persian province of Fars, he was attracted to an ascetic way of life at an early age. Not being satisfied with having learnt the Quran by heart, he developed a strong urge to understand its deeper and inner meanings, for which he underwent instructions from a highly respected Sufi in Baghdad, al-Junaid (d. 910). He travelled extensively (as far as India) preaching, teaching and writing about the way to mystical relationship with the Divine. His thought and activity were particularly provocative at a time when the Sufi movement, in general, was arousing a great deal of opposition from the civil and religious authorities. In one of his moments of ecstasy, he uttered the statement, *Ana al-Haqq* (meaning, 'I am the Truth'—i.e., God: Truth being one of the ninety-nine attributes of God), which led to the accusation of blasphemy and his consequent arrest. But he was, for later mystics and poets, to become the 'martyr of Love' *par excellence*, an enthusiast killed by the orthodox theologians.

Al-Hallaj's tomb in Baghdad is regarded by many to be that of a saint.

Sufism

Sufism grew out of early Islamic asceticism, which itself grew, on the one hand, as a puritanic reaction against the sumptuous luxury and licence prevalent among the wealthy classes of the Umayyad period, and, on the other, from dissatisfaction with the formalism of orthodox Islam. Although the ascetic movement had taken its shape in the beginning of the eighth century (the most distinguished among the early ascetics being al-Hasan al-Basri, d. 728, who was also a religious scholar), the tendency had emerged much earlier (a prominent critic of the third Caliph, Uthman, was Abu Dharr, a Companion who practised asceticism).

Towards the middle of the ninth century, the ascetic movement gave way to mysticism proper, that is, experiences which might be described as ecstatic leaps of the spirit into oneness with God, 'passing away (*fana*) into God'. The way to this ultimate goal of the Sufi life was by self-denial, purifying the soul and mystical knowledge of God, as distinguished from formal knowledge. But *fana* was thought of in various ways: in the extreme, some would abandon themselves and be filled with the Glory of God. This transcendental bliss of abandonment was called 'intoxication', a dying-to-self. In the progress towards *fana*, some mystics described their experiences in such extravagant language as to appear heretical and un-Islamic to the *ulama* ('learned men', the body of religious and legal scholars). Abu Yezid al-Bistami (d. 875) used to utter in a state of trance 'Glory be to Me! How great is my Majesty!', and claimed to have ascended to Heaven in a dream. It was a spiritual union with God, attained through ecstasy, in which the Sufi claimed to become himself God. To distinguish between 'I' and 'God' is to deny the unity of God. However, the more sober Sufis such as Muhasibi (d. 857), Dhul Nun (d. 861), Kharraz (d. 899) and al-Junaid (d. 910) expressed their mystical experiences in less intemperate language and thus avoided giving fatal offence to the orthodox, although even they did not escape suspicion and disapproval.

There have been pantheistic tendencies within Sufism, but the normal Sufi is faithful to his Islamic theology, however difficult it may be to reconcile the idea of union with God with the Islamic doctrine that God is altogether different from His creation. However, in their defence, they could claim Quranic sanction in a number of passages in the Sacred Book which assert, e.g., that God is 'closer to him (man) than the vein of his neck' (sura 50:15). But the characteristic tendency of the Sufis to disregard outward conformity with Islamic laws, and their theopathic utterances made them obnoxious to the orthodox Sunnis. It was the great Persian jurist, philosopher and theologian, Abu Hamid al-Ghazali (1058–1111), who finally succeeded in reconciling Sufi doctrine with the formal framework of Islam, and after his time 'Sufi' was not a term of reproach. Al-Ghazali wrote in Arabic.

Sufism has always been a great stimulus to, and a persistent strain in, Islamic literature, especially in poetry. Almost all first-ranking Persian poets, in particular, were mystics. It can be seen, for instance, in the work of the great Persian poets Umar Khayyam (c.1048–c.1124), Rumi (1207–73), Sa'di (c. 1184–c. 1292) and Hafiz (c.1325–c.1390).

The term *sufi* (from the Arabic word *suf*, meaning 'wool') was applied to these mystics because they wore a robe made of undyed wool as a symbol of their renunciation of the world and its pleasures.

923

The Death of al-Tabari

Al-Tabari (full name: Abu Jafar Muhammad ibn Jarir al-Tabari), a remarkable historian and commentator who was a native of the province of Tabaristan (south of the Caspian Sea) as his name suggests, died in Baghdad at the age of about eighty-four. He is famous for his great chronicle *Annals of Apostles and Kings*, covering the period from Creation to the year 915, in which he condensed the vast wealth of historical erudition of the previous generations of Muslim scholars. It was written in a typical Arabian style, describing events in chronological order. The Islamic era was covered year by year in the Muslim calendar. He travelled far and wide in Persia, Iraq, Syria and Egypt in his search to collect and verify the material covered in his book, which consisted of several volumes*. The other great work of this prolific and versatile scholar was a commentary on the Quran which was written before he embarked on the historical work. All his writings were in Arabic.

*The monumental work of al-Tabari is the chief primary source of information on early Islamic history. This was drawn upon by later Muslim historians such as Miskawayh (d.1030), Ibn al-Athir (1160–1234) and Abu al-Fida (1273–1331). The well-known Leiden edition published during 1879–1901 is only a brief version of the original, which is thought to have been ten times as long, but even so, it spreads over twelve volumes. Many of the earlier works which al-Tabari made use of in his history are not extant in their original form.

His commentry on the Quran, which in one printed edition occupies thirty volumes, was also originally written on a much larger scale. In it he made a distinctive personal contribution and at the same time preserved a large amount of the work of previous scholars.

925

The Death of Rhazes

Rhazes (Arabic name: Abu Bakr Muhammad al-Razi), the first outstanding Muslim physician (b. circa 865 in Rhages, modern Rayy near Tehran), died in his native town. Although one hundred and thirteen major, and twenty-eight minor, works by Rhazes (the Latinized version of his name) are listed in the *Fihrist* compiled by Ibn al-Nadim in 987, he is best remembered as the author of the first book on smallpox, in which smallpox and measles were clearly distinguished for the first time. It was translated into Latin in Venice (1565) and later into other modern languages, which established his reputation as being one of the most original physicians of the Middle Ages. Another of his great works, *al-Hawi*, compiled posthumously from his papers, was later translated into Latin by the Sicilian Jewish physician Faraj ben-Salim (1279) as *The Continens* or *The Comprehensive (Book)*. It is not only an encyclopaedia of medical science as then known, but a comparative study of the views of Greek, Syrian, Indian, Persian Arabic physicians on each disease. To all this he added his own clinical observations and final opinion. It was repeatedly printed from 1486 onwards and had a remarkable influence on the development of medical science in Latin Europe. In all, over seventy of Rhazes' works are extant.

He also had the special gift of describing his experimental work so methodically that it could be repeated by other scientists and his results checked.

A stained glass window in the Princeton University Chapel commemorates the contribution of al-Razi to medical science.

929

Title of Caliph Taken by Abdur Rahman III

So far, the Umayyads of Spain had been content with the modest title of Amir, thereby tacitly leaving the title of Caliph to the Abbasids. But now, Abdur Rahman III (r. 912–61) assumed the combined title of Caliph and Defender of the Faithful in opposition to the threatening claims of his rivals—the Fatimids—in north Africa. It was not meant to be a claim to be ruler of the whole Islamic empire, more of an assertion that he was independent of all higher Muslim authority. This new digniy gave him some additional diplomatic weight in north Africa in his political manoeuvring there; he also felt that it was in keeping with his military and political achievements. There thus existed three mutually hostile Caliphs in the world of Islam; the Abbasid in Baghdad, the Umayyad in Spain and the Fatimid in Ifriqiya, each competing for the allegiance of the Muslims.

The Death of Albategnius

Albategnius (Arabic name: Muhammad ibn Jabir al-Battani), one of the greatest Muslim astronomers and mathematicians, died near Samarra at the age of about seventy. Born in Harran (now in Turkey), he lived for the greater part of his life, and from 877 carried out his famous scientific work (including remarkably accurate astronomical observations), in Raqqa on the Euphrates (Syria). He checked and improved upon the astronomical calculations of

Ptolemy* (c. 75–?) by replacing his geometrical methods with a new type of calculation involving trigonometry, in particular the use of a table of sines** for the first time. The most famous of the four main books he wrote was *Kitab al-Zij*. This work contained, among many astronomical computations and useful tables, his own observations of the sun and the moon and an emendation of their motion as given in Ptolemy's *Almagest*, which had, of course, been previously translated into Arabic. His other main contributions included a more accurate estimate of the length of the year than the Greeks had managed with their inferior instrumentation and excellent value of 23° 35' for the angle of the earth's axis which it makes with its plane of revolution. His value for the length of the year was so accurate that it was used seven centuries later in the Gregorian reform of the Julian calender. The contributions he made in the field of spherical trignometry were no less impressive.

Al-Battani's contributions were so valuable, not only in themselves but also for the mathematical techniques he employed for deriving them, that they were extensively used by later generations. In western Europe, they were quoted from the fifteenth to the seventeenth century by such outstanding astronomers as Copernicus (1473–543), Kepler (1571–630), Tycho Brahe (1546–601) and Galileo (1564–642).

> Besides medical science for its obvious practical use, astronomy had a special fascination for the Muslims, if only because the study of heavenly bodies was an indispensible aid to religious observance. It helped to determine the month of Ramadan, the hours of prayer and the orientation of mosques towards the Kaba. Moreover, the Quran enjoined the faithful to contemplate the Glory of God in the construction of His universe. And besides all this, a knowledge of astronomy was essential in sea navigation, in which the Muslims were deeply involved through their commercial and military activities.

*This Ptolemy (Latin: Claudius Ptolemaeus) is not to be confused with any of the Ptolemies who were Macedonian kings of Egypt and ruled the country from the death of Alexander the Great in 323 BCE to 30 BCE, when Egypt became a Roman province.
**The word 'sine' comes from a Latin translation sinus of the Arabic word jayb (meaning 'pocket').

930

Sacking of Mecca by the Qarmatians and Removal of the Black Stone

The Qarmatians, an extreme sect of the Ismailis who had built up a prosperous small state in Bahrain, had been terrorizing the caravans of pilgrims to Mecca for several decades. In 930, they attacked the holy city itself, plundering it and killing thousands of the faithful. So great was their contempt for traditional religious values that they littered the sacred Zamzam with the dead bodies; when returning, they removed the sacred Black Stone from the Kaba and carried it off to their capital al-Ahsa, regarding it as an object of superstition. It was returned twenty years later but only at the request of the Fatimid ruler al-Mansur (r.946–53).

935

The Death of al-Ashari

Al-Ashari (full name: Abu al-Hasan Ali ibn Ismail al-Ashari), famous theologian, died in Baghdad at the age of about sixty. Born in Basra of a noble and ancient Arab family (it was one of his ancestors, Abu Musa al-Ashari, who had represented the cause of Ali in the arbitration after the battle of Siffin in 657), al-Ashari became a zealous Mutazilite as a pupil of the greatest living exponent of Mutazilite doctrines, al-Jubbai (d. 915), in his home town, which was a centre of religious controversies. However, at the age of forty, he broke away from the Mutazilite position and went over to the opposite camp of the orthodox to champion their standpoint, holding several disputations with his old teacher, al-Jubbai. Al-Ashari was a prolific writer on varied subjects dealing with the Quran and the Traditions, but above all attacking heretics and unbelievers of all kinds.

The importance of al-Ashari lies in the fact that he was the first major intellectual figure to employ the dialectic method in the defence of orthodox doctrines, those lines of reasoning which the rationalists had previously made use of so effectively, instead of just doggedly repeating the Quranic texts and Traditions (both of which al-Ashari, of course, devoutly believed in) in answer to all arguments and questions. He attracted followers who developed his doctrines and formed a school of their own bearing his name. His formulation of orthodoxy was later to become the standard for the Sunni framework.

940

The Death of Ibn Muqla

Ibn Muqla (full name: Muhammad ibn Ali ibn Muqla), one of the leading calligraphers and a *vizier* of the Abbasid period, died in his native city of Baghdad at the age of fifty-four. Calligrahpy was the highest ranking among the Islamic arts for two reasons: it was a medium for a Muslim both to perpetuate the Word of God and to express his aesthetic feelings, which could not be expressed through depicting living beings because that was forbidden by the religion. Ibn Muqla is credited with being the first to invent the cursive style (with curved lines and rounded forms) of Arabic lettering, called the *naskhi* script, which was gradually to replace the angular Kufic as the standard Islamic calligraphy.

Although *naskhi* was originally intended for copying the Quran, which in itself was a profoundly meritorious act, by the eleventh century it had also become widely used in correspondence and as architechtural decoration.

944–6

The Death of al-Maturidi

Al-Maturidi (full name: Abu Mansur Muhammad ibn Muhammad al-Maturidi), a leading figure of the Hanafi school in Samarqand and an almost exact contemporary of Al-Ashari (d. 935), died in 944. He was as orthodox in his basic outlook as al-Ashari but with slight differences. Al-Maturidi, like al-Ashari, held that all acts were willed by God but, unlike him, maintained, as is generally accepted in the Muslim world, that evil acts occur by God's will but not 'with His good pleasure'. Like al-Ashari, al-Maturidi also gathered enough disciples to establish his own school of theology in Sunni Islam.

The Outbreak of the Berber Revolt against the Fatimids

The second Fatimid ruler, al-Qaim, died in 946. He came to power in 934 on the death of his father, Ubaidullah, and proved to be even more fanatical in his religious views and aggressive in his expansionist policy. In the year following his enthronment, he launched a third Fatimid expedition to capture Egypt but it was again unsuccessful, as had been those of the two previous occasions (914 and 921). During his reign of twelve years, he strengthened the Fatimid fleet, raided the coasts of France and Italy and plundered Genoa; the Fatimid power was feared all over the Mediterranean.

The cost of all this fell on the people in the form of heavy taxation, which added to the resentment already felt by the orthodox against the heretical rule (the vast majority belonged to the Sunni or Kharijite faith). In 944, a holy war led by a Kharijite ascetic from Tahart, Abu Yezid, was waged by a seething mass of enthusiastic Berbers against the Fatimid rulers. The rebellion swept through irresistibly, and the helpless al-Qaim remained stranded in his fortress at Mahdia for ten months till the autum of 945, when the insurgents withdrew to Qairawan. In 946, Al-Qaim died and was succeeded by his thirty-one-year-old son, al-Mansur (r. 946–53), who inflicted a heavy defeat on the rebels, who had almost succeeded in destroying the Fatimid power in Ifriqiya. He was greatly assisted in putting down the rebellion by the Sanhaja tribe of Berbers, who had already helped in relieving Mahdia. Abu Yezid escaped but was pitilessly hunted down, and a year later his body was brought in triumph to al-Mansur.

The failure of Abu Yezid's rising left the Fatimids far stronger than before and with a much firmer grip on the rein. The new ruler felt secure enough to move out of the coastal fortress at Mahdia, and in 947 he started building a new complex of palaces for his court on the outskirts of Qairawan.

The Seizure of Baghdad by the Buwayhids

The revolt in the west by the Berbers coincided with the invasion of Baghdad by the Buwayhids (or Buyids) originally from Daylam, a mountainous region south-west of the Caspian Sea. The Daylamites were fierce highlanders who, like the Turks, provided mercenary troops to the Muslim world, including Baghdad. The Buwayhid dynasty derived its name from Abu Shuja Buwayh, leader of a Daylamite tribe, and rose to power by the parallel efforts of his three sons, Ali, Hasan and the youngest, Ahmad. After the assasination in 935 of Mardawij ibn Ziyar, another powerful local adventurer who had seized a large part of northern Persia from the Samanids and extended it to as far south as Isfahan and Hamadan, his territory (except the Caspian region) fell into the hands of the three brothers. In the confusion of the following year or so, the three brothers kept expanding the area they controlled; Ali consolidated power for himself in Isfahan and Fars, Hasan occupied Rayy and Hamadan while Ahmad took Kirman in the southeast and Khuzistan in the southwest.

In December 945, Ahmad marched on Baghdad itself and occupied it without any oppostion, for the Abbasids had by now sunk to the lowest depths of humiliation under their own Amirs and were in no position to put up any defence. And the Amirs, mostly Turkish generals, were themselves engaged in power struggles, leaving no one with a firm grasp over civil and military affairs. The helpless and frightened Caliph al-Mustakfi (r. 944–6) came out of hiding and handed over supreme control to Ahmad with the title of Amir al-Umara* (Chief Amir) and the honorific title of Muizz al-Dawla (strengthener of the state). At the same time, Ali and Hasan received the titles of Imam al-Dawla (pillar of the state) and Rukn al-Dawla (support of the state) respectively. The new power in the capital was complete, and a permanent Amirate with hereditary rights within the Buwayhid family was established. A few weeks later, in January 946, the tribal barbarian Muizz had the unforfunate Caliph blinded, and replaced him by a son of al-Muqtadir (r.908–32) under the throne-name of al-Muti (r. 946–74); he was allowed a mere daily pittance as pocket money.

All this created a peculiar situation. The Buwayhid conquerors were of Shi'ite faith and therefore did not recognize the religious basis of the office of Sunni Caliphs, but retained them for political reasons, practically stripped of their remaining sovereign functions and privileges. While the real power was excerised by the Persian Shi'ite Amirs, orders were issued in the name of the Abbasid Caliphs, Commanders of the Sunni Faithful, who were humiliated by being granted a personal allowance and kept as puppets at the mercy of these Amirs. The provincial rulers who acknowledged the Caliphate as a religious institution, but who were otherwise independent, indicated it by mentioning the name of the ruling Caliph in the *khutbah* (serman) at the Friday congregational prayer and other ceremonial occasions. But the *khutbah* at Baghdad was also a symbol of political supremacy. Even this prerogative of the Caliph was now encroached upon, and the custom was started of having the name of the Amir mentioned along with that of the Caliph in the *khutbah* from pulpits at the capital. The Buwayhids even had their names inscribed on one side of the coinage minted at Baghdad, a clear symbol of sovereignty. Shi'ism, which had suffered for lack of political prestige, was protected and encouraged by the Buwayhids during the period in which they retained power in Baghdad (until 1055). As soon as Muizz al-Dawla (r.945–67) had established himself firmly at Baghdad, he tried to bring the Shia element, which constituted a small portion of the population, into prominence.

The first recipient of this title was Muhammad ibn Raiq, governor of Basra, for whom it was especially created by the helpless Caliph al-Radi (r. 934–40) to gain his approval. Ibn Raiq soon became the real ruler. Even before the arrival of the Buwayhids, almost all the temporal authority of the Caliph had been taken over by various Amirs who had risen to power in Baghdad, and who held the Caliph in utter disregard.

950

The Death of Alpharabius

Alpharabius (Arabic name: Muhammad ibn Muhammad ibn Tarkhan ibn Uzalagh al-Farabi), the Aristotelian and Neoplatonist philosopher-theologian, died. Born in Transoxiana (c. 870) of Turkish parents, he received his education in Baghdad under a Christian physician and a Christian translator. He accepted an invitation from the Hamdanid ruler Sayf al-Dawla (r. 945–67) to take up residence at his brilliant court in Aleppo, where he flourished until the time of his death.

In the ninth century, the Arab al-Kindi (d. circa 873) was the first notable scholar to use the Arabic language in a general introduction of mainly Aristotelian philosophy, and endeavoured to harmonize Greek philosophy with Islam. This process had been continued and expounded upon by Alpharabius (Latinized version of al-Farabi), whose system of philosophy, as expressed in his numerous works on Plato and Aristotle, earned him the exalted title of 'the second teacher' (Aristotle being the first). His philosophical thinking was nourished in the heritage of the Arabic Aristotelian teachings of tenth-century Baghdad. His great service to Islam was to take the Greek heritage, as it had become known to the Arabs, and show how it could be used to answer questions with which Muslims were struggling. Besides several commentaries on Aristotle and other Greek philosophers, Alpharabius wrote extensively on politics, metaphysics, medical science, mathematics and music. Inspired by Plato's *Republic* and Aristotle's *Politics*, he wrote a book entitled *The Perfect City* in which he represented his conception of a model city, which, as a hierarchical organism, resembles the human body. The ruler corresponds to the heart and is served by functionaries who are themselves served by others lower down the scale. Its main object is the happiness of its citizens, and the ruler is morally and intellectually perfect. *The Perfect City* is an essay on what might be called ethical urbanism—the ideal city should be founded on moral and religious principles, and from there would flow the physical infrastructure. The book is an indication of the degree to which Muslims had first assimilated Greek ideas and then capped them with their own indelible stamp. A renowned musician of his time, Alpharabius is also considered to have been the greatest Arab music theorist.

961

The Byzantine Revival; Capture of Crete by Nicephorus

Unfortunately for the Muslims, the rapid decline of the Abbasid empire caused by internal strains coincided with a great revival of Byzantine military strength, particularly under Emperor Constantine VII (r. 912–59) and his successor Romanus II (r. 959–63). While the Muslims were suffering from successive *coups d'etat* in Baghdad under the Turkish mercenaries, and the Qarmatians were ravaging lower Iraq and Syria, the new aggressive Byzantine Emperors were busy strengthening their defences and equipping themselves with a powerful army and navy. The Byzantines were presented with an opportunity for revenge after suffering terrible disasters for nearly three centuries at the hands of the Muslims, both in major battles and in the traditional annual raids conducted by the dedicated frontier troops with the honourable title of *ghazi*, meaning 'campaigner' (against the infidel). After securing and fortifying the strategically important Taurus passes, the Macedonian emperors took the offensive against the Muslims and inflicted many reverses on them on the plains of northern Syria and Iraq, which lay undefended at their mercy.

In 961, Romanus turned his attention to the Mediterranean where the Muslims had a strong presence. He gave the command of a wartime expedition to Nicephorus Phocus, the future emperor (963–9), to liberate Crete, which had been under Muslim control ever since 827, several attempts to recapture it having failed in the past . Nicephorus mobilized the entire Byzantine fleet and nearly 24,000 men for the enterprise, and gained the island by breaking all Muslim resistance in a pitiless general massacre. This gave the Byzantines an advantageous position from which to launch further attacks in the Mediterranean; the island remained, from then on, in Christian hands till 1669, when it fell to the Ottoman Turks.

The Death of Abdur Rahman III

Abdur Rahman III of Cordova died at the age of seventy-two after a glorious rule of forty-nine years. In 912, he had inherited a country divided among chieftains and with no effective control from the capital, whose reigning family was about to disappear. During his long and fruitful reign, he recovered the lost provinces, consolidated the central government and created internal peace. A recognized international statesman, he exchanged embassies with the Byzantine Emperor as well as with the monarchs of France, Germany and Italy; Muslim Spain emerged a Great Power. All three communities of Christians, Jews and Muslims flourished during his tolerant reign, contributing to the intellectual life and prosperity of Spain. The country enjoyed a hitherto unknown level of prosperity, rooted in a well-diversified agriculture (which was as ingenius as it was productive), industrial production, flourishing horticulture and lucrative overseas commerce. Considerable reserves in the public treasury allowed the Caliph to give his reign a display of splendour and a patronage of the arts. Cordova with its twenty-one suburbs, seventy libraries, numerous bookshops, scholarly circles, nine hundred public baths, beautiful mosques and gardens, rivalled Baghdad. It had miles of paved and illuminated streets.* If the rulers of the Christian north needed a surgeon, an architect or a master singer, it was Cordova that they turned to. Near the capital, he built a magnificient palace, which was called al-Zahra (the Bright One) after his favourite slave girl, and on which 10,000 workmen are said to have worked for twenty years. Later to be regarded as the greatest ruler of the Spanish Ummayad dynasty, he raised the prestige of Umayyad rule to a new level in his territory, which included all but a thin strip of land in the northernmost part of Spain.

He built up a strong army and navy, and launched a series of invariably successful campaigns against the Christians of the north. Abdur Rahman's army was the strongest and best-disciplined of his time, and consisted of Arabs, Berbers, and 'Slavs', the name given to young boys bought as slaves in France, Germany or Italy, converted to Islam and recruited as soldiers. The presence of a foreign element in the army was a powerful instrument in the hands of the Caliph for enforcing peace and order in the country. Hated as much as dreaded by the proud Arab nobility, the foreign military slaves, who were blindly devoted to Abdur Rahman, prevented the very thought of disobedience or treason from any side, and protected the peasant, artisan and tradesman from oppressors and brigands. This, of course, was the same technique as had been employed by the Abbasids, but in their case with disastrous consequences; exactly a hundred years earlier Caliph al-Mutawakkil had been killed by his own slave soldiers. But the mistake made by the Abbasids had been to fill their armies with mercenary Turks to such an extant that the Turks ultimately became aware of their own power. Abdur Rahman III was, however,more prudent and kept the 'Slavs' to about one-third of the army, which was sufficient to ensure stability but not enough to be dominated by them.

London had its first street lamp c. 1680.

962–3

Introduction of Shi'ite Ceremonies

With the Buwayhids at the helm of state affairs in Baghdad, the ritual cursing of Muawiya and 'the doers of wrong against the family of the Prophet'—a thin reference to the first three Caliphs—wasordered in 962. In the following year, Muizz al-Dawla (r. 945-67) established Shi'ite festivals. In particular, he introduced the customs of public mourning on the tenth of Muharram to commemorate the anniversary of Hussain's massacre in 680 at Karbala, and the feast of Ghadir Khumm* on 18 Dhu al-Hijja.

A spring between Mecca and Medina, where, according to Shi'ite beliefs, the Prophet Muhammad, on returning from the last Pilgrimage, appointed Ali ibn Abi Talib as his successor before the vast crowd that was accompanying him. The Shi'ites celebrate the event to this day as a major religious festival marking the day when the right of Ali to succession was established; this, of course, is the basic tenet of Shi'ism.

965–9

Sayf al-Dawla's Resistance against the Byzantines; Invasion of Syria by Nicephorus

The Byzantine military revival which had commenced nearly half a century earlier was maintained and then increased under Emperor Nicephorus Phocus (r. 963–9), the conquerer of Crete (961). In 965, he recovered the island of Cyprus, which gave him command of the sea and was a severe blow to the naval supremecy the Muslims had enjoyed for so long in the Mediterranean. Cyprus remained in Christian hands for the rest of the Middle Ages till 1571, when the Ottoman Turks captured it. The Ottoman rule in the island was to last for more than two hundred years.*

On land, the only opposition to the aggressive Nicephorus had been that offered by Sayf al-Dawla, the most prominent member of the Hamdanids (905–91 in Mosul; 945–1004 in Aleppo). The moderately Shi'ite Hamdanid principality had been founded (905) in al-Jazira (the northern area of land between the Tigris and the Euphrates), with its capital at Mosul, by the Arab tribe of Taghlib, whose members were intensely proud of their pure Arab descent. In 944, Sayf al-Dawla advanced into Syria and wrested Aleppo and Hims (Homs) from the Ikhshidids of Egypt, who were then ruling the country, thereby establishing in the following year a separate branch of the dynasty.

Sayf al-Dawla (r. 945–67) was later to become famous for his gallant struggle against the armed might of the Byzantine empire. Most of his reign, in which he received no help from any other Muslim ruler, was taken up in defending his lands in Syria. He suffered many setbacks but nevertheless succeeded on the whole in safeguarding a large part of his domain. After his death at the age of fifty-one, however, no effective opposition was left to prevent Byzantine inroads. In 968, Nicephorus entered Syria, sacking Hims mercilessly and laying waste the Lebanese coast from Tripoli back to Tarsus. Towards the end of 969, the ancient city of Antioch (founded c.300 BCE by Seleucus I), the former Greek and Roman capital of Syria, was seized only a month before Nicephorus, one of the greatest soldier-emperors the Byzantines had produced for centuries, was himself murdered by his nephew, John Tzimisces, who then became emperor. For a while, it looked as though all northern Syria would be restored to Byzantine rule. But Sa'd al-Dawla, the son and successor of Sayf al-Dawla, managed to hold on to his territory by playing off against one another the Byzantines and the Fatimids; the Fatimids had occupied Egypt in the same year and thereafter extended their dominion through Palestine into central Syria. Eventually, in 997, a treaty would be concluded between the Fatimid ruler al-Hakim (r. 996–1021) and the Emperor Basil (r. 976–1025) which would give most of Syria to the Fatimids. The Hamdanid dynasty would finally be extinguished in 1004.

Besides being a warrior, the fame of Sayf al-Dawla also rests on his having been a great patron of the arts, especially literature. The decentralization of the Muslim empire had given rise to several provincial centres in which literature flourished. One of the most brilliant such centres was at Aleppo, receiving generous encouragement from Sayf al-Dawla, himself a poet. The celebrated philosopher al-Farabi (d. 950), the poet al-Mutanabbi (d. 965), literary historian and author of the monumental work *Kitab al-Aghani* (Book of Songs) and al-Isbahani or al-Isfahani (d. 967) were just three of a group of outstanding figures which belonged to the intellectually active 'circle of Sayf al-Dawla' at the magnificient Hamdanid court.

The Fatimid Conquest of Egypt

Having overthrown the Aghlabids, Rustamids and Idrisids in north Africa, the Fatimids tried in earnest but unsuccessfully, on no less than three occasions (914, 921 and 935), and under two rulers, to seize Egypt. In 958, the fourth and greatest Fatimid ruler, al-Muizz (r. 953–75), decided to establish his complete authority over Ifriqiya and al-Maghrib before re-embarking on the cherished plan of conquering Egypt. He entrusted the task to his commander-in-chief, Jawhar the Sicilian, a former Greek slave bought from Sicily, who built a strong army which chiefly consisted of the Sanhaja Berbers, whose loyalty had already been tested in the campaign to put down Abu Yezid's rising (944–5). After completely destroying any residual resistance in the former Rustamid territory, he moved further west and recaptured Fez, the former capital of the Idrisids (789–926). And the land as far as the Atlantic coast was subdued in one continuous sweep.

After sixty years of struggle, the Fatimids had acquired sufficient resources and stability in north Africa to be able to return once more to the first stage of their cherished plan of expanding eastward. They hoped it would eventually lead to the overthrow of the Abbasids, leaving the Fatimids solely holding the Caliphal rein. The Ikhshidids, under nominal allegiance to Baghdad, had been ruling Egypt since 935, but their power had declined rapidly after the death in 968 of their fourth ruler, Kafur, with anarchy and political instability having got a strong grip over the country. And the Abbasids, themselves being mere puppets in the hands of the Buwayhids in Baghdad, were in no position to come to the rescue; to make matter worse, the country was suffering from severe famine. The timing of all this could not have been more fortunate for the Fatimids' ambitions. Consequently, the country became an easy prey in 969 to their well-planned attack under the brilliant general Jawhar, its capital Fustat offering virtually no resistance.

No sooner had Egypt new rulers than any recognition of the Abbasid Caliphs was abolished; the currency was replaced and it was the name of al-Muizz which was now mentioned in the Friday prayers, though Shi'ite forms (including the prayer call) wereintroduced gradually. As a monument to their triumph, Jawhar began, in the same year, 969, the construction of the new city of Cairo (al-Qahira, meaning the victorious) near Fustat, which was made the capital of their empire in 973. The elated Jawhar then marched on to occupy Palestine and part of Syria. By the time al-Muizz made his grand state entry into the new capital of Cairo, the Fatimid empire stretched from Morocco to Syria, and for a time the Abbasid power seemed on the the the verge of being desroyed by their arch-rivals, but that was never to happen. However, before al-Muizz could enjoy the moment of glory, the Fatimids had to face another but much more formidable power, that of the Qarmatians, who were in control of Arabia and were alarmed at the arrival of a new power so close to them. A fierce battle took place near Cairo (972), in which Egypt was saved but not without considerable cost.**

Although the Fatimids did not succeed in converting the bulk of the Egyptians (who, apart from the Copts, were Sunnis belonging to the Maliki school, with a sizeable minority of Kharijites) in their brilliant rule of two centuries, they did create a widespread missionary network in many other lands for their movement. Similar situations existed at other places in north Africa under their domination; the inhabitants of the coastal planes remained Sunni, whereas those of the Atlas were Kharijites, staunch republican puritans.

Egypt under the Fatimids*** enjoyed an era of great prosperity; trade with India, Italy, the western Mediterranean and even, at times, with the Byzantine empire flourished. The tolerant attitude of the regime (al-Hakim's reign from 996 to 1021 was exceptional in this respect in the Fatimid period as a whole) created great intellectual vitality in the country.

*Cyprus was first taken by the Muslims as far back as 649, lost in the civil wars and then recaptured in 804.
   All the major Mediterranean islands were conquered and lost several times by both the Muslims and the Byzantines in their struggle for territorial expansion.
**This may reflect the independence of the two movements at this early period in the formation of Ismailism; both the Qarmatians and the Fatimids professed the Ismaili form of Shi'ism. The Fatimid rulers, however, were shrewd enough to avoid pursuing the extremist policies of the fanatic Qarmatians, who may have regarded this as a betrayal of Ismaili ideals.
***From 996 onwards, north Africa was divided between various Berber dynasties, and the authority of the Fatimid Caliph extended no further west than Barqa.

970

The Foundation of al-Azhar Mosque

The great Mosque/University of al-Azhar in Cairo was founded by the same Fatimid general, Jawhar, who had started building the city itself the previous year. Originally built to serve only as a mosque for the new city, it gradually developed into a major centre of Islamic scholarship, providing education for students of all ages. As late as 1925, the subjects taught remained exclusively religious, based on the Quran, the Traditions and their interpretations.

973

Expulsion of Fatimids from Morocco

Al-Hakam II (r.961–76), Umayyad Caliph of Cordova, drove the Fatimids out of Morocco and thus put an end to their power in north-west Africa, after which they were concentrated in Egypt.

974–5

Invasion of Northern Iraq and Syria by John Tzimisces

The successive waves of Byzantine incursion into Muslim Syria and northern Iraq continued under Emperor John Tzimisces (r.969–76). In 974, he launched a full-scale invasion of northern Iraq, and the following year marched into Syria virtually unopposed, mercilessly laying waste the whole country, taking Damascus, Sidon, Beirut and other important cities. However, the conquered cities did not remain under the tight control of the Byzantines for very long because of their lack of manpower. The death of John Tzimisces in 976 brought relief to Syria from the relentless Byzantine invasions.

976

Consolidation of Buwayhid Lands by Adud al-Dawla

From the start, the Buwayhid power was very much a family affair and always remained so, with various relatives sharing the land it collectively controlled and giving recognition to one another. This was both a strength and weakness, since it tended to fluctuate with family loyalty. After the death of the three brothers, in-fighting broke out, but the Buwayhid authority was saved by Adud al-Dawla (r.949–83), the third and perhaps the most outstanding in his line, who in 976 defeated all his main rivals and became the sole master of the family fortunes. After his death in 983, however, the Buwayhid state fell apart for good, and numerous local dynasties of Persian and Kurdish rulers sprang up. This fragmentation eventually led to its eastern half being conquered by the Ghaznavids in 1029 and the rest by the Seljuqs when Isfahan was captured in 1051. In 1055, the Seljuqs seized Baghdad and had their rule confirmed by the Caliph.*

The Death of al-Hakam of Spain

Caliph al-Hakam II of Cordova died after a reign of fifteen years.

Himself a man of letters and patron of the arts and sciences, he made Cordova a pre-eminent centre of learning. He amassed a library of some 400,000 volumes, established numerous schools, sponsored and attracted to the local university, founded by his father, Christians and Muslims, not only from Spain but also from western Europe, Asia and north Africa. The widespread availability of, and encouragement in, education raised the level of literacy among the masses to an amazingly high degree. On hearing that some poor families were unable to educate their children, the enlightened Caliph opened twenty-seven primary schools in which children from poor parents were educated free of charge. This was at a time when just across the Pyrenees in Christian Europe, even kings and nobles were often illiterate; learning there was rudimentary and confined largely to members of the clergy. A contemporary library at the monastery of Saint Gall (Switzerland) was the largest in Europe; it boasted a grand collection of less than fifty volumes, while the catalogue alone of the Cordovan library filled forty-four volumes. Many centuries were to elaspe before Western Europe would reach the educational standard achieved by the Muslims of Spain in the tenth century.

Seizure of Power in Spain by Chamberlain al-Mansur

Al-Hakam was succeeded by his son Hisham II (r. 976–1009), who came to the throne as a minor, so the regency was jointly exercised by his Basque mother, Aurora (known to the Arabs as Subh, which the word Aurora means in Arabic), and a certain Muhammad ibn Abi Aamir (b. circa 938) of Yemenite Arab descent, who gained her favour by his social talent. Gifted with exceptional administrative and military skill as well as the power of manipulation, he was finally raised to the position of Hajib (meaing,

Chamberlain), the highest office in the state. Disbanding the Caliph's guard of Slavs, replacing them with Berber mercenaries from north Africa and substituting for the traditional tribal structure, he thoroughly reorganized the army, making it a strong and flexible instrument in his hands. Within a few years, he became *de facto* ruler of the country, assuming the honorific title of al-Mansur ('the Victorious') in 981 and exercising supreme power in Cordova till his death in 1002.

Throughout his period in office, al-Mansur (Almanzor in Spanish) conducted a series of successful campaigns against the Christian states of northern Spain; the most notable of his feats of arms included the invasion of Leon (981 and 988) and Barcelona (985) and the destruction, in the wild mountains of Galicia, of the well-defended shrine of Santiago de Compostela (997), thought to be the burial place of Saint James the Apostle. The saint's tomb itself of the most famous place of pilgrimage in Spain was, however, spared. During his twenty-five years of untiring offensives, he reduced the Christian kingdoms to trembling subservience; but this was marred by excessive ruthlessness in his zeal, which left a lasting desire for revenge. In northern Morocco too, he continued and reinforced the Umayyad influence by his several military interventions, including the capture of Fez (986). He died on his way home from his fifty-second campaign, and such was his enthusiasm for the cause that in his tomb was put, according to his will, the dust of many battlefields which he had collected off his armour. This was meant to serve as evidence, on the Day of Judgement before the recording angels, of his devotion to fighting the Christians.

Besides being a soldier, he was extremely active in promoting the material welfare of the people by improving roads, irrigation, commerce and industry. But in one respect his absolute power also sowed the seeds of the eventual ruin of his country. He completely overshadowed Caliph Hisham and thus undermined the Umayyad house, with the result that even after his death, when he bequeathed the office of Hajib to his son, the real sovereign, Hisham, was unable to exert his authority, and Spain fell into anarchy. After a rapid succession of Umayyad pretenders, the dynasty finally melted away in 1031, and the country was broken up into thirty or so petty states, each centred on one of the towns and with its own princeling.

*Both the Ghaznavids and the Seljuqs emphasized their association with the Sunni cause and with the freeing of the Abbasid Caliphs from the clutches of the Shi'ite Buwayhids. This ensured them orthodox sympathy as they advanced against the Buwayhids.

977

The Establishment of the Ghaznavid Dynasty

When the Samanid ruler Abdul Malik died in 961, a new power had begun to
rise in the Kabul area. It was led by a Turkish slave commander of the Samanid
forces, Alptigin, who founded a small state-city in Ghazna (962) on the
periphery of the Samanid state. He was now succeeded by his son-in-law,
Sebuktigin (r. 977–97), who was even more of an adventurer, extendeding his
dominions and establishing the Ghaznavid dynasty (977–1186), named after its
capital city at Ghazna (modern Ghazni, sixty-five miles south-west of Kabul, in
Afghanistan). He was succeeded by sixteen Ghaznavid rulers, all his lineal
descendants. During the next twenty years, he conquered a large part of
Khurasan from the Samanids in the west and an area as far as Peshawar in the
east. It was under him that the tradition was established of raiding India, which
was continued with much more vigour and regularity by his son, the most
celebrated member of the dynasty, Mahmud (998–1030).

   After losing their Persian territory to the Seljuqs (1038–1194), the
Ghaznavids were finally driven out from Ghazna by the Ghurids (c.1000–1215)
from central Afghanistan, who in 1186 annexed their remaining lands in
Punjab.

987

Publication of *Fihrist*

Ibn al-Nadim (d. 995), a bookseller, completed after painstaking effort the
compilation of a scholarly work *Fihrist* (meaning, *Catalogue*) which contained
a vast number of books, together with biographical notes on the authors, and
other materials. The *Catalogue* covered all kinds of publications, ranging from
philology to alchemy, and it gives an idea of the profusion and variety of the
literature that was currently in circulation.

996

The Accession of Fatimid al-Hakim

After the prosperous and peaceful reign of al-Aziz (r. 975–96) in Egypt came the turn of his eleven-year-old son, al-Hakim (r. 996–1021), and the consequent long period of unrest. Al-Hakim was later to be noted for his eccentric, arbitrary and cruel policies; he was possibly unsound in mind. He tended to oscillate between one extreme and another in his proclamations affecting public life. His religious persecutions affected Sunni Muslims as well as Christians and Jews.

Above all, he entrenched himself more and more into an extreme Ismaili stance and eventually started claiming to be a divine incarnation, which gave rise to the Druze* religion, whose ahherents beieved he was really God.

*The founding figure of this new sect, from whom it derived its name, was a Persian by the name of Muhammad ibn Ismail al-Darazi (d. 1019), an Ismaili, who came from Bukhara to Egypt in 1017 and started preaching that the divine spirit, transmitted through Ali and the Imams, had become incarnated in al-Hakim, who was thus deified. This led to riots in public when he escaped to the Lebanese mountains where the primitive hillmen gave a receptive response to his teaching. The Druze religious sect, which has survived to this day, is a closed, tightly-knit, Arabic speaking community concentrated in parts of Lebanon and Syria. Knowledge of Druze faith is uncertain since its adherents tend to conceal the tenents of their religion; in fact, most of the Druzes themselves have only a superficial knowledge of their religion. The society is divided into the uqal (meaning, sages or knowers), who make up ten percent of the population, and the juhal (meaning, ignorant). The Druzes have their own customs as well as their beliefs, which have no resemblance with those of the Sunni or Shi'ite doctrines. The sect reveres to this day the half-demented al-Hakim as the incarnation of God and expects his return in the last stage of the world; in fact, the Druzes can hardly be regarded as Muslims.

998

Seizure of Power by Mahmud of Ghazna

Yamin al-Dawla Mahmud (better known as Mahmud of Ghazna, d. 1030), one of the great figures of Islamic history, became ruler of the kingdom of Ghazna (comprising of Afghanistan and northern Persia) at the age of about twenty-seven for the next thirty-two years, after driving out his elder brother Ismail, his father's heir to the Ghaznavid dynasty (977–1186). Like the rulers of other petty kingdoms which had sprung up in the Muslim empire, he became autonomous in every respect but paid nominal allegiance to the Abbasid Caliph al-Qadir (r. 991–1031) in Baghdad, in return for which his rule over the lands he occupied was formally legitimized. Al-Qadir conferred upon him the title of Yamim al-Dawla (the right arm of the state).

Mahmud, who was an ardent Muslim and champion of Sunni orthodoxy (like all Turks), as well as an outstanding military and political leader, proved himself to be the scourge of the heterodox and the infidel. He concentrated his efforts especially in India, where Islam had first been introduced as far back as 711 by the Arabs, but had so far made no significant advances; there were only two isolated petty Muslim states, around the area of Multan. The Arabs, coming from Makran, had conquered the southern Indus valley up to Multan, but they had never occupied the northern Punjab which, in the year 1000, was ruled by Jaipal, the Hindu ruler of Lahore. It was Mahmud, a man of dauntless will and tremendous driving force, who was neither an Arab nor belonged to an Arabicized people, but a Turk, whose ancestors had been converted to Islam by the Persian Samanids, who opened the way into India for Islam. From 1001 to 1026, he led about seventeen raids into India, the first being in the northern state of Punjab (November, 1001), where he defeated Jaipal near Peshawar, after a fearful massacre of the massive Indian army. After the battle, Jaipal threw himself on a funeral pyre and burned to death to escape the humiliation of defeat. In these raids, he destroyed Hindu temples, forced conversions to Islam and carried off immense booty and an enormous number of slaves. The most famous of his campaigns was in January 1026 against an extremely wealthy temple dedicated to the deity Shiva, situated at Somnath in the Kathiawar peninsula (now part of Gujarat state in India). Nearly a dozen Indian states had pooled their resources to protect the shrine and give him battle who had the disadvantage of being separated from his main base in Ghazna by nearly a thousand miles of enemy territory. Despite the reckless bravery of the Indian soldiers, fired with religious enthusiasm, Mahmud won the day after a fierce battle in which fifty thousand Indians were killed. He returned in triumph to Ghazna three months later, laden with the incredible riches of the temple. So much hatred had he for idol worship that, in spite of a desperate plea by the Hindus, the deity image was destroyed and a part of it carried to Ghazna, where it was laid under the threshold of the great mosque, that it might be for ever trampled under the feet of the Muslims. He took great pride in professing to be an 'idol-breaker'. Mahmud's ruthless methods, and especially his contemptous destruction of Hindu holy places, left a strong desire for revenge and sowed the seeds of hatred between the Muslims and Hindus of the sub-continent.

Significantly, under Mahmud and all subsequent rulers, it was Islam and not Arabism which took root in India.

Having gained the lands south of the Oxus from the Samanids (999), he had a secure base from which to expand westwards. In 1029, he pushed the Buwayhids west of the Persian plateau, extending his rule over Rayy and Hamadan; the boundaries of Mahmud's empire by the time of his death were stretched to include Punjab and the Indus valley in India, and the whole of Afghanistan and eastern Persia. However, there was a sudden loss of the Persian provinces soon after his death, when the Seljuqs began to spread rapidly through Khurasan during the reign of his son Masud.

Although Mahmud's main preoccupation throughout his rule had remained the military expansion of his kingdom and the resultant propagation of the Islamic faith, he did patronize literary talents and embellished his capital Ghazna with the vast riches yielded from his Indian campaigns. Many renowned men of learning were invited to his court; the most notable of these were the celebrated Persian poet Firdawsi (c.934–1020)*, the scientist-historian al-Biruni (973–c.1050) and the Arab historian al-Utbi (d. 1036). A Persian by birth, al-Biruni produced his writings in Arabic, though he knew, besides Persian, no less than four other languages: Turkish, Sanskrit, Hebrew and Syriac. Later to be regarded as one of the most comprehensive scholars to emerge in the Islamic world, he made significant contributions in the fields of the natural sciences, mathematics, mathematical astronomy and chronology. He also went to India, a country he was interested in and whose Hindu philosophy had a deep fascination for him. In 1030, he wrote *Tarikh al-Hind* (*A History of India*), which was a comprehensive and informative book about the country based on native sources and his own observations, and dedicated it to Mahmud. Al-Biruni belonged to the Shi'ite faith, but with agnostic tendencies.

Mahmud established an academy at Ghazna and adorned the city with many magnificient buildings, including a grand mosque of granite and marble.

It was under Mahmud's patronage that the Persian national epic and one of the greatest classics of world literature, the Shah-nama (Book of Kings) *by Firdawsi was finally completed in 1010. It is a poem of some 60,000 verses, and has remained one of the most popular works in the Persian language. This lengthy work is full of romantic and heroic tales based more on legend than on an accurate history of the Persians before Islam; its heros are Zoroastrians and Sasanids. It was a source of inspiration to later Persian poets as well as to such western authors as Mathew Arnold, who retold one of the finest of the tales in his poem* Sohrab and Rustum (1853); *in this episode, the hero Rustum unknowingly meets his son in battle and kills him.*

Index

Except for the pages 1–4, the indexing is done according to the date under which a subject is mentioned. In arranging the entries in alphabetical order the Arabic article (al-) is overlooked.

Tr to cir

Ref
new

DATE DUE

NOV 0 7 2001	
JUN 3 2002	

GAYLORD   PRINTED IN U.S.A.